The Abingdon Guide to Funding Ministry

An Innovative Sourcebook for Church Leaders

Volume 1
1995

EDITORS

Donald W. Joiner
Norma Wimberly

ABINGDON PRESS
NASHVILLE

THE ABINGDON GUIDE TO FUNDING MINISTRY:
AN INNOVATIVE SOURCEBOOK FOR CHURCH LEADERS

Copyright © 1995 by Abingdon Press

This book is printed on recycled, acid-free paper.

ISBN 0-687-00477-2
ISSN 1081-4957

Most Scripture quotations are taken from the New Revised Standard Version Bible, Copyright 1989 by the Division of Christian Education of the National Council of the Churches of Christ in the USA. Used by permission.

Those noted RSV are from the Revised Standard Version of the Bible, copyright 1946, 1952, 1971 by the Division of Christian Education of the National Council of Churches of Christ in the USA. Used by permission.

Those noted LB are from *The Living Bible,* copyright © 1971. Used by permission of Tyndale House Publishers, Inc.,
Wheaton IL 60189. All rights reserved.

Those noted REB are from The Revised English Bible. Copyright © 1989 Oxford University Press and Cambridge University Press. Used by permission.

Those noted NKJ are from The New King James Version. Copyright © 1979, 1980, 1982, Thomas Nelson Inc., Publishers.

"An Accountable Reimbursement Plan" by Wayne Barrett in Part 7 is reprinted by permission of *Clergy Finance Letter.*

"A Closing Worship" by Fran Craddock, "Prayer for the Offering" by Karen E. Warren, "Prayer of Dedication" by Alec J.
Langford, "A Stewardship Carol of Christmas" by Dan Conway, "Everybody's After a Buck" by Jack and Lynda Johnson-Hill,
"Poor God" by Diane E. Caughron, and "Time and Financial Management" by Dan P. Moseley are reprinted from *The Gifts We
Bring: Worship Resources for Stewardship and Mission* by permission of The Christian Church (Disciples of Christ).

"Putting It Together: A Year-Round Approach" is from *Stewardship: Congregational Program Planning Manual* by Paula K.
Ritchie, Christian Board of Publication, St. Louis, Missouri. Used by permission.

"Stewardship Challenges" by Don McClanen, "I Hate Money" by Dale Stitt, and "The Stewardship of Enjoyment" by
Robert Cooper are reprinted by permission of *Ministry of Money.*

"Prayer Before a Twenty-Dollar Bill," from *Prayers* by Michel Quoist, is used by permission of Sheed and Ward, Publishers.

Kudzu cartoons are reprinted with permission of Doug Marlette, *New York Newsday.*
Father Faber cartoon by Robert Portlock is reprinted by permission of Thomas Nelson Publishers.

96 97 98 99 00 01 02 03 04—10 9 8 7 6 5 4 3 2

MANUFACTURED IN THE UNITED STATES OF AMERICA

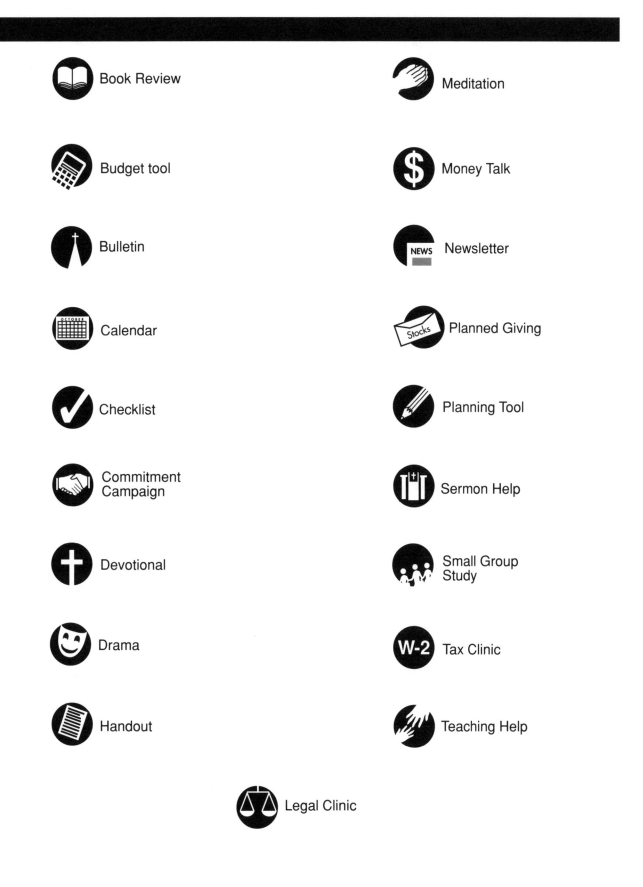

Book Review		Meditation	
Budget tool		Money Talk	
Bulletin		Newsletter	
Calendar		Planned Giving	
Checklist		Planning Tool	
Commitment Campaign		Sermon Help	
Devotional		Small Group Study	
Drama		Tax Clinic	
Handout		Teaching Help	
Legal Clinic			

For quick reference, see the Index of Funding Tools on p. 158.

CONTENTS

OUR COVENANT

Donald W. Joiner is director of local church funding for the General Board of Discipleship of The United Methodist Church. He also directs the Planned Giving Resource Center for that agency. He is an ordained clergyman from the Detroit Conference of The United Methodist Church.

Norma Wimberly is a teacher, freelance writer, author, and speaker at seminars across the country. She was formerly a director of stewardship education and resource development for the General Board of Discipleship.

JOINER: Financial ministries involve more than money. Such ministries invite Christians to act out their faith in exciting ways through the church.

Christian stewards begin with the affirmation that all we have, are, and can be is a trust from God. That trust invites us to discover our purpose in God's world and to decide how we are to use what is entrusted to us for God's purposes.

Christian stewards are financial stewards. However, when we define stewardship as a method of persuading people to give, we skew the biblical story and send people away. When a church begins from a stewardship perspective, the congregation moves from a fundraising focus to an emphasis on funding ministry.

A fund-raising mindset raises money, regardless of what it does for or to the steward. To put it in business terms that many church leaders will understand, fund-raising is often more concerned with selling a product than with the benefit we seek for others. A perspective on funding ministry helps the steward in the journey of receiving and giving. For a fundraiser, money is the goal. For the church, the steward's response to the good news of God in Jesus Christ is the goal.

When a local congregation focuses on funding ministry, the message changes from giving *to* the church to giving *through* the church. The message centers on what is happening through the church, as each individual responds to the call to ministry.

WIMBERLY: I believe that all we are, all we have, and all we do begins with God. We are called to be "servants of Christ and stewards of God's mysteries." That brief passage from First Corinthians 4:1 probably tells more about me, my perspective on stewardship, and my teaching than anything else I can say. I begin with God and the Scriptures. My relationship with God is primary in my life as a steward. My thoughts, attitudes, actions, and relationships reflect my spiritual condition—sometimes faithful, sometimes not. That idea often comes as a surprise to those who consider stewardship synonymous with fund- raising!

We are called to be willing to change and grow, and move toward God's final victory. Our process for accomplishing this goal is found in honestly examining our relationship with God each day and discovering how the Scriptures intersect with our personal experience.

Stewardship is a relationship issue—with giving and money as symbols of the quality of that relationship. The way I feel about giving, and the purposes for which I use money reflect my spiritual condition, my relationship with God. Do I persist in trying to control money? Do I think I need more and more? Do I live in fear—protecting what I have or thinking I'll not have enough? When I fall into any of these traps, I am not putting God first in my life, not being grateful for God's gifts, not trusting that God will provide for all my needs. Those attitudes do not make room for generosity!

TOGETHER: We hope to help people look at the critical issues of their relationship with God, their relationship with money, and for faithful ways to practice generosity and healthy church finance. We believe that developing Christian givers is a process rather than a program, that it takes practice and that it is a journey rather than a destination.

A Vision

Our vision of funding ministry is like a painting that appears blurry from a distance, but assumes clarity as we approach it step-by-step. Our vision is that pastors and church leaders will begin, or continue to develop, a perspective on giving, that they will teach giving consistently and effectively and will proclaim the joy of giving.

To achieve that vision, to step ever closer to the picture, we present "an almanac for good stewards," which will tell stories of giving and offer suggestions, sermons, tips, tools, worksheets, and much more for developing generous disciples. Our aim in Volume 1 of *The Abingdon Guide to Funding Ministry* is to provide a resource to encourage pastors and leaders to examine and continue to develop their perspective on giving.

This publication on finance is informational and motivational. We want it to help leaders look not only at themselves, but beyond current programs, for tangible results.

We assume a diverse readership, and we know that reliable and faithful Christians disagree about money as often as they do about doctrine. Some of you have significant experience in financial stewardship, which makes you hungry for new ideas. Others have little or no history of exploration in this discipline, and we hope to delight you with usable tools and practical suggestions. As we assemble the parts of this "almanac," we imagine a diversity of age, denomination, theology, geography, church size, and "comfort zone" with the topic.

We believe that growth in giving is an ongoing, lifelong process. The *Guide* is compiled to suggest, as well as to direct each of us to the next steps of the journey. The next step may be clear for some of you. For others, it may include a question, a doubt, more searching. In some instances, the next step may offer a choice. What is God leading you to do?

How This Guide Will Help You

1. It will reveal how to motivate people to give more generously.
2. It will offer tips for eliminating waste.
3. It will include ways to enjoy better tax advantages for staff compensation.
4. It will provide the latest information on legal challenges.
5. It will suggest ways to attain better accountability. And much more . . .

Volume 1 of this *Guide* is focused on developing a perspective on giving. We will concentrate on "teaching giving" in Volume 2 and "proclaiming the joy of giving" in Volume 3.

A COVENANT WITH THE READERS

The Abingdon Guide to Funding Ministry is committed to:

1. Open dialogue with you. Each of us is a learner and a teacher. We will listen. We will impart. We desire to be co-searchers.

    What are some of your questions, concerns, insights?

    What topics would you like to have addressed?

    What experience, strength, and hope can we share?

2. Providing a leading edge of direction and information on church finance in North America.
3. Being inclusive—theologically and denominationally.
4. Being accessible. We want to hear from you.

   Norma Wimberly
   Donald W. Joiner
   Abingdon Guide to Funding Ministry
   c/o Abingdon Press
   P.O. Box 801
   201 Eighth Avenue South
   Nashville, TN 37202-0801

PART ONE

HELPING CHURCH LEADERS TALK ABOUT GIVING

Building a Perspective on Giving

Introduction

DONALD W. JOINER

"Do not talk about money unless it is absolutely necessary, or until there is a crisis, whichever comes first."

An Unwritten Rule in Many Churches

The way a congregation talks about money, or avoids the subject, is a barometer of its financial health. How we feel about money directs how we respond to financial issues. When you hear a person say, "Our church is always talking about money," or "The only time the church visits is when they want money," the complaint is directed more at *how* a church speaks about money, than about the *frequency* of money talk.

Joe Walker, in *Money in the Church*, says that "there is only one thing more enjoyable than raising money for the Kingdom of God, and that is spending money for the Kingdom of God." One sign that a church is on its way to a healthy financial ministry is that it is beginning to see money not as a "necessary evil," but as a religious tool to accomplish God's purposes.

Everyone, including Murphy, seems to have some kind of law or other. When you hear such principles, you think how simple they are, and how true.

Why didn't I think of it myself? Haven't I heard that somewhere? Joiner's Law is just that simple: "Where the leaders lead, the congregation will follow!" The way church leaders, clergy and lay alike, think and talk about money, will lead the congregation.

> *"What we do for ourselves dies with us— what we do for others remains and is immortal."*
> —ALBERT PIKE

The goal of this part of the *Guide* is to build a base upon which to talk about money, and to encourage church leaders to construct their own "money talk." Brian Bauknight invites church leaders to build a new theology of giving, based not on fund-raising gimmicks, but on what God has done for us through Jesus Christ— that it is an act of discipleship, not a dues-paying collection. Betsy Schwarzentraub picks up on the same theme from First Peter 4:10-11, that we are stewards not merely of money or possessions. We begin by being "stewards of the manifold grace of God."

In "I Hate Money," Dale Stitt puts into words the paradox about money that each of us faces at some time: "I can't live with it and I can't live without it." And David Heetland challenges each of us to develop a theology of stewardship that will direct our journey of faith.

Don McClanen reminds us that all of us are affluent—when compared to someone else. In the last thirty years, North American societies have gone from survival to comfort. What was once a luxury is now a necessity, or a right. How can Christians deal with this affluence, in our own life, as well as with those with whom we are in ministry? At some point, faith values and social values intersect. How are we Christians prepared to deal with that intersection when it dovetails, and when it hints at cultural war?

Ron Reed helps us move from paying bills to being givers. He also points out that the gift carries with it a continued involvement by the giver.

Dan Conway closes Part One by relating stewardship to a Scrooge in the Christmas parable. Your responsibility is to Build a Perspective on Giving. Stewardship talk goes on throughout the year—after the campaign is over, the budget is approved, and there is no upcoming crisis.

 MONEY TALK

An Encouraging Word About Giving

BRIAN BAUKNIGHT

The time has come to approach Christian stewardship in a manner that is distinctively different from the approaches of the past generation. We must make the bold and clear declaration that stewardship is a part of the call and claim of God upon our lives. True stewardship is an act of discipleship. It is a response to the grace and the prompting of God.

True stewardship is not fund-raising. It is not dues paying. It is not well-intended manipulation. It is not charity. It is not an itemized deduction on Schedule A of Form 1040. It is not legalism. And it is not almsgiving. Giving is a response from a growing awareness of God in our lives. It is fundamentally an act of discipleship! Why is it that we are constantly looking for gimmicks in order to raise money for the ministry and mission of the church? The story is told of a special-order offering plate that you can buy:

> **For sale: Hallelujah Offering Plates**
> If you put in $20, it plays the "Hallelujah Chorus." If you put in $5, it rings a bell. If you don't put in anything, it takes your picture!

Avoid gimmicks, because gimmicks prey upon inappropriate forms of self-interest, such as pride or guilt! Instead, treat people as followers or would-be followers of Jesus Christ.

We are living at a time when the next generation apparently hasn't learned about giving in the same way I learned about it. I "caught" Christian giving from my parents, and I caught it very early in life. The experience was highly contagious.

> "Giving to live is, in fact, the only way to live fully. When each of us shares what has been given to us, we gain a new life. If each of us hangs on to what we have, it will never seem enough. Even the richest people in the world think they have to have more if they do not have the habit of sharing what they have. They are letting what they have determine who they are."
> —DOUGLAS M. LAWSON

How do we teach and pass on the theology and practice of giving today? I am quite sure that I do not have all the answers, but I will share a few.

1. No Apology Necessary

Let us not apologize for talking about money in the church. Many of us know friends in ministry who seem to apologize for every money talk given or stewardship sermon preached. It is as though our friends need to say, "I am really sorry for having to talk about this today, but you knew it was coming."

Jesus did *not* say, "I'm really sorry to have to tell you this, but do not lay up for yourselves treasures on earth." Jesus did *not* say, "Now this next statement might offend some of you; and if it does, close your ears. But a person's life does not consist in the abundance of possessions." Jesus did *not* say to the rich young ruler, "I don't mean to offend or unduly complicate your life, but you need to go and sell everything that you have, give to the poor, and then come, follow me."

Jesus talked about money in 16 of the recorded 38 New Testament parables. Jesus spoke five times as often about money and earthly possessions as he did about prayer. A careful researcher can find 500 verses in the Bible on prayer, and a few more than 500 on faith. But more than 2,000 verses in the Bible are concerned with money and possessions.

Clearly, money is a part of our Christian formation. The only subject Jesus mentioned more often than money is the kingdom of God. Surely, however, the kingdom of God and money are in the same general category of spiritual concern. Let us no longer be ashamed to talk about money in the church.

2. Growing Somewhere

Let us help people, in their stewardship journey, grow from wherever they are toward wherever God is calling them. Many people already are trying to find their way in this area. They are looking for help. They are asking to be challenged. They want some direction.

I remember a conversation with a newer member of our congregation a few years ago. I had invited him to a breakfast meeting to talk about his giving to a particular project. I was a bit nervous because I didn't know him well. When he arrived, we exchanged a few pleasantries, and then I said, "I want to talk to you about your giving in relation to the project currently underway at our church."

Before I could get the next sentence formulated, he said, "I am so glad you asked me about that. For some reason, God has given me the ability to make quite a bit of money in the past few years. And I need to be very sure that I use that gift of God appropriately."

We should give people visual images, "steps" they

> "There is a tendency to make money negative if it isn't positive. We need to be careful to make 'security' not negative, threatening. Find other expressions of security; see some form of expression, but realize that the 'form' isn't the way."
> —*ANDY CANALE*
> *Opening Ourselves So God Can Fuss with Us*

can take along the way. We need to help them in their quest to stretch forward. Our people are "straining forward" to that which lies ahead.

It is never high pressure. It is never any kind of bartering for God's favor or an entry pass into heaven. Have you heard the story of a wealthy man who was dying? He called the minister to his home and said, "Preacher, I know I don't have long to live. Do you suppose that if I gave $50,000 to the church, I could get into heaven?" The minister replied, "I don't know; but it's worth a try."

We ought always to be challenging our people toward growth. Somewhere I read a statement, paraphrased like this: The record is clear. Generous givers are typically more spiritually vigorous and happier than those who are not generous. And that record has nothing whatever to do with the size of the gift!

Work for the long haul, not for the immediate need. Our cultivation of stewardship in our people ought not to be for the current budget crisis or for the current year's general operating budget. We are about *discipleship* growth in this church of ours. We are about training troops for the Kingdom.

3. Tithing Is a Spiritual Goal

Let us offer tithing as a spiritual goal. Not as a law! Not as a rule! But as a spiritual goal! We must not back away from guiding our people toward tithing simply because it may cause some discomfort along the way. Let us invite our people to take a step each year toward, or even beyond tithing.

I was very fortunate. I saw and heard about tithing in my childhood home. It was understood from the beginning. There was no big issue made of it. Tithing was simply the way things were.

But most of us do not have that kind of experience. Many people are suspicious and afraid of tithing. So our responsibility as church leaders is to provide stories about those who have learned to tithe.

One man shared his witness about tithing at a Saturday evening service. He did it with grace and humor, and it was a fine statement. He talked about tithing while he and his wife were both employed, and then told how they were able to continue after one of them, and then both, retired. I thanked him.

When we got home from the service that evening, the phone was ringing. "Brian," this same man said, "I forgot to say the most important thing about tithing."

"What was that?" I asked.

"I forgot to say that tithing has taught us to discern the difference between what we need and what we want."

Let us challenge our people toward tithing!

4. Cheerleaders for Good Giving

Let us encourage our people regularly. Let us be cheerleaders for good giving, good stewardship in the church. We tend to hear and speak such discouraging words today about giving in the church.

We tend to put a ceiling upon ourselves. We tend to say, "We can go so far, and no farther." But God puts no ceiling upon us. A noted church consultant has said, "Not one church in a hundred has any notions of its power."

Someone else has said, "God's work done in God's way will always yield God's supply." I believe that.

Do you know what may be the greatest text on stewardship in the New Testament? The words from Ephesians 3:20! In fairly accurate paraphrasing, it reads: "God is able to do far more abundantly through us than we can imagine." The overstated redundancy of Paul's style is very apparent here. Paul often used a string of words to make a key point. That's why the King James Version renders the phrase "far more abundantly" as "exceeding abundantly."

God is able to do exceeding abundantly through us—far more than we think or imagine. I truly believe those words. I trust you do as well.

✝ DEVOTIONAL

I Hate Money

DALE STITT

Like many people, I have a love/hate relationship with money. I know that I need it to provide for my family and cover my expenses. It is really essential when I go to the grocery to purchase food. Even my bank wants chunks of it to apply to the loan I've taken out on the house we live in. Most everywhere I go, even to church, people want some of it.

But I also hate all the worries and complications it brings into my world. Money has an impact on every significant relationship I have. Sometimes I even fight over it. I certainly have to struggle with money issues when negotiating a salary package or determining how much money I want to give to the church during the next calendar year. Sometimes, my worry about money gets in the way of my desire to be compassionate in my response to human suffering.

I love the things money can do in my life; the kind of doors it can open; the places it can take me; the education it provides; the cultural stimulation it makes

"My main philosophy is that my money is a loan from God. I'm in charge of it. I'm responsible for giving some of it away, providing for my family, investing it, and protecting it."

—OREL HERSHISER IV

possible. I love exploring this wonderful world that God has given us to enjoy, yet almost every time I go somewhere to enjoy it, it costs money. It even costs money to cash in one of those hard-earned frequent-flyer coupons.

I've decided that money is one of the paradoxes in life. We cannot live without it. Some of us have a hard time trying to live with it. I've frequently considered the benefits of becoming a Roman Catholic priest, joining an order, and taking a vow of poverty! My priest friends tell me they have never felt more secure or had fewer money worries. Except for some of the obvious limitations (like marriage and family, for example), it sounds wonderful!

But I am not going to become a priest. I must find another way. So what am I doing in order to find a measure of peace with money?

1. I found a place of employment where I can talk about money all the time. My work with Ministry of

Money (a mission of the Church of the Saviour in Washington, D.C.) doesn't make me an expert with money. It does allow me to work with the issue I most need to confront.

2. I now am able to confess the ways I've been confused about money. As they say in Alcoholics Anonymous, moving out of denial is the first step toward health.

3. I must embrace the ways that money is both **very important** and **not important** in my life. I've picked up this distinction from Gordon Cosby, the pastor of Church of the Saviour. For some very good reasons, the paradox about my relationship to money leads to health. Somewhere between the two extremes of important and not important is where truth and health reside.

So, **how is money important** in my life? Obviously, you can add to this list, based on your own experience. *First,* money is needed to live. I need some of it to provide shelter, food, medical care, transportation, and education. Almost everything I need to provide for a human existence costs money. *Second,* it is also a symbol of my worth to the organizations I serve. People show me that they value my time and creative energy by giving me money. *Third,* it provides a measure of security to know that some of my money is invested in health insurance (so that I can see a doctor if something is wrong with me), and there will be some money to pay my expenses when I am no longer able to work. I should pay attention to all these legitimate needs. Any attempt to avoid these realities is a form of denial that destroys the possibilities in my life.

But this is where the power of the paradox comes into play. Just as money is important in all the ways listed above, it is, at the same time, **not all that important.** *First,* even though we need money to live, money cannot guarantee life nor happiness. Money is not life. It just enhances the living of life in ways that really count: being present with our loved ones and nurturing their life and growth; and

paying attention to the inner journey. Money is not a substitute for life itself. *Second,* while it does provide a measure of security for those moments when we cannot provide for ourselves, our ultimate security is not to be found in money. Our ultimate security is to be found in God. That is what I believe Jesus was talking about when he said, "Look at the birds of the air; they neither sow nor reap nor gather into barns, and yet your heavenly Father feeds them. Are you not of more value than they?" (Matt. 6:26).

Third, our ultimate value can never be measured by what we earn or have accumulated. The current system of paying people for their labor based on some measure of their worth is ultimately bankrupt.

In my experience, the people who contribute most to the health of our society frequently are paid the least for their time and labor.

I have learned much about money from some of the people who have the least of it. We label these people *poor.* I have been privileged to spend significant time with "the poor," and in the process have developed several wonderful friendships. As friendships blossom, I have discovered an incredible freedom and joy in many of their lives. While their need for money is greater than mine, they are able to hold on to it loosely, realizing that they are only stewards of the resource: The money doesn't belong to them. If someone has a greater need for it, they are willing to pass it on.

They hang on to their money lightly. How much richer our world would be if all of us could learn this lesson!

And even with all the above in place, I still worry. I still struggle for my serenity about money. I still need to go to meetings (in this case the meeting that means most to me is Sunday morning worship) where I can confess my brokenness about the worship of money and find healing and encouragement. I know that I cannot serve two masters.

I want to serve God, not money.

> "Money, neutral or demonic? Both may be true. Jesus' statement about serving two masters is just a statement of fact."
>
> —*ANDY CANALE*

"Dealing with money is an individual issue which we come to every moment with an openness and freshness to learn. Who has the most pain, the wealthy or the poor? The wealthy are so used to being used, they can't accept 'gifts' . . . the power that gifts have. Look at the 'we' psychology of Fritz Kunkel—creative ego response—we know when we 'light up,' respond creatively—Jesus never repeated himself—we need to remember that willingness to take creative steps—we don't have answers, only willingness—**enter** into the 'I don't know' relationship with others. *Then God can fuss with us,* and that's an incarnational sentence to me!"

—*ANDY CANALE*
Opening Ourselves So God Can Fuss with Us

 DEVOTIONAL

Stewards of God's Grace

I Peter 4:10-11

BETSY SCHWARZENTRAUB

We are "good stewards of the manifold grace of God"—what an odd phrase! At times you may think of yourself as a steward of things, especially of money—but not very often as a steward of God's grace!

Yet the bedrock of our lives is grace. Despite how hard you and I have worked, how deeply we are committed to providing for those we love, and how dedicated we are to helping people along the way, the fact remains: We own nothing. We have nothing by our own efforts. Our entire lives are gifts from God. And these gifts are not trivial, from a Christian point of view, because every breath we receive and exhale is a sign of grace, a continual gift of life for us.

So there's a purpose to our stewardship. God does not expect the kind of sacrifice that takes place during war, such as D-Day on the beach, nor does God expect us to pursue a perpetual repetition of the cross. God wants us to have an abundant life that spills over with joy and fullness, through our giving and receiving. So the purpose of our stewardship is to glorify God in all things, through Jesus Christ. It's not a matter of giving 10 percent but of responding with 100 percent of who we are and what we do.

Good stewardship begins with the mystery of the Triune God. All around us, we see God's activity, in whatever is life-giving, whatever is life-saving, whatever is life-fulfilling.

We know God's manifold grace through God's ongoing creation. In response to God's creative love, we give of what we have been given: time, talent, possessions, and care for our cosmic home.

God's redeeming love continually saves and heals us from our own killing tendencies to play god. For some crazy reason, God has chosen to invest in human life, despite our broken covenants. So we are stewards also of the Good News itself.

As God fulfills us, we receive individual spiritual gifts to build up the church, in this specific time and place. But the entire Christian community is a gift as well, as a community of stewards to reconcile a needy, bleeding world.

As we come to consecrate our commitments to God through the church, we give back the time, money, and individual gifts we can offer for our common ministry. It is a small thing in God's cosmic scheme, in a way—but also a very great thing! God has chosen to create and sustain us, to love and redeem us, and to empower and fulfill us! You and I are the only ones who can love God fully in return, in our unique and cherished way. It is upon this foundation of steward-ship—whatever we do with the gospel in our lives—that we can be the community of stewards that God has called us to be.

 # SMALL GROUP STUDY

Caretakers of God's Undeserved Love
Responsible Handlers of Grace
DAVID HEETLAND

Leader's Introduction

I find that a theology of stewardship increasingly influences my work. I am attracted to the words in First Peter 4:10, as a wonderful summary of what I'd like my ministry in this congregation to be: We are to be "good stewards of God's varied grace" (RSV). Or, as stated in other versions, we are called to be "responsible handlers," "good managers," or "faithful dispensers of the magnificently varied grace of God." If I had to put it in my own words I would say we are called to be caretakers of God's undeserved love. Our calling is not simply to receive God's undeserved love for ourselves, but to demonstrate God's caring love to all of creation.

This, of course, has wide-ranging implications for every aspect of our lives—how, as caretakers, we "take care" of our environment, our bodies, our sisters and brothers, our time, our talents, our treasure. A theology of stewardship should be understood in the broadest possible terms, if it is to have the necessary power to change lives. This small-group study deals with only one aspect of stewardship: financial resources.

1. How a theology of stewardship influences work.

First, a theology of stewardship helps you see each person as a child of God. Each person is a whole person, an important part of God's creation, regardless of financial resources. He or she is not a means to an end, someone to be manipulated for some "greater purpose." A theology of stewardship reminds you that persons should not be regarded or referred to as "Mrs. Bigbucks" or "Mr. Deeppockets," but as full human beings, who may have the gift of financial resources along with many other varied gifts.

Second, a theology of stewardship invites you to know and appreciate these people in their fullness, so that you can be a more responsible caretaker of their gifts. A theology of stewardship encourages you to develop relationships of mutual care and respect for all God's creation. Thus, your relationship with persons is not so much a one-shot attempt to "get a gift" as a long-term commitment to know others as persons, with their own unique needs and aspirations. It is only when you come to understand their hopes and values as fully as possible that you can be a "good manager of God's different gifts," bringing together the dreams of individuals and the goals of an institution.

Third, a theology of stewardship helps you understand your role. You are not a "professional beggar" whose job is to extricate a gift from an unwilling donor, but rather a leader whose vocation is to provide opportunities and invite responses. Some observers suggest that lack of financial resources is the major impediment to eradicating hunger, developing self-help programs, and spreading the gospel of Jesus Christ. What could be more rewarding than being "faithful dispensers of the magnificently varied grace of God," helping to provide adequate resources to enable ministries of relief, development, and proclamation to be carried out in Christ's name?

The invitation extended to persons is more than an invitation to glorify God and serve neighbor. It is also an invitation to find personal fulfillment by investing ourselves in something greater than ourselves. As we grow in our giving, we often discover that we also grow spiritually, with our lives taking on new purpose and meaning.

Fourth, a theology of stewardship helps you recognize that if you are to be a "responsible handler of God's many-sided grace" your invitations to give must reflect God's own nature. Such invitations, in other words, should reflect genuine care for the donor, which obviously is evident in compassion, integrity, and honesty. Your motives should not reflect greed, fear, or guilt—even though there may be a strong temptation to imitate the secular culture that attempts to use these psychological needs.

No doubt your ministry is influenced by a similar understanding of stewardship. However, we all know leaders who want nothing to do with the stewardship of financial resources. These persons look at the development of financial resources as dirty work, something beneath their calling and less important than other ministerial tasks. Such an attitude is based on the misuse of money in our culture, but we cannot avoid the task, especially given Jesus' own emphasis on the subject. But the danger of lost ministry is much greater when church leaders fail to develop a theology of stewardship that places a high priority on the stewardship of financial resources.

DISCUSSION QUESTIONS

1. How do you feel about the wealthiest persons in your congregation?

2. Do you find it difficult to talk about money?

3. Think of and discuss some occasions when you were influenced to buy something because it appealed to your guilt. Your greed? Your fears?

4. Think of and discuss a time when you gave to a church cause out of guilt or fear.

5. More than 2,000 verses in the Bible are related to money, property, or possessions. Read the following texts and discuss the implications for your study group.

Text 1—II Corinthians 8:1-4

Text 2—Malachi 3:6-12

Text 3—II Corinthians 9:7-10

---

2. When Leaders Despise Money

First and foremost, the work of the church is diminished. The church has barely tapped its full financial potential—largely because people in the church have not been adequately informed, inspired, or invited to give. Some sobering research from empty tomb, inc. (see "Discipleship for Affluent Churches" in part 7), suggests that while the incomes of church members are rising, the percentage given to the church is declining. We church leaders should face the fact that we have played a role in this decline by abdicating our role as strong leaders in financial stewardship. One can only wonder what the profound positive impact on the mission of the church would be if we began to take our stewardship more seriously.

Second, we miss opportunities for spiritual growth. Many church people do not see their pattern of giving as related in any meaningful way to their own spiritual growth. An essential part of the Christian message, however, proclaims that the two are intricately related. When this message is not taught boldly and with conviction, we often are not motivated to grow in our giving, and an important part of our spiritual growth is stunted.

Third, the lack of church leaders willing to emphasize financial stewardship creates a vacuum which is quickly filled by charlatans. Such persons do not seek gifts based on God-given reasons for stewardship. Rather, they prey on the unwary and unwise, using tactics of manipulation and coercion, seeking to motivate gifts through guilt, greed, and fear. Several examples in recent years remind us all that such charlatans exist, and that, regrettably, people respond. Again, one can only wonder whether the givers would be so prone to respond if they were grounded in a strong theology of stewardship? Thus we contribute to the effectiveness of charlatans by not leading people to understand the reasons for their gifts.

Why is it that some leaders recognize the importance of financial stewardship and provide exemplary leadership in this area, while others want nothing to do with it? One important reason for the difference in attitude and ability can be traced directly to training in stewardship. Those who have had strong training in stewardship tend to be strong leaders, and those who have had weak or no training tend to be weak leaders in a congregation.

Thus, the follow-up question becomes, "How do we receive such training?" Stewardship training is a long-term process, rather than a one-time event. One comprehensive stewardship program was called a "Twenty-Year Program of Stewardship Training," which probably is realistic, if we are expecting to develop committed leadership.

Reading in the area of stewardship can be part of a long-term education process. (See Part Nine in this *Guide* for a list of books and resources.)

Stewardship education should provide opportunities to practice stewardship. This may well be the most important—and the most difficult to implement. We all know that we learn best by doing, rather than by simply hearing, and that we are most likely to make changes in our lives if we are supported by others who are making similar changes. Thus, the communities in which we live and work should provide daily opportunities for us to practice—as well as discuss—stewardship. Covenant groups and action groups can be developed to help us prophetically address what it means to be a steward in today's world.

Perhaps our most important responsibility is to raise awareness of what it means to be a responsible steward. If we can continue growing in the area of stewardship ourselves, we will, I think, nurture a people who are more committed and effective in their stewardship. I can think of no greater gift that we could give the church.

Discussion Questions

1. Have you ever given money to a ministry, and then later felt that you had been deceived?

2. When do you think you have given enough of your resources to grow spiritually?

3. If you have ever tithed (given 10 percent of your income), describe what happened to your lifestyle.

4. Has your percentage of giving (your annual contributions divided by your annual income) risen in the last five years, or decreased?

To provoke discussion, have each person in the study group write last year's percentage of giving on a slip of paper, collect the anonymous slips, and make a chart of percentages, based on last year's contributions in your study group. Average it, and discuss.

5. Do you think Christians should be afraid to disclose their monetary wealth when in the presence of other Christians? Why do we keep such matters private? Why do we expect government-paid workers (e.g., educators and police) and politicians to disclose their income publicly? (See article by Don McClanen below, to stimulate discussion).

 MONEY TALK

Ministering to Affluent Persons

DON McCLANEN

We can help people who are unwittingly trapped and crippled by affluence to move into freedom, joy, and a growing self-giving, only after we can comfortably acknowledge our own wealth. Too often, we limit stewardship to the "giving of money," failing to see that the giving follows from our enlightened understanding that we are holistic stewards of all that has been entrusted to us. In fact, money is but one small piece of the pie of holistic stewardship. Because money and our use of it are such visible portions of life, we can learn to use money as a tool for growth in discipleship, to minister to wealthy people. Stewardship is then an exciting and challenging adventure.

1. Money Forms Identity

We need to understand that money is in itself neither a disease nor a cure. Rather, money and our use of it reflect our innermost values and choices; money forms our very identity. The possession of large amounts of money simply magnifies our total makeup. Wealthy persons have problems common to all economic levels, but the effects may be more dramatized, complex, and far-reaching.

The best way to understand our wealth, then, is to understand ourselves, our own attitudes, feelings, and values concerning money. Even those of us in other economic levels are defensive and easily threatened when the conversation turns to money—a taboo subject. Until we can deal with and freely discuss our own finances, we can hardly expect persons of greater affluence to do so.

2. Align Money with God's Order

For pastors and church leaders, the key problem of stewardship is not how to motivate people to give more, but rather, how to help them develop into disciples who, in gratitude, compassion, and justice, are eager to align their money with the needs of God's created order.

> "Money is like an arm or a leg. Use it or lose it."
> —HENRY FORD
> *New York Times*

In a word, fund-raising, or "putting the bite on" people and making them like it, is not the issue. That is precisely the problem when we equate stewardship with giving, making it seem sterile and dull, on the one hand, and manipulative, on the other. When we speak of stewardship, but in effect we are actually looking for money to underwrite the budget, we are the very people the rich defend themselves against.

Few persons become truly wealthy without developing sensitive radar equipment against being used. A fresh look at our past relationships with persons of wealth, from whom we sought funds, may lead us to a healthy confession that we have sometimes made the raising of money, rather than the enlistment of persons, the central issue.

The real issue is how to begin with ourselves and our money—how to see money as a vital and exciting means of personal growth and ministry, not as a finite resource to be acquired and protected. Then we will not need more "up-to-date techniques" for motivating the affluent to give. Instead, we will have new freedom and changed lives, which will enable us to reach out to others, who, despite their extraordinary prosperity, are immobilized and unfulfilled.

3. The Support System

When we accept the serious challenge to change our way of working with money and affluence, a support system is essential. A role model, very likely the pastor or lay leader who offers example and encouragement, is crucial for sustaining growth over the long term. A community (whether another person, a group, or a church) must provide both support and confrontation.

Remember that sudden inspirations or insights concerning money can quickly cool and fade because of the resistance in this fortresslike area of our lives. Also, be aware that to be converted of soul may leave the pocketbook essentially unchanged. A very real second conversion, involving our money and possessions, is necessary.

The sustained encouragement, and even gentle confrontation of a trusted group or person, help us to grow in our relations toward money and toward one another. A place where our feelings can be shared, honest fears admitted, and others' responses heard, builds relationships that free us to see our wealth and make a response. More significant than our growing freedom with money, however, is our growing spiritual life. Working with money is primarily a spiritual challenge: The more mechanical processes, such as giving money or simplifying lifestyle, follow authentically from a life of discipleship.

4. Breaking Our Shell

Special nurturing in the areas of gratitude, compassion, and justice is also essential to awaken us. Because the issue of money is both exceedingly difficult and tricky, we need to integrate the varied ways of working with it. For example, although the biblical aspect is a vital focus, it cannot be separated from getting in touch with and owning our emotional response (guilt, fear, insecurity) as we deal with money. Furthermore, our growing understanding of God's Word and of our own relation to money must expand to include a sociological dimension—the global impact of money. Only then, with this broad base of enlightened stewardship, can we look at the mechanical dimensions traditionally associated with stewardship (giving a tithe, determining assets/liabilities, writing a will, establishing endowments) from a freer and more joyful perspective.

To grow in a spirit of gratitude, we must understand what wealth is and how each of us measures it in relative terms. For example, Mother Teresa ministers to the "poorest of the poor," people with no family, job, housing, health care, not even a place to die. In the United States, we are aware of another level of poverty, an existence that is often substandard but does give the "ordinary poor" limited access to income assistance, housing, food, or health care.

For a basic awakening of gratitude, we who have access to jobs, housing, food, and health care must be able to say that we are indeed fortunate, indeed "wealthy." It is another important step for those who have more than sufficient income, housing, investments, and possessions to acknowledge that they are the "wealthiest of the wealthy." To deny our wealth status (wherever it lies) is to avoid reality and to deceive ourselves, preventing our growth, freedom,

and gratitude. Yet, as the Bible warns us, our hearts are "desperately corrupt" (Jer. 17:9 RSV).

Denying our wealth in turn suppresses our spontaneous gratitude to God for all that has been given to us. By viewing our wealth as resources we have earned and deserved, we cut ourselves off from being part of the totality of God's creation, and we build a shell of isolation around our hearts. Our materialistic, consumer-oriented, narcissistic society encourages us to live within this shell and focus on ourselves, oblivious to the needs of others and to our own real needs. Our souls wither. Stewardship becomes a nagging drag. Money, which is so all-pervasive in our daily lives, becomes a taboo; we talk about it only in secular terms of getting, not giving.

This shell of isolation must be shattered before compassion can begin to grow. The most effective way to break out of this shell is to touch the reality of poverty. The tougher the shell, the more dramatic that reality must be. Working alongside Mother Teresa's Sisters in Calcutta or visiting the refugee camps in Thailand can break open the shell. So can walking through an inner-city neighborhood, visiting the local jail, or volunteering at a soup kitchen. Being in the midst of such unsolvable despair brings home the gratitude for life that explodes the shell and opens our hearts to compassion.

Strengthened by the new security of gratitude (seeing and believing how much God has given us) and softened by new pockets of compassion (seeing and believing others' great needs), we begin to comprehend justice. Now knowing the world as a global community in which all people are interrelated as brothers and sisters, we feel the suffering of war-torn Latin America, unemployed America, and starving Africa as our own. We also become aware of the role that money plays in inflicting this pain and the role money can play in healing it. Our response in generous, just, and compassionate giving then follows authentically.

5. Giving Follows

Once the degree of gratitude, compassion, and justice has grown strong enough to replace the old insecurity, isolation, fear, and greed, giving follows spontaneously. But for the wealthy, giving presents a unique problem.

Wealthy people may say, in all sincerity, that they cannot afford to give significantly. Typically, their resources are tied up in land, stocks, and other investments not readily available. They have surrounded themselves with lawyers, accountants, and advisors who confirm their accumulation. Also, they often take a limited salary from their business, turning the rest of their income (profit) back into the business. From a balance sheet of income and expenses, a wealthy person may believe that generous giving is out of the question. Yet they have failed to tap their vast resources.

Part of the nurturing of spiritual growth, then, is helping wealthy people to see the many options of stewardship inherent in their wealth—not only the magnitude of assets but the creative ways to use those resources must be realized. For example, the businessman who owns four hardware stores in the city may be helped to understand that he has options other than simply selling one store in order to have liquid assets to donate. Possibilities abound—providing jobs more creatively, managing a neighborhood center as well as a business, exploring new management practices and employing the poor, considering equal salaries and rotational managers—but he may never see these possibilities. The pastor or lay leader can initiate the dreaming, brainstorming, prayer, and support necessary to enable a wealthy person to make more resources available.

Stewardship, then, far more than just the giving of money, is a pastoral and lay ministry. The holistic sense of stewardship lies like a "diamond in the rough," waiting to be developed. Counseling a couple in anguish and disagreement over money and tithing is just as much a duty and opportunity as ministering to the couple about their prayer life or other marital problems. Preparation for this vital ministry begins with our own growth, enabling us to lead and nurture others into awakening gratitude, compassion, and justice. The money then given may appear to be the same product as traditional fund-raising stewardship, but in truth, the ultimate result is a new inside-out freedom and salvation in Jesus Christ, as Lord of all!

Now I want to tell you what God in his grace has done for the churches in Macedonia.

Though they have been going through much trouble and hard times, they have mixed their wonderful joy with their deep poverty, and the result has been an overflow of giving to others. They gave not only what they could afford, but far more; and I can testify that they did it because they wanted to, and not because of nagging on my part. They begged us to take the money so they could share in the joy of helping the Christians in Jerusalem. (II CORINTHIANS 8:1-4 LB)

"Money inevitably causes guilt. Let's deal directly with guilt; darkness and evil can attack us there if we don't understand this consciously. In becoming free, we need to examine all aspects. For example, we tend to use money terms to define feelings, 'I feel poorly,' when we mean we feel valueless/worthless. Tap into feelings of value rather than into guilt. Play with the words we use; move into the imagining of richness; focus on the abundance God has given to us, rather than the consumer/competitive/materialistic words the world uses to tell us we haven't enough. Even John D. Rockefeller, when asked how much is enough, answered, 'Just a little bit more.' And, of course, you must respect the donor's right to say 'yes' or 'no' to the invitation."

—ANDY CANALE
Opening Ourselves So God Can Fuss with Us

NEWSLETTER DEVOTIONAL

Seeing Myself As a Giver

RONALD REED

Some years ago, while I was living in Philadelphia and commuting to New York, where I worked in stewardship education for The Episcopal Church, I came upon a big problem about myself and giving. Here is what happened.

For some reason I had worn a clergy shirt and round collar on the train to New York that day.

After I got off the train at Penn Station, I needed to use "the necessary." This was before the remodeling of Penn Station, and to go downstairs to the men's room was roughly the equivalent of entering Dante's Inferno, where the banner read "Abandon All Hope, Ye Who Enter Here." It was dirty and noisy, crowded with bums and other unsavory characters. The problem was that I, as they say, couldn't wait or suffer the public consequences. So down into hell I went.

Toward my destination I walked, all starched up in my natty clergy attire, as a group of the homeless ones stood, hands out for some change. Approaching them, I did what I call my "crab" walk, moving my feet straight ahead while my eyes, head, and arms seemed to be going another direction. This was intended to avoid any contact whatsoever with these guys. Whisking into the men's room, I did the job and started back out, still

> ## "In the fabric of gratitude are woven the threads of unselfishness."
> —STEVEN VITRANO

"crab" walking. Unfortunately, for one brief (if seemingly eternal) moment, I did make eye contact with a young African American whose hand was held out.

He looked at me, no doubt discerning my fear of him, and moved his outstretched hand up in a wave, saying, "Have a good day, Father!"

Needless to say, the remainder of the day was not good. I felt awful, guilty, convicted of my inhumanity toward these and the other street people. Here I was, just like a biblical temple priest, strutting around Jerusalem in disregard of, if not out-and-out contempt for, the beggars. It was a pretty sorry image I had of myself. Consciously, out of fear and concern for the efficiency of my commuting day and having such an important position in the church, I had failed to even acknowledge another human being, let alone give a helping hand of some sort. I really felt convicted by an angel of God visiting me as a street person.

My decision was to confess this sin of mine to God and find a way to make amends by planning for future encounters. After some prayer and reflection, I simply resolved to follow Jesus' words: "Ask and ye shall have . . . ."

> I figured, "Well, if I am asked, I will give whatever comes not out of my pocket but out of my wallet."

From then on, whenever I was asked, I did not count the cost, but merely pulled out dollars from my wallet.

The effect was both wonderful and interesting. I felt liberated from my guilt. I began to look into the faces of the recipients of my charity, and even engage them in some conversations. Soon I started having some fun with the giving, for I had completely lost my worries about "what those people did with my money." I just gave when asked.

Something else began to happen. As a reforming giver, I began to find that my actions raised new questions and possibilities. If it felt so good and pleasant to give when I was asked, what would happen if I gave *before* being asked? I was beginning what later dawned on me as a deep spiritual recognition—that life can become a wonderful experiment for a giving person. New and interesting behaviors can be investigated, if you are not trying to hold on to your money.

I began to think more about Jesus' behavior and how I might learn from him and his stories in the New Testament. Did he count the cost of giving? Well, if he did, he still gave it all away, his life included. And why? Because he, like his God, came to save us sinners. Why couldn't I give not only my tithe in church, but also my gift right on the street corner, sort of like Jesus?

Finally, the right opportunity came. Late one day, I walked from my apartment in Philadelphia down to South Street to see a friend. It was dusky outside, the light at that special time when magic does seem to happen, when the spirit of the day gives over to the spirit of the night. Maybe I felt the mood of something special soon to take place, a little hint that the eternal was coming through to me. Then it happened.

Just as I was about to knock on my friend's apartment door, a shadowy figure across the street came to my attention. An old man walked out from the dark recesses, he himself being of dark complexion and wearing drab clothes, and in the light from a sign, I saw that this man was totally blind, no eyes in his skull's sockets. He walked with a cane, shuffling up the street, totally oblivious to my existence. The time had come.

I could not resist the urge to walk over and carry out with this man my experiment in giving. I would give him money without his even being able to see me. Rushing over, making my excuses to stop him, I grabbed some money from my billfold, took his hand, gave him the money between his hand and mine, and said, "Please, sir, this money is for you just because I want you to have it."

He said, "Oh, thank you, how nice." Then he said something quite simple, which, for me, became profoundly important: "What is your name?"

And I said, "Ron, and what's yours?"

"Jake," was his answer.

We talked a little longer until, realizing the time, I announced, "Jake, I guess I'd better go. My friend across the street is expecting me."

Jake replied, "Yes, and thank you again. God bless you."

I responded, "And God bless you, Jake."

He said, "I'll pray for you, Ron."

I answered, "Thank you, Jake, I need your prayers. Good-bye."

I crossed the street, then turned around and discovered the strange humor and irony of the situation: We had been standing under a lighted sign, advertising one of my favorite eating spots in Philadelphia —Ron's Barbecue Pit. That's the truth.

God gave us two hands: One to receive with and one to give with.

Had I only walked across the street? Or had I walked from here to eternity and back? I knew my little experiment in giving had taken me a greater distance than I could ever have imagined. In the few weeks that followed, I began to think more deeply about what had happened in that short encounter. There occurred to me some profound meaning in Jake's simple question, "What's your name?" as I thought over God's lesson for us in Genesis, concerning the naming of things and people. Naming is creating, giving life by identifying something as uniquely personal and individual. I thought about how we name persons to be baptized and, in so doing, identify them with Christ in his baptism, death, and resurrection. "Ron, and what's yours?" Jake was his name. What special something had we given each other?

Then it came to me, the zinger of all the spiritual thoughts and emotions brought on by the conversation. As we departed, Jake had offered, "I'll pray for you, Ron." "Thank you, Jake, I need your prayers." You see, I was the rich man, dispensing money from my excess to those in need. Or am I so rich after all? And what of poor Jake? He was so rich in prayers that he had some to give away to me. Yet he couldn't even see to whom he was giving these precious prayers. Who was rich, and who was poor? Who was blind, and who could see?

Having asked all these questions, the most serious answer of all came to me. At last I realized that peeling away the layers to expose the heart of this experience exposed a soulful reality. God really doesn't care who is giving and who is receiving. God only cares that we love one another as God has loved us, without reference to condition or position. Seeing myself and others as God's children—that's what it's all about.

NEWSLETTER DEVOTIONAL

Everybody's After a Buck

Acts 2:45

JACK & LYNDA JOHNSON-HILL

We have grown up hearing it: "Everybody's after a buck!" and "Money may not be the most important thing, but it's way ahead of what's in second place." As missionary educators in the Fiji Islands, we can attest to the fact that there are places in the world where people's values are different.

Here is Jack's tale about an experience that he and a Tongan colleague recently had while teaching in Kosrae, a remote island in Micronesia:

"After eating lunch at one of the island's few restaurants, Toa and I pondered whether we should tip the waitress. Tipping is considered rude in the Pacific Islands, but Micronesia has been influenced by American values. Better to tip and risk embarrassment, we decided. Toa put down a dollar. It was returned with a smile.

"On the way to the church where we were teaching, we stopped at a roadside fruit stand to buy some limes. A young woman gathered up the 15 or 20 limes she had left and handed them to Toa.

"When he asked, 'How much?' and extracted his dollar, she waved him off.

" 'These are old limes,' she said. 'They are too small. I couldn't take money for them!' "

Everybody's after a buck? No, not everyone; not yet. We have been impressed, as well as humbled, by the spirit of giving and sharing that is normative throughout the Pacific. In Fiji, it is called *keri-keri*. People in rural villages take for granted that "what is mine is yours." Malaysians call it *wantok*. The one who earns the money expects to support the whole family and all the friends who are not earning money.

What is the significance of keri-keri for us Christians in North America? In our highly individualistic society, what is mine is mine. We've worked hard to accumulate things, and sometimes it seems as if a host of forces is conspiring to take them away from us. Yet, living in Fiji, we are jolted by how large the gap really is between those of us who are comfortable and the majority here. It may sound trite, but it's also true that though the majority has almost nothing, they willingly share even the little they have.

MONEY TALK

A Stewardship Carol for Christmas

DAN CONWAY

We all remember the scene from old movies and TV specials. Two "portly gentlemen," as Charles Dickens calls them, enter the offices of Scrooge & Marley, hoping to raise money "for the poor and destitute who suffer greatly at the present time of year."

They make their case, pointing out that "hundreds of thousands are in want of common comforts," but Scrooge is not impressed.

"Are there no prisons?" the old miser asks. "Aren't the workhouses still in operation?" he snarls.

"Yes," one of the gentlemen replies, "I wish I could say they were not." Undaunted, the two gentlemen continue. "What shall we put you down for?"

"Nothing!" says Scrooge.

"You wish to be anonymous?" the gentlemen ask.

"I wish to be left alone!" says Scrooge.

The gentlemen leave with hearts full of sadness. They grieve for the poor and the homeless "who would rather die" than suffer the humiliation of a nineteenth-century English workhouse; but they also grieve for old Ebenezer Scrooge, whose self-centered misery has blinded him to the simple joys of Christmas.

How many times have we heard similar versions of this same old story? How many times have we found ourselves playing the part of Scrooge—saying to those who ask for our time or our money, "Please don't bother me. I wish to be left alone"?

Though he never uses the word, Charles Dickens' wonderful story, *A Christmas Carol,* is about stewardship. It is about the joy of giving and about learning to care for (and be responsible for) all of God's creation. And, as Mr. Dickens makes very clear, *A Christmas Carol* is about much more than just the sentimental (or commercial!) "Christmas spirit" that comes and goes each holiday season.

Scrooge is not a good steward. He hoards what he has been given (time, talent, and treasure), and he buries his gifts deep within himself. He cannot give or share, and the result is a twisted, self-absorbed misery. Along with his gifts and talents, Scrooge accumulates and hides all the hurts, resentments, and disappointments of a lonely lifetime. In the end, nothing makes him happy. Nothing gives him peace.

Only one thing can save this miserable old man from the hell he has made for himself. *Giving.* Open, generous, unrestricted giving is the only cure for the likes of Ebenezer Scrooge. As long as he holds back—asking "What's in it for me?"—Scrooge is condemned to live the life he has fashioned for himself through many years of lonely self-centeredness.

Fortunately, Mr. Dickens believed in a God who is generous and forgiving. Old Scrooge is given one last chance to experience life as it is truly meant to be lived. The spirits who visit Scrooge (including Jacob Marley, a former business partner now condemned to haunt the spirit world in chains of his own making) help Scrooge to face painful truths about himself. And by caring enough to confront him with his selfishness, the spirits give Scrooge something far more valuable than all his gold; they give him a glimpse of who he was, who he is now, and who he could become—if only he would let go of his bitter resentment and embrace the joy of giving.

Recall that following his change of heart, as he hurries to join his nephew's family for Christmas dinner, Scrooge encounters one of the two "portly gentlemen" who had asked him for a contribution the day before. After greeting the gentleman so warmly that the man barely recognized the old miser, Scrooge whispers in his ear the amount of his pledge to help the poor and destitute.

"My dear Mr. Scrooge, are you serious?" cries the gentleman, as if his breath were taken away.

"Not a farthing less," says Scrooge. "A great many back-payments are included in it, I assure you. Will you do me that favor?" he pleads.

And then the most amazing thing happens. As the astounded solicitor tries to express his gratitude, stammering from both appreciation and disbelief, old Scrooge says it for him.

"Thank you," says Scrooge. "I am much obliged to you. I thank you fifty times. Bless you!"

In *A Christmas Carol,* Dickens wants each of us to discover what old Scrooge had to learn the hard way: The only way to hold on to something is to give it away. This is the paradox of giving: The one who gives (from substance and without counting the cost) is the one who is most grateful. Besides being a donor, the generous person is also a beneficiary. That's why Scrooge says, "I thank you fifty times," and also why he asks the gentleman, quite sincerely, to do him a favor by accepting the gift.

Ever afterward, Mr. Dickens says, it was said of Scrooge "that he knew how to keep Christmas well." Like any good steward, Scrooge kept it well by giving it away. And so, as Mr. Dickens observes at the conclusion of his story, "May that be truly said of us . . . every one!"

PART TWO

FOR PASTORS AND WORSHIP TEAMS

Introduction

NORMA WIMBERLY

A pastor is called to be the spiritual leader of a congregation, in matters of the spirit, of service, and of sharing. The congregation and community perceive, as well as observe, the manner in which spiritual leadership is lived out. That leadership is often planned with the help of the persons who form the worship team in a congregation.

How can the pastor help others to develop a generous perspective on giving, to grow in generosity, to affect change in the worshiping community, and in the regional culture? Practicing faithful stewardship in the context of worship; preaching and talking about giving, and writing about it in all available vehicles for communication; counseling those who seek to live as wise stewards; using the Scriptures as the basic resource; and believing in the power of bold prayer—all are tools offered to the pastor.

I believe that a pastor who uses these tools daily, one who offers a variety of opportunities for response to God by giving and serving, has taken a giant first step toward helping others realize that all areas of spiritual growth are ongoing in a process. For dramatic change, however, one also needs to be continually evaluating one's own life, way of living, accumulation of resources, and use of time. As we remember where we came from and assess where we are now, we can sow the seeds of faithful stewardship "extravagantly."

John Bannerman, a pastor with the Presbyterian Church of Canada, told us of an experience with his small daughter as a reminder of the need for pastors to sow extravagantly: John and his family had moved to a new pastor's residence. There was a patch of lawn which should be reseeded. Having purchased the grass seed, John proceeded to sprinkle seed in the bare area of lawn. His daughter, watching her father very carefully, reached into the bag of seed, clutched two handfuls, and spread the seed on the ground thickly. John scolded her. Later that spring, however, new grass was growing only where that little girl had sown so "extravagantly."

Praise God that people don't always do as they are led! What if pastors reach in with both fists, grab the tools that are available, and sow "extravagantly" as spiritual leaders!

In Part Two, Ralph Taylor recalls the ways his first congregations helped him to develop a healthy stewardship perspective. The vital role of stewardship in the context of worship is outlined by Thomas Rieke and William Miller, with Patricia Wilson-Kastner offering a deepened view of the stewardship elements in Holy Communion.

A sermon outline by Betsy Schwarzentraub serves as an example of the possible exegetical rewards of examining scripture through the lens of stewardship. A complete sermon by Ken Gallinger reminds us that however we approach or avoid money issues, we respond to a trust that God has shared with us.

More sermon outlines, two chancel dramas, offertory prayers, an outline for a more dynamic offertory time, examples of newsletter material, and several prayers, as well as specific ways to encourage planned gifts, complete this section.

Pastors, worship leaders, and worship committees are encouraged to use the selections for information, for encouragement, as motivation for personal reflection, and as suggestions that lead to more ways to "sow extravagantly."

 MEDITATION

A Stumbling Steward

11 Lessons Learned on the Job

WM. RALPH TAYLOR

This feels like the September essay you knew was coming when school started, "What I Did on My Summer Vacation." Back then it was a chore that had to be completed as soon as possible, with as little fuss as possible, to gain as much ground as possible with the new teacher—a new teacher you didn't know because your father worked for the railway and you had moved again that year. Everything was new.

Many pastors approach stewardship with the same sense of duty. It has to be done. It is new every year. You must get as much as possible with as little fuss as possible. You may not have had any past lessons in this subject, just as nobody told you what to do with summer. If you remember your training in seminary, you may have had one afternoon Practical Theology class on the offering.

That class probably contained several cautions: be careful with it; don't expose yourself to unnecessary risks; if someone wants to give to the church when you are out visiting, have them put it in an envelope, sign their name, and make sure it goes directly to the treasurer. And, oh yes, when you announce the offering, do it with some dignity, as befits the occasion. A prayer of dedication is expected and appropriate, along with a doxology.

I also seem to remember some things being said about your own offering. "Set an example" was the way I remember hearing it. (This happened in the first-year class, when you were being instructed how to conduct public worship, and what order you should follow.) From what I have heard from other travelers in the ministry, I may have had quite a bit of instruction. Of course, when I went to school, the assumption was that you had experienced a "Christian family upbringing," which included discussions about regular support of the church!

Well, away I went to my first full-time pastorate, a circuit that, within the first year, grew to eleven small rural churches. It was exciting. My spouse, who had supported us as I completed the last two years of seminary, did not expect to find employment, and we planned to continue with one income. We also planned on making some regular payments on the car loan and my student loan. We budgeted our offering to be an example by looking up, on the last financial statement of the pastoral charge, the list of contributors and the amounts they gave. We did what it took to be in the top 5 percent!

Unexpected lessons in management and stewardship soon started. At the end of the first month, I was invited to drop by the treasurer's house. It was to be payday and, as we were a little anxious to pay the bills, I went promptly. When I arrived, the treasurer went to a spare bedroom, pulled out a sturdy cardboard box from beneath the bed, and placed it on his dining-room table. He then showed me some

numbers on a slip of paper: gross minus pension, minus tax, minus health insurance, minus this and minus that, plus travel, equals net. Who was I to confront the powers of high finance? The net was then produced from the sturdy cardboard box, with a running total called out as each contribution envelope was examined as to what was written in the space provided: $1.15 + $1.00 = $2.15 + $1.25 = $3.35 + etc.

That wasn't the whole picture. When the tally was completed, these envelopes (still unopened), were placed in a paper sack with the slip of paper and handed to me, and I was bid, "Good day." Do you know that it takes a pastor and spouse three hours to open, sort, stack, and roll one month's pay? This money then had to be transported to a regional bank miles away, so that the banker's call for payments could be answered. (It was a good time to do some shopping at the regional store, as well.)

Stewardship lessons one and two and three were not by design, but by accident and default. I knew, as did my spouse, without having to consult the annual report, the giving patterns of many of the members on a rather basic level. I knew that the church was exposing a trusted and faithful member to unnecessary risk, along with members who transported this money from their church to his home.

I knew that with ten congregations to serve, I could not afford the eight hours of my time, plus three hours of my spouse's time, to get paid each month. Just because they had always done it this way was not an obstacle in making the changes that would allow for acceptable counting, accounting, and banking procedures. It had never been suggested.

Some time later, as the end of another month approached, I received a call from the treasurer, whom I had gotten to know fairly well. He asked if I could drop by for a few moments when I was down in his community. I knew the request was not extended without thought, so I set aside some time in the late afternoon. The news was not great. Insufficient money was available to make the required payment at the bank for the mortgage on the manse, as had been the case the previous two months. In addition to these three monthly payments in arrears, there was not enough money to pay the salary.

Lessons four and five were being taught. I had a responsibility to see that the church's financial information was shared. If I did not do this myself, I had to see that it was done. Members of the church had a right to know the financial story along with the Christian story. The personal lesson was how to get along with less and still satisfy the financial commitments I had made. Budgeting with close attention to the resources available, and a willingness to be a receiver of the generosity of others—these are still valued.

Lesson six was self-discovered. I had to address the whole issue of support for the budget of the church; and the sooner I did it, the better it would be for the church and for our family finances. It is amazing how well I remembered the lessons that had been taught in biblical studies, particularly the New Testament courses on Paul's letters to the Corinthians and the great collection. I discovered the necessary basics of a fund-raising program: Tell the story; suggest a possible level of giving; expect a response. The story was the current picture of financial shortfall; the possible level of giving was putting aside a fixed amount at the first of the week, whether the minister was there or not. The fixed amount suggested was a minimum of $1.00 a week. With eleven churches, the chances of the minister being there was 2 to 3 *against*. (The second part of this lesson was ten years away!)

Lesson seven was putting this discovery of fund-raising into regular practice. We did, and we increased our support of missions beyond ourselves, as well as discontinuing our reliance on denominational support for our local budget.

While this was happening to us as a pastoral charge, some of the individual churches were in need of replacement or major capital repairs. Lesson eight was from members who proved that capital things can happen. In addition to the regular support of the church's ongoing budget, regular over-and-above gifts were made to repair and build places for the church family to gather and worship. It didn't happen without an effort, but by the will and work of many.

> "Frugality is enjoying the virtue of getting good value for every minute of your life energy and from everything you have the use of."
> —JOE DOMINQUEZ AND VICKI ROBIN
> *Your Money or Your Life*

> "It is being graced in ways that are unexpected. God might just have had a hand in it, along with some others who love as God loves."
> —JOE WALKER

Somehow, I was invited by a regional church officer to attend a workshop on the Commitment Plan. There I *stumbled* upon the word and concepts of stewardship. I must admit that I found many possibilities in the practical stuff that was covered: A way of getting at the evangelism that was always talked about; a way of finding entry for the newer and younger members to become involved in the business part of the church; and a way to find the members and needed leaders for the church schools and groups.

Someone had structured a way to deal with all this stuff that I had been *stumbling* over! Faith-action connections were being made—that's why my grandparents kept that box of church envelopes on the kitchen shelf, and why they placed money in it every time they received a few dollars! The biblical understandings grew, as if someone had just provided warmth and water for an already seeded lawn. There was a library of five or six titles, and I bought them all!

Why I had not seen this material before was not an issue. It was like the time during my high school education, when a teacher's spark had ignited within me a discovery of "learning for the joy of learning." Not only were there practical applications, but now there was a way that what had to be done, could be done, and in a richer, fuller way. Biblical connections were made clear as I helped church people deal with all that God has entrusted to us. This was a part of the faith that we are called to live, not something to be completed as soon as possible, with as little fuss as possible, to gain as much as possible.

And many more lessons were discoveries of joy! Lesson nine came when I was invited to go back to my first pastoral charge. As I visited with some of the people, I discovered that they were in financial difficulty. One father, who was my age, was reflecting on the time I had spent in ministry with them, and how the practice of regular weekly givings, with the minister there or not, had been started.

Number nine came as he said, "That was a good lesson, and our family still carries on with the practice. We have not missed a Sunday." That made me feel great until I was bold enough to ask how the amount had changed, and I discovered that it was still $1.00 a week! If I had only encouraged 1 percent, rather than $1.00, the financial difficulty would not have been a crisis. Percentage or proportional giving makes a lot of sense.

At another pastoral charge, they flatly refused to make any kind of visit that asked for money. They would make one that asked for a person's time, talent, and energy, but not money. It took some time in Bible study, in worship, and in regular visitation to come to the discovery that money was just our time, talent, and energy in the form of coin of the land. It could have far less value than the life commitments we had been asking. It was their insight that the people who were visited made commitments of their money with their time, energy, and talents, but they grew to see the interconnectedness of their money and their life, both gifts from God.

Evangelism is telling the Christian story so that others may discover its reality. Stewardship is retelling the Christian story to ourselves, so that we can live its reality.

I am not sure how many more lessons there are for me, but when I visit a religious bookstore, and sometimes a regular bookstore, the number of good stewardship books and related materials that have been written and developed in the last few years lead to constant discoveries. They would have made my early lessons a little less haphazard. They continue to help me make the biblical life connections that we need, as people who live in today's world.

At one time, I could not find material to help me. Today, my challenge is to budget my time to become familiar with all that is available and get it to where it will be used.

Lessons of a Pastor:

1. It helps to know the giving patterns of the members.

2. Make sure there are safeguards for the members who handle money.

3. Counting, recording, and banking practices are essential.

4. The pastor needs to ensure that financial information is shared regularly, in ways that can be understood, and in ways that are related to the gospel we live.

5. Personal budgeting is important.

6. Learn how to receive, so that you know better how to give.

7. Encourage and expect regular giving from those who know Christ. Stewardship is necessary for the Christian. Fund-raising may be necessary for the church's development.

8. Capital and special offerings are not in conflict with regular budgeted giving.

9. Percentage giving has many advantages and growth possibilities.

10. In the eyes of many, it is debatable whether the heart or the money comes first in importance. Chances are, if you get one and make the connections, you will get both.

11. Many solid, useful stewardship materials are available.

There is joy in stumbling and getting up, for Christ is there.

 SERMON HELP

Possible Sermon Titles

Life Is God's Gift of Grace
Partners with God
A Scary Story
   of Half-Commitment Giving
   (Acts 32:-5:11)
The Dishonest Steward
The Sermon on the Amount
The Secret of Living Is Giving

Possible Sermon Titles

You Are the Benchmark
Creative Christian Stewardship
How Much Is Enough?
Principles of Stewardship
Commitment Is Central
Growing Through Giving
The Christian Philosophy of Giving
The Gift Without the Giver Is Bare

 SERMON HELP

Giving Feels Good

DONALD W. JOINER

Few television shows make me stop what I'm doing in order to watch what's happening. Even in reruns, "Night Court" is one exception. If you have seen the show, you know that the star is Harry. He is sometimes a magician, sometimes a comic, and sometimes a judge. Another key actor is Bull, a large, bald bailiff.

In one particular episode, Bull is helping an electrician string some wire. He is on the roof of the courthouse when lightning strikes. His shaven head and his height draw the lightning. He is hit and knocked out. The scene opens with Bull lying on the couch in the judge's chambers. His face is blackened, his clothes are torn and smoking. A doctor is looking at him in wonder.

"He should have died when the lightning hit him," the doctor declares. "In fact, he was technically dead for a brief time, but it looks as if he is going to be all right."

When Bull recovers, he relates that he heard a voice and saw a bright light—which he interpreted as God. The voice said, "I'm not ready for you yet—go and give everything you have to the needy." It sounds like something God would say, doesn't it? So Bull had removed his life savings from the bank and begins handing it out to anyone in need. A long line forms in the courthouse cafeteria, where Bull is truly enjoying his new role.

When all but one crumpled bill of his entire life savings has been given away, Harry confronts Bull with the news! It wasn't God he heard! In the confusion when the lightning struck, Bull misinterpreted what the electrician was saying to him.

Saddened that he had given away almost all his life savings, Bull is later seen in a darkened courtroom. His large head is in his hands. Then a rather undistinguished old man in rumpled clothes, with long unkempt hair, covered only by an old hat, comes into the courtroom. He asks Bull to show him where he can find the man who is giving away the money. The man is obviously in great need.

Bull pulls his long body up, reaches into his pocket, and pulls out a crumpled bill. As he stretches out the last $100 of his $27,500 in life savings toward the man, he says, "I was saving it for food—but here, you take it."

As the grateful man leaves the courthouse, the scene pans to Harry, who had entered the courtroom in time to witness the whole scene. He calls out to Bull, "It's a hard habit to give up, isn't it—giving, that is?"

POSTSCRIPT: After Harry leaves, Bull begins talking to God, clearly a new relationship for Bull. He explains to God that he really thought it was God speaking. He thought he was doing God's will. Besides, it *felt* good! Now what should he do? He had given away his life savings. Could God give him a sign? There is a long silence in the dark courtroom as Bull stares at the skylight.

Just then, another man enters the courtroom. He represents the city, which is anxious to avoid a lawsuit because of Bull's electrical accident. The attorney offers Bull $20,000 to sign the papers releasing the city from any liability. Bull hesitates while he considers the offer. The attorney says, "O.K., then, $27,500, but that's our final offer." Bull grabs the papers and signs as the attorney fills out the check. When the attorney leaves, Bull walks quietly across the dark courtroom, staring at the check. Then he stops, looks up, and simply says, "THANKS!"

The Tragedy of the Chameleon

There was a little girl who had a chameleon. She would bring it out whenever guests arrived to show how it changed colors. One day, a guest asked about the chameleon.

"Oh he's dead," she exclaimed. "Last week I put him on Mom's scotch-plaid blanket, and he couldn't decide which color to become, and he exploded."

 SERMON HELP

Tina's Will

A True Story

Micah 6:6-8; II Corinthians 9:7-10 (or others)

TERRY WAYNE ALLEN

Tina was a very important and loving part of the church. Having no children of her own, she "adopted" many in the congregation. She asked questions, celebrated successes, and remembered important dates.

Last fall she became ill. Cancer was the diagnosis, and it didn't seem fair, yet she continued with as much energy and gusto as she had at her command. While visiting one day, we discussed her death and her funeral arrangements. All had been cared for. She was an organized, detailed person, with a sense of responsibility. It never occurred to me to ask.

Following her sooner-than-expected death, her family bombarded me with questions about her attorney, her papers, her wishes, and in particular—where was her will? We searched everywhere. It was not to be found. I was now hearing stories of Tina's wish to leave the church a "substantial gift." Where was the will?

It was never made. Planned for . . . yes. Outlined. Never executed. Tina's will was strong during life. Her wishes were heard and usually respected. We couldn't believe she hadn't followed through. As her pastor, I couldn't believe I hadn't asked. I had "assumed." Too bad that Tina's wishes were not legally binding.

Make sure that this doesn't happen to someone you love and admire. Talk about wishes for a will.

Outline for Sermon

- Story
- Too often we assume things
- Embarrassed to ask
- Not wanting to seem to "hasten" death
- Reality—denying people a chance to give and do what they really want to do
- Helping that individual, the family, and the church
- Lift up concept of a permanent Endowment Fund
- Principal retained—truly a gift that will continue to give!
- God will make it grow and produce a rich harvest from your generosity (see II Cor.).

Hymn: "Take My Life and Let It Be Consecrated"

SERMON HELP

The Adventurous Steward

Romans 8:18-19, 24-25

DONALD W. JOINER

Beginning Illustration

Elie Wiesel shares a memorable Hassidic tale in his *Gates of the Forest*. When the great Rabbi Israel Baal Shem-Tov felt the Jews were in danger, he would go to a special place in the forest to meditate. There, he would light a fire, say a special prayer, and the miracle would be accomplished, the misfortune averted.

Later, a disciple of the great rabbi felt the same urgency to intercede with heaven on behalf of his people. He went to the same place in the forest and said, "Master of the Universe, listen!" And again, the miracle would be accomplished.

Still later, another revered rabbi, in order to save his people, ventured into the forest. "I do not know how to light the fire, and I do not know the prayer," he confessed, "but I know the place, and this must be sufficient." And it was, and the miracle was accomplished.

Then it fell, in much later times, upon another trusted rabbi to overcome grave misfortune. Sitting in his armchair, his head in his hand, he spoke with God: "I am unable to light the fire, I do not know the prayer; I cannot even find the place in the forest. All I can do is tell the story, and this must be sufficient!" And it was sufficient.

But what are we to do in an age like today, when the location of the woods is lost, the ability to light the fire is gone, the prayer forgotten, and the story is no more? I believe that lurking beneath the dull, rather unassuming, sleepy word *stewardship,* is hidden a journey that points the way.

1. "The Steward" concept is a misguided thought in contemporary church life. Stewardship is not just about money, or time, or what we do with them, but a journey—an adventure of faith.

2. The concept of the steward begins not with giving but with receiving (see John 3:16). You cannot be a giver until you are a receiver.

3. Philanthropy is giving of what one has to the benefit of another. That is not a natural act, but a learned act. As Christians, we learn to give from God.

4. The concept of the steward goes on to affirm God's ownership. Today's philosophy is summed up on some T-shirts: "The one who dies with the most toys wins."

5. The steward celebrates a partnership with God (see I Cor. 3:9). Meaning in life, and our part in this partnership is discovered in the "gifts" God shares with us.

6. Ephesians 3:20 NRSV: "Him who by the power at work within us is able to accomplish abundantly far more than all we can ask or imagine."

7. The steward knows the story, is able to pray the prayer, can light the fire, and leads us beyond the point of today's crisis to God's adventurous journey.

> "God does not place hope in you for which God has not already provided possibility."

✝ SERMON HELP

Living As Seeds

Isaiah 55:10-11; Philippians 2:12-13; Mark 4:26-29

BETSY SCHWARZENTRAUB

Introduction

The surprise of the scriptures is like breaking through an ice crust, suddenly up to my hips in snow, a new reality!

I. The Seed Growing Secretly

A. Walking on the icy crust: Often I'm like the farmer who experiences new life as sheer gift from God, and who tries to tend it into fruitfulness.

B. Suddenly a new perspective: What if I'm also the seed? We are living seeds, with the literal life of God within us. God has risked big-time and invested in us, so that we are not only in Christ (as Paul says), but also God-in-Christ is in us (John 17).

> "Religion is, first, an open hand to receive a gift, and second, an acting hand to distribute gifts."
>
> —*PAUL TILLICH*

II. Stewardship Is Agrarian

A. We're created to be stewards of the Good News (I Cor.; I Peter). A "steward" is a manager and distributor, one who receives the gift of God's love, knowing God through Christ, and is allowed to share this treasure with others.

B. That's a business model. Mark 4 is an agricultural model of stewardship: The life of God the Giver is in us. It's our joyful task to grow from the inside out, from the tiny seed of faith within us to the fruitfulness of action.

C. Stewardship is not so much a task as a becoming. It's the way I grow in relationship to God, and the signs of this growth are in how I use my time, money, and human relationships, in the priorities I live out, and the ways I show my care.

D. Like Philippians 2:12-13 NRSV: "Work out your own salvation [wholeness, maturity] . . . for it is God who is at work in you, enabling you both to will and to work for [God's] good pleasure." So faithful stewardship is a process, a matter of growth. God gives us not only the will to share God's love, but also the power to fulfill this will. We have all we need, in seed form within us, to bear incredible fruit!

III. Living As Seeds

A. Anthony de Mello's story of a woman's dream of a brand new shop, where she finds God behind the counter: "What do you sell here?" . . . "Everything your heart desires."

She asked for peace of mind, love, happiness and wisdom, and freedom from fear—and then added, "Not just for me. For everyone on earth."

God's response: "You've got me wrong. We don't sell fruits here—only seeds."

B. God has given us the seeds of all that already, seeds of abundant and eternal life (John 20:31).

C. I admit this sounds pretty crazy, that God chooses to work through human beings! It's not just to get certain tasks done (as if God couldn't do these things alone). It's to bring about a transformation within us, not by overpowering us, but by inviting us to freely accept our stewardship and match our actions and will to God's own.

D. What a marvelous gift this invitation is!—that God would choose to transform creation, not despite us, not because of us, but willing it through us!

IV. Breaking Through Crusty Soil

A. This is the point of Jesus' story about the seed growing secretly: the sureness of growth. We can depend upon the fruitfulness of God's Word or Life within us! (Isa. 55:11).

B. We also will accomplish our purpose, when we live as God's seeds. We were created to be fruitful, to put God's love into action, and this ability to bear fruit comes as sheer gift from God!

C. We can only marvel at this seed business!

1. Imagine the little seed, buried into the dark soil all alone, thinking it had been left to die.

2. But God's nature breaks through, and our hard shell cracks open with suffering and vulnerability. We begin to care, to put our compassion to work through a tiny new green shoot. With practice, it grows, and our gift of time, resources, and priorities becomes life-giving in return.

3. Then at last we break soil into a whole new reality of air, of entire fields, a community of faith across space and time, growing toward harvest! Life becomes joyous and fruitful, and it's as much a mystery to us as it is to others who see it!

D. This growth as stewards is astounding (I Cor. 3:6).

Conclusion

A. What does this story do to our understanding of ourselves as stewards? It says that:

1. Giving always begins with God, with the life of God's love put within us, as we're continually showered with God's blessings.

2. God has entrusted us with God's greatest gift of love in human terms—Jesus himself—and in a growing, living relationship with him.

3. We were created to be fruitful, to live out God's will, with the power to fulfill it.

4. We can depend upon the Life of God within us, to prod us to greater growth, from faith into action.

B. We are God's seeds. We can trust this growth process (Isa. 55:11). Snow. Whoever thought that Jesus' little seed story would teach us about stewardship? Then there we are, up to our hips again.

How Much Is Enough?
Luke 12:15-21, 34
Donald W. Joiner

The problem for the rich man in this parable, and for us, is not "how you get your wealth," but "how it gets you!"

1. Rich in material things;
2. Poor in soul;
3. Rich toward God.

The question remains, then—"Not how much is enough, but what have you done with what you have?"

SERMON HELP

The Sentiment of Gratitude

Matthew 10:8; John 3:16; Deuteronomy 8:17-18

DONALD W. JOINER

1. "A true Christian is a person who never for a moment forgets what God has done in Christ, and whose activities have their root in the sentiment of gratitude."   —John Bailey

2. "As I view life and creation from the biblical perspective, the picture I see is of an endlessly giving God."   —Donald Heinze

3. "The flowing out of God always demands a flowing back."   —Jan Van Ruysbroeck (1293–1381)

4. "All you have shall someday be given; therefore give now, that the season of giving may be yours."   —Kahlil Gibran *(The Prophet)*

DRAMA

Not Just Another Offering

GILSON MILLER

Cast of Characters

Rich Man ....
His Entourage ....(six or seven people)
Minister...
Widow ....

Costumes

Rich man: medieval-type long, flowing gown with robe and hat.
Widow: rummage-sale dress and worn coat, hat, and purse.

Props

Broom, play money (coins and 2 buckets of bills) kazoos, cymbals, tambourine, drum, offering plate, shabby purse with 2 coins.

"As Jesus looked up and saw rich prople dropping their gifts into the chest of the temple treasury, he noticed a poor widow putting in two tiny coins. 'I tell you this,' he said: 'this poor widow has given more than any of them; for those others who have given had more than enough, but she, with less than enough, has given all she had to live on' " (Luke 21:1-4 REB).

This sketch is presented as an integral part of a stewardship-emphasis program. The scripture is read earlier in the service. Careful staging for this sketch is necessary to communicate the desired effect. The minister, or whoever announces the offering, should not indicate that anything will be different from the usual procedure.

Use a customary announcement, such as: "Will the ushers please come forward to receive our morning tithes and offerings, gifts to the God we love." However, when the offering is called for, several people burst through the doors of the sanctuary, making considerable noise with kazoos, tambourines, and other simple rhythm instruments. Following this initial fanfare, one of the group, dressed in flowing robes says: "You want money? I have money, lots and lots of money!"

With this comment, spoken so that everyone is aware of this obnoxious and showy braggart, the rich man begins strutting through the sanctuary, occasionally tossing play money (or real, depending on how much realism you can afford!). His entourage follows him, playing the instruments to emphasize his importance. One person

35

may even walk before him with a broom, sweeping a path, followed by two people with buckets of bills.

Following a couple of "sweeps" of the sanctuary, the entire party arrives at the altar. The minister heartily welcomes the guest and his money. The rich man takes center stage. The minister is at his left. At this point, the rich man tosses coins in the air; as he does this, the tambourines shake. The minister catches the coins in the offering plate, the cymbals clap, and the drum bangs. With every successful catch, the tambourines snap and the entourage "ohhs" and "ahhs." The rich man happens to be a magician! He pulls coins from behind ears and out of thin air.

> "The rich young ruler, we'd call prudent. Jesus called him a fool!"
> —*PAUL TILLICH*

After a brief show, the rich man announces he doesn't have time to stay for the service and starts to leave. The minister escorts him down the center aisle to the door, expressing gratitude for his generosity and thinking out loud of all the projects that can be accomplished because of the rich man's offering.

As they reach the door, a woman, humbly dressed, enters from a side door. People begin to shift attention from the rich man to the woman. She proceeds slowly and prayerfully to the front of the church. Upon arriving at the altar, she pauses and looks upward. She deliberately empties the contents of her purse; two small coins fall on the altar. At this point she removes her coat, lovingly places it on the table, and leaves.

Note: Following this sketch in our congregation, we experience a sobering mood which requires no commentary. We sit for several minutes in the impact of the scene. We then proceed with the customary offering—although, because of what we have experienced, it is not just another offering!

 **SERMON HELP**

Creative Christian Stewardship

Matthew 25:14-30

DONALD   W.   JOINER

Introduction

A. If each of us were given $10, $50, or $100 to invest for the church, and in three months we were asked to return the principal and the interest, how would we respond? What would we do?

B. Today is Stewardship Sunday
   1. Most of us think that stewardship means money, and we turn off our ears when the word is mentioned;
   2. John Wesley taught: "Get all you can, save all you can, give all you can";
   3. One definition of stewardship: "acting responsibly with what God has given to you."

Points:

A. Stewardship begins with a recognition of God's generosity.

   1. It celebrates God's gift of love;
   2. It affirms that all we have is from God.

B. Stewardship is a covenant, a partnership, with God. Jesus' story of the rich farmer was not about accumulation, but about ownership. A steward affirms God's ownership and our partnership (trusteeship).

C. Stewardship is not about an inventory of what we have, but about a journey in life.

D. What we need today is a Creative Christian Steward, who:
   1. Knows that God loves me;
   2. Knows that all I am and have is from God;
   3. Accepts God's gift with fear and excitement;
   4. Accepts God's invitation.

 SERMON HELP

That Isn't Fair

Acts 5:1-11

KEN GALLINGER

GRANDMA DYING OF AIDS the headline of the *Daily Sun* declared in four-inch red letters. The words were superimposed on a picture of a middle-aged woman tearfully embraced by members of her family, while the story told the tale with all the blubbering pathos that only a tabloid can muster.

The tragedy had begun when this unfortunate woman had a blood transfusion in the 1980s, before AIDS testing was an established procedure in Canada, and now the slow and awful death of an AIDS patient seemed her inevitable fate. The story, it's true, was a sad one—just as sad as the stories of the ten or twenty other residents of our city who, that same day, if annual statistics are to be believed, were told they had cancer that would lead to their deaths. But their stories weren't anywhere in the papers, and hers was on the front page. Why? Well, it just seems so . . . so *unfair* for a grandmother to have AIDS.

It is, of course, the Magic Johnson phenomenon revisited. It's not right, not fair for a nice guy like Magic to have AIDS: heterosexual, married to a photogenic wife, promiscuous (but aren't all athletes?), generous to charity, always flashing that winning smile worth millions of dollars. We "understand," don't we, why drug addicts get AIDS: They're always shooting foreign substances into their veins to avoid life and, hey, if you keep doing that long enough, what can you expect? We "understand" why homosexual males get AIDS. We "understand" why Haitians have AIDS, and why parts of Africa have infection rates as high as 40 percent; those are poor and unsophisticated places, where they don't have the knowledge, the sanitation, or the health care we do; and we know how promiscuous those people are.

Of course, we never say any of those things out loud; we're far too polite, far too genteel, far too "Christian" a society to express our racism or our homophobia or our elitism out loud in most circles. But they're in our minds, firm and steady, and we

know that "fair is fair." So when one more gay dies on the AIDS ward, it warrants, if anything, a paid obituary; word of the rapid spread of HIV in Africa gets one square inch on page 17. But when Magic is infected, it's front-page news, and when Grandma has AIDS, the red letters are four inches high. Because? Well, because it's just so unfair that nice, innocent people like them should meet such a fate. And unfairness sells.

Such a strange notion is this concept we love so much, this cherished illusion we call "fairness." Many homes, particularly those with children, are built on that concept and its pursuit. If Dr. Spock taught us one thing, it was that in dealing with children, we must strive to be, if nothing else, absolutely fair. So refrigerators across North America sprang up with dishwashing charts: Johnny washed last night, so Janie must wash tonight, because that's, well, only fair. The fact that Janie has a science-fair project due tomorrow is too bad, but doesn't really matter—after all, it's her turn.

"When Janie was 12, she got to stay up until 10:00. Now I'm twelve, so I should, too." "You made *him* a chocolate cake on *his* birthday." And it's not just with children. "How come every time we make love, I have to start it?" "Why do *I* have to put the garbage out every week?"

So much about fairness is attractive. It appeals, on the one hand, to all our egalitarian instincts, while ironically, at the same time, it allows us to manufacture countless opportunities to feel abused and badly treated. It removes from us the need to make thousands of decisions for which we have neither the time nor the energy: If a wedding in our church costs $500, and everybody pays $500, then it removes the need to make countless individual decisions about who should pay what. Fairness provides a continually renewable resource of excuses for not doing things we didn't want to do anyway: "Well, I would baptize your baby, but I said no to someone in the same circumstances last week, and it just wouldn't be fair." And it supports the image of God that we have constructed: a God who, all things being equal, would have all things being equal.

Fairness. Intellectually, we know that life on this planet is not fair, and we've all seen enough irrational suffering to prove the point. Yet deep in our guts, since the day we agreed that if he got the little red wagon today, I should have it tomorrow; if I had to set the table tonight, she should at least do the dishes, we've had a conviction that, darn it, if the world is, in fact, not fair, it should be. Surely fair is the way God intended life to be. Surely, insofar as it's not, that's a violation of God's plan.

That, of course, is why we love the principles that lie behind the tithe. Tithing is a wonderfully effective way to handle giving in the church, and those like me who come from liberal denominations covet, in the murky depths of our souls, the financial stability and ease of interpretation and marketing, which seem so much more available in churches with a tithing tradition. Tithing works. If I could get everyone in my congregation to give 3 percent of their gross income, we literally wouldn't know what to do with the money. And 3 percent (or 5 or 10 percent, or whatever number a communion sets as appropriate) is obviously fair, in that it applies equally to the rich and to the poor.

And this is why we find Luke's brief story of Ananias and Sapphira so upsetting. By all accounts, Ananias and Sapphira were a nice young couple who were highly thought of in the community. They were clearly touched by Peter's powerful preaching, so, as Peter invited them to do, they were baptized and quickly became plugged into the church in Jerusalem. Among the members of that new young church, however, there was a tremendous outpouring of generosity; some of those new Christians weren't wealthy, to

> ## "God is the first and the last. Until we find God and we are found by God, we begin at no beginning and work to no end."
>
> *—H. G. WELLS*

say the least, so the whole community pitched in to share their resources.

This posed a real problem for our young heroes. Because they really didn't understand what the church was about, and because they were very much locked into the bartering culture of which they were a part, this whole notion of being truly generous was foreign to them. When you bartered, you always held a little bit back, never told your whole story. That was not cheating. That was just the way it was done. That was how you made a "fair deal" in those days (as in these). Still, Ananias and Sapphira wanted to appear to be really generous and caring, to uphold their reputation by doing the best they could for the cause, and all that good stuff.

So they came up with a scheme. They would sell a prime piece of property, and then, in front of the whole congregation, they would make a big show of presenting the proceeds of the sale to the church. Everyone would think they were wonderful. And that's what they did. They sold the land and pocketed 50 percent.

Then Ananias, being the man of the house and therefore in charge of the money, brought the rest to the church, and when the plate came around, popped in the proceeds. When the offering plate hit the front, and the doxology had been sung, Peter called Ananias up and asked him, right there in church, in front of everyone, "Now, my friend, is that the whole proceeds of the sale?"

"Oh, yes indeed," lied Ananias.

Peter looked him square in the eye and said, "Liar," at which point, according to Luke, the shock was too much for Ananias, and he fell over dead.

"This," says Luke, in one of the most wonderful understatements in literary history, "made a profound impression on the congregation."

Poor God

A mother was trying to teach her daughter about tithing and the importance of giving to God. She counted out the little girl's dollar allowance in ten dimes. Then she separated one dime from the end of the line. "This is for God." she said.

The little girl looked at the dime for a moment, then commented, "Poor God. It's not very much, is it?"

—*DIANE E. CAUGHRON*

The point here is not simply that if you lie in church, God will strike you dead. There are times when we might wish that were the point, but it isn't. Fundamentally, this story was one part of the early church's protest against the notion of fairness, which was taking hold even in those earliest days—the notion that if everyone just did their fair share, the church would prosper and the world would be saved. Ananias and Sapphira didn't need to sell their land—there was no rule requiring them to do so—and if they did, they certainly weren't required to give it all to the church. The biblical standard was 10 percent; that was their fair share; that's all everyone had the right to expect of them. They were "plus-que-tithers," and there's not a church treasurer in our time who wouldn't welcome them.

But what they couldn't bring themselves to be was generous—generous not only of money, but generous of spirit. Their gift was calculated and calculating, rather than free and unrestrained. They wrote their check on the basis of their relationship to those around them, rather than their relationship to God. Real generosity, the spontaneous outpouring of a grateful spirit, was beyond their understanding. And what happened to them, tragically, was typical of what happens to most people whose spirits never experience the meaning of generosity; they wove an elaborate web of deception so that they would seem to be better than they were. Unable to be genuinely and deeply generous of spirit, they lived in a world of pretense, trying to convince themselves and others that they were O.K.; and when the walls of their glass house came tumbling in upon them, they died, because there was nothing else for them to do.

One of the struggles of the early church, a struggle that continues to this very day, is the struggle of help-ing people understand how the gospel works—indeed, what the Good News is. The Good News is this: All that we are, all that we have, all that we do—it's all a gift from God. Jesus says it's all a gift: sun and rain; seed time and harvest; the little bird that falls out of the nest, and the hairs that fall out of our head until there are no more to fall; the love of one who holds us in her arms and washes our feet with her tears. All a gift. This life we receive, and the grace of God by which it becomes worth living—all a gift. Whether we're honest or dishonest; whether we give $5,000 a year to the church or not a cent; whether we're Christians or golfers, it's all the same—all a gift.

If we don't understand one other thing about the death of Jesus Christ on that Calvary cross and his resurrection a couple of mornings later, we must understand this: By those events, our lives were changed in some fundamental way, and that change was not of our own crafting or of our own deserving—that change was a gift from God. It had nothing to do with fairness, for God owed and owes us nothing; it had everything to do with generosity and with grace. When we choose to measure our response to that grace just by the standards of what's fair, we miss the point altogether, and when we allow ourselves to believe that life is governed by standards of fairness, we set ourselves up for the kind of shock that can be fatal. God never asks us to be fair in our living or in our giving, whether that giving be of time, or talent, or money. God calls us, in the name of Jesus Christ, to be generous.

It would be nice if everyone in the church did their fair share; then those who are generous wouldn't be so tired all the time. But if the world were fair, there'd be no need for a crucified Jesus, or for the outrageous love of a God who knows no limits and holds us up, even in the midst of self-inflicted brokenness. We need to give up on all this fairness stuff, which means, sadly, that we may need to give up on the tithe. Not because it's too difficult for people to accept. But rather because the principles of fairness and equability, which lie at the root of tithing, simply will not stand the test of the gospel and will not encourage the kind of grace-filled response that the church in our time will need to flourish. In its place, let us cultivate the spirit of generosity that lives amongst us, nurtured and inspired by the grace of God.

SERMON HELP

How Much Is Enough Today?

DONALD W. JOINER

Leo Tolstoy tells of a man who was offered all the land he could encompass in one day's travel by foot. The only condition was that he return on the same day to the hill where he started.

He began his journey, and after a considerable distance, made his first turn. He wanted to go farther before he made his second turn, and still farther before making his third.

He was a long way from the finish line when the sun began to set. So he struggled on and reached the hill, but died from exhaustion. The only land he could use was his six-foot grave.

That is an old story, but the question it poses is just as modern and real as if it were asked today: "How Much Is Enough?"

 DRAMA

David B. Boomer Talks to God

DEBORAH FISHER AND THOMAS PETTY

DAVE: Hello . . . ? Hello . . . ?

GOD: Hello, is this David B. Boomer?

DAVE: Speaking.

GOD: David, do you consider yourself a faithful Christian?

DAVE: Wait a minute . . . is this one of those dumb telephone surveys . . . or worse, one of those televangelist solicitations? . . . Listen, pal, I am *very* busy right now. I don't have time to answer a lot of idiotic questions!

GOD: No, this is not a survey, Dave. This is the Lord calling you. I haven't heard from you for years and years. In fact, I haven't heard from you since you were 12 years old. You're 35 now, so that makes it 23 years since I have received any kind of communication from you at all! I just thought I would call and see how your faith is doing these days.

DAVE: RIGHT! This is God, and I'm Bugs Bunny. Come on, tell me the truth—who are you really, and what's your scam?

GOD: No scam, Dave. I really am the Lord your God.

DAVE: Well, now, listen . . . God doesn't use *phone lines* to talk to people—that surely must be a violation of some Federal Interstate Communications Act . . . some violation of the separation of church and state—some violation of *something!* Besides, God just doesn't *need* to use the *phone!*

GOD: Settle down, Dave; your blood pressure is going off the charts. Now, how do you know so much about what I do and don't do?

DAVE: Well, I just *know* these things! And I know that God can't just go around bugging people's phones—even the CIA can't do that! At least they're not supposed to.

GOD: I am *not* bugging your phone, as you put it. I'm *calling* you on the phone!

DAVE: Besides, *no one*—absolutely *no one I know* believes that God is a woman!

GOD: Well, at least now you are settling down to facts—you are *right.* I am not a woman.

DAVE: Now at least you are making *sense!*

GOD: But I am not a *man* either!

DAVE: Whoa! Wait a minute . . . penalty flag—fifteen yards! I tell you, *everybody—absolutely everybody* I know—*knows* that you are a *man!*

GOD: Well now, David, I'm not surprised that you are having trouble dealing with this! The fact is that the way people *hear me* depends a lot more on how *they listen* than on how *I speak!*

DAVE: Wait a minute. This is just *too much!* I'm getting a headache! Wait! I have a call coming in on the other line. I'll be back in a minute. *(Dave clicks phone.)* Hello? Frank! Oh, am I glad to hear your voice. Why? I'm on the other line with a real loony-tune. *(loud crack of thunder played over PA system)* Ah, gee, it's going to rain. . . . What do you mean, there's not a cloud in the sky? . . . Where are you anyway, Frank? In your office? That's just two blocks from here. Didn't you hear that huge crack of thunder? *When?* When I was telling you about the crazy broad who . . . *(louder crack of thunder).* Listen, Frank, like I said, I have someone on the other line. Can I call you back in ten minutes or so? O.K. Catch you later. *(Dave clicks phone again)* Hello? Hello?

GOD: Hello, Dave. How is Frank today?

DAVE: You *do* have my phone bugged!

GOD: No, Dave, I sincerely have *not* bugged your phone. I just wanted to call and see how your faith is these days. What church do you and your family attend?

DAVE: Church? Listen, Gaaa . . . or whoever you are. We just don't go to church. If you were *really* God, you would know what our life is like. I work 6 days a week, 12 hours a day; my wife works outside the home; and we have two children to raise. I tell you, we're so busy during the week that *Sundays* are the only day we have to get caught up on all the work around the house! No way we can go to church—we're just too *busy!*

GOD: You don't need to talk to me about busy, Dave. I created the world in just six days. Talk about busy weeks! But I still had time to rest on the seventh day. It's not good for you or your wife or your children to always be rushing around, busy, busy, busy, and take no time to talk with me. I can guarantee that you would be a *lot* happier if you would take time for me. I can provide you with a whole list of references—people who would be more than happy to tell you that Sunday mornings spent with me are worth more than a trimmed yard, a waxed car, or money in the bank!

DAVE: I cannot believe that I am having this conversation! I am standing here, talking on my phone to . . . talking on my phone to—to God knows who.

GOD: Yes, Dave.

DAVE: O.K., O.K. For the sake of discussion, let's just talk about church for a minute. I suppose it would be good for my children to go to church. I would like them to have the same good experience in Sunday school that I had. Church would be good for my wife, too—heaven knows she *needs* to go! She needs to learn to be more loving, forgiving, and unselfish! And besides, she has been saying, every since Sarah was born, that we should go back to church. Hey! Did you catch that name? *Sarah!* We didn't just pull that name out of the air, you know. We thought it would be good to name her after the wife of one of Jesus' disciples.

GOD: Abraham.

DAVE: What?

GOD: Abraham. Sarah was Abraham's wife.

DAVE: Whatever. We did get the name out of the Bible. That says something for us and our faith—doesn't it? *(long pause)* Doesn't it? Jesus!—cut me a little slack, why don't you?

GOD: Remember, Dave, I'm God, not Jesus. You admit that you haven't had much time for church. I respect your honesty. I am very delighted to know that you will make a sincere effort to go to church in the future.

DAVE: *Effort?* Not just an effort—we are talking *commitment* here! We are going to begin . . . this very Sunday! And we will be there *every* Sunday from now on!

GOD: That is excellent, Dave. I will be glad to see you there. What about your money, Dave?

DAVE: What about it? *(very suspiciously)*

GOD: Have you been giving any of your money to the church?

DAVE: Oh no, here it comes! The old bottom line—"How much money do you give?" I *knew* this wasn't really God. You're a fund-raiser for that church down the street, aren't ya?

GOD: No, Dave. . . . Listen, do you hear that?

DAVE: What?

GOD: You have a FAX coming in.

DAVE: *Jesus H. Christ! (Dave looks around.)* Oops, I didn't mean to say that. I meant, "Gosh darn, I have to hurry to catch the FAX." *(Dave moves into the chancel and takes a piece of paper from the altar.)* Let's see, who is this from? . . . Real cute! . . . It's from you, isn't it?!

GOD: Yes, Dave, it is. Would you care to read it?

DAVE: "All the tithe of the land, whether of the seed of the land or of the fruit of the trees, is the LORD's; it is holy to the LORD. If a man wishes to redeem any of his tithe, he shall add a fifth to it. And all the tithe of herds and flocks, every tenth animal of all that pass under the herdsman's staff, shall be holy to the LORD. A man shall not inquire whether it is good or bad, neither shall he exchange it; and if he exchanges it, then both it and that for which it is exchanged shall be holy; it shall not be redeemed. These are the commandments which the LORD commanded Moses for the people of Israel" (Leviticus 27:30-34 RSV). . . . A *tithe?* Isn't that 10 percent of my income? . . . *I can't do that!*

GOD: What do you do, Dave?

DAVE: Well now, you know how it is! . . . You know we're just starting out and all. We just live paycheck to paycheck, and there is *nothing* left over in the bank account at the end of the month. I'll tell you, I break out in a cold sweat whenever I think about sending my kids to college. Why, our best friends just finished putting their only child through college—they said it cost almost $80,000! We need to start saving for that real soon. And I don't know how we'll *ever* be able to save enough to *retire* . . . like I said, there's just nothing left at the end of the month!

GOD: How much did you pay for your new car, Dave?

DAVE: My car? . . . That little thing? . . . Let's see, I think $14,500. *(loud thunder)* No, no, wait, it was $19,500—that's right, $19,500. *(loud thunder)* No, no, it was $21,000. *(loud thunder)* . . . O.K., O.K., so I paid $28,900.

GOD: No wonder you have no money left at the end of the month! How about your boat, Dave?

DAVE: My boat? That little fishing boat I got so I could take my son fishing? You know, picture this scene. . . . There my son and I are, early in the morning, out on the lake fishing—with the crisp, clear, cool fresh air all around us, the fog gently lifting off the water, and the glorious beauty of the sun peering up over the clouds on the eastern horizon. . . . There we are, sitting with our fishing poles draped over the side of our little boat!

GOD: *Little* boat? You call a 38-foot C-Ray a *little boat?*

DAVE: Oh, you've seen it, huh? . . . Yeah, of *course* you've seen it!

GOD: And, Dave, how about your big-screen TV? How about your CD players (one in your four-year-old's room? Really, Dave!). . . . How about your snowmobile?

DAVE: OK! OK! I get your point. . . . I have a lot of toys. So shoot me! *Oops!* I didn't mean that! What I meant was, I am going to begin to try to cut back on how much I buy for myself and, maybe, probably, start giving some of my money to you. *Wait! I cannot believe I am having this conversation with someone I cannot even see, and making promises to do things I never before this minute ever considered doing! Am I losing my mind?*

GOD: Maybe you are just *finding* your *soul!* . . . Go check your computer screen, Dave.

DAVE: My computer? My computer had a *complete crash* 48 hours ago! No matter what I do, I can't get it going again. I'll probably have to get a new one. Ah, I mean *after* I give some money to the church, of course!

GOD: Just check the computer, Dave. *(Dave walks to pulpit.)*

DAVE: It's on! *Wow!* Look at these phosphorescent *fonts!* These are *incredible!* I've never seen anything like them! . . . You know, Lord, you really disappointed me with that FAX! I figured that surely *you* would not send a FAX on that crummy, crinkly old FAX paper. I expected at least a *plain paper* FAX. But these phosphorescent fonts are *fantastic!* You sure more than made up for that FAX with this!

GOD: *Read* what it says, Dave.

DAVE: "Hear, O Israel: The LORD our God is one LORD, and you shall love the LORD your God with all your heart, and with all your soul, and with all your might. And these words which I command you this day shall be upon your heart; and you shall teach them diligently to your children" (Deuteronomy 6:4-7*a* RSV). I guess this and the FAX and the thunder are what you call *signs*—right, God?

GOD: Signs are my specialty, Dave.

DAVE: I haven't been doing a very good job of loving you with all my heart and soul and might, have I? But you must love me. Why else would you go to all this trouble, when you have so many other people to watch out for? I guess I've been sort of self-absorbed when it comes to money, too. All of a sudden I feel real crummy about that. But that's going to change. I mean *really* change—my check to you will be the first one I write—no leftovers for a God

who loves me this much! And that part from the computer screen about telling your children? I'm going to start that, too—tonight, right at the dinner table—between the overcooked hamburgers and the undercooked pork and beans! My wife will be shocked . . . but I think she'll be glad, too. And . . . God, can we talk again? I mean, I really liked this! It was . . . cool! . . . And I . . . I really liked it. . . . Can we talk again soon?

GOD: *Any time,* Dave. I'm always here, ready and anxious to listen to you. And, Dave, if you need any help with those changes . . . well, I'm here for that, too!

 # SERMON HELP

Scripture Starters

DONALD W. JOINER

Many passages in the Old and New Testaments could be called stewardship scriptures. These include especially the parables of Jesus and stories of an individual's struggles with faith. Those in the following list are not intended to be exhaustive, but only touchstones to spark your creative faith:

Old Testament	New Testament		
Genesis 1:1ff.	Matthew (the tax	12:15-21, 34	16:2ff.
Leviticus 2:7ff.	collector!)	16:1-13	II Corinthians 4:1-2
Deuteronomy 8:17ff.	6:19-21; 6:25-34	21:1-4	8:1-7
Deuteronomy 16:17ff.	15:18-19	John 15:1-5	9:6-8, 11
Psalm 24:1ff.	16:24-28	Acts 20:35ff.	Ephesians 3:1-13
Psalm 37:1-26	25:14-30	Romans 12:1-2	4:1-6
Malachi 3:1-10	Mark 10:17-26; 10:39-45	I Corinthians 3:9ff.	I Timothy 6:6-12
	12:41-44	4:1-7	James 2:14-17
	Luke 6:38ff.	12:1ff.	I Peter 4:1-11

 # SERMON HELP

Bible Sources for Stewardship

THE CENTER FOR PARISH DEVELOPMENT (CHICAGO, ILL.)

Consider these biblical sources when preaching or teaching about stewardship.

The Gifts of Creation

Luke 9:57-62
Colossians 4:5

Ephesians 5:16
Matthew 25:1-13
Romans 8:24; 4:18
Hebrews 11:1
I Corinthians 13:7
I Corinthians 6:19-20
Matthew 22:34-40

Matthew 5:3-16
Luke 10:29-37
Luke 19:1-10
II Corinthians 8:1-4
Psalms 24:1-2
Isaiah 40:12-31
Genesis 1:1-31

The Gifts of Redemption

Matthew 25:14-30
I Corinthians 2:6-7; 4:1-7
I Timothy 1:19; 6:3, 20
II Timothy 1:13; 4:3
Titus 1:9-11
I Peter 4:10-11
Romans 12:4-8
I Corinthians 12:12-28
Ephesians 4:4-6

The Gifts of Empowerment

Isaiah 11:2
Galatians 5:22-23
I Corinthians 12:1-13
Ephesians 4:11-16
II Timothy 1:3-14
I Corinthians 1:1-9
Romans 12:6-8
I Corinthians 13:1-13
I Corinthians 3:21-22; 4:1-2
I Peter 1:1-10
I Peter 2:1-10
Romans 12:1-5;
II Corinthians 6:3-10
II Corinthians 5:16-19

 PRAYER

We gave what we could, or at least, what we would. Bless, with your grace what we have brought. Multiply it with your wisdom. Increase it with your strength and power. Enhance it with your vision. Sweeten it with your precious love. And, O God, may our hearts be filled with the joy of giving in the name of Jesus, our brother. Amen.

Karen E. Warren

 PRAYER

Last Sunday, there was $4,827 on the altar when I prayed. I know this money comes from grateful worshipers, and I am certain that again this morning, these people here are saying that they love you.

Hilbert Berger

 PRAYER

Prayer Before a Twenty-Dollar Bill
MICHEL QUOIST

Lord, see this bill! It frightens me.
You know its secrets, you know its history.
How heavy it is!
It scares me, for it cannot speak.
It will never tell all it hides in its creases.
It will never reveal all the struggles and efforts it represents, all the disillusionment and slighted dignity.
It is stained with sweat and blood,
It is laden with all the weight of the human toil
   which makes its worth.
O Lord, I offer you this bill with its joyous mysteries,
   its sorrowful mysteries.
I thank you for all the life and joy it has given.
I ask your forgiveness for the harm it has done.
But above all, Lord, I offer it to You as a symbol of all
   the labors of men, indestructible money, which
   tomorrow will be changed into your eternal life.
Prayers (Kansas City: Sheed & Ward, 1985)

 PRAYER

Prayer of Dedication
ALEC LANGFORD

God of the universe, transform our love into thought, our thought into concern, our concern into action, and thus make our lives an expression of your sacrificial dealings with humanity. To seal our resolve, O God, we present our gifts to make action possible. Amen.

PRAYER

Offertory Prayers

HILBERT BERGER

❧

Grant that this offering might be a response to your love and not a function of duty. Let it be a sign of grace and not a dictate of law, an act of freedom and not a gesture of compulsion. Create in us the joy of the generous heart and the spirit of self-giving that is in Jesus Christ.

❧

All that we have, we have from you, Creator and Preserver of all. Accept these gifts which we now offer, and help us to make the whole of life an offering, and every thought a prayer.

❧

So often we do not speak to you at all. Grant us grace to praise you. So often, we give from duty, obligation, and pressure. Grant us grace to offer you, not only our financial gifts, but our humble repentance. Thank you for hearing our prayers and receiving our gifts.

❧

We give you our material, earthly gifts, a symbol of our willingness to know you more fully, to love you constantly.

❧

Thank you for your Holy Word, which patiently teaches us that our ways are not always your will. As we offer these gifts to you today, we ask again for the willingness to do your will, to love and do justice, to live righteousness.

No matter what we say
or what we do,
Here is what we think of You.

PRAYER

Offertory Prayers

NORMA WIMBERLY

We are reminded again that you are love. Our gifts are offered to you now, with renewed desire to do justice, to show love, and to live in humble fellowship with you.

❧

We come before you now, reminded that we often fail to hear Jesus' words calling us to love and obedience. We offer these gifts as a symbol of our desire to love you with all our hearts, minds, and strength, and to love and serve our neighbor.

❧

We have come before you today singing. We have tried to worship you with joy. We know we are yours, and we praise you. We give to you now with thanks.

TEACHING HELP

Adult Study Questions

1. What are some of your memories, feelings, and thoughts when you hear the words *offering? sacrifice?* Name and describe the times and places when those feelings and thoughts occur in your worship experiences.

2. Describe the offertory time in your congregation. What parts would you like to do differently? Why?

3. Consider the time of offertory and communion as a drama, a reenactment of Christ's life, death, and resurrection, offering himself for us. What are some ways you offer yourselves to the world?

4. Name some ways the offering may be more realistically symbolic of our lives. What else might we offer as symbols of our response to God and the giving of ourselves to the world?

5. In your congregation, name some ways you might specifically celebrate the sharing that is implicit in communion? Name ways of sharing yourselves, your goods, your time, your witness.

TEACHING HELP

Why the Offering Is Part of Worship

THOMAS RIEKE AND WILLIAM MILLER

From time to time, some pastors hesitate to include time for the offering in the midst of worship. Some church leaders have decided to mention nothing about money, while relying on a collection box at the back of the sanctuary. This sort of doubt, which springs from a desire to avoid worshiping both God and Mammon, can be overcome when we look at stewardship in the context of worship, or when we experience worship in the context of a life of stewardship.

Gathering

The people of God come together in the Lord's name. There may be greetings, music and song, prayer and praise. The people gather, from settings where priorities of daily living command attention, into a community of faith, gathered primarily to exalt Jesus Christ as Lord.

Separate and diverse persons come to one assembly, physically symbolizing the whole Body of Christ, the church. These are loved and gifted persons, coming from the places their gifts have been used to a place of renewal. Bringing individual insights, persons develop and celebrate a vision of the church that motivates and inspires.

Worship may be understood as rehearsal (preparation) for the drama of life experience. What we bring to worship, our basic pattern of worship, and how we incorporate the Word (received and celebrated) into daily stewardship are uniquely related.

We, being many, are one body in Christ.

Praise

This is the privilege and joyful task of the Body of Christ. Worship is corporate and mutually supportive. The community of faith joins in many rich expressions of joy and thanksgiving for the acts of God in history, in nature, in our lives, and in the future. We confess failures, accept pardon, and celebrate the good news of Christ's love and acceptance of us.

Praise is an act of turning life toward God.

To plan for the progress of Christ's Body, to set goals and dream creatively, to experience the sound, sight, and environ-

> ### *Attitudes of Offering*
>
> Psalm 51:15-17 (offer praise, broken heart, contrite spirit)
> Hosea 6:16 (God desires love and knowledge of God)
> Amos 5:21-24 (desire for justice, righteousness)
> Micah 6:6-8 (justice, kindness, humility)
> Mark 12:33 (love of God, self, neighbor)
> Psalm 100 (gladness, praise)

46

ment of corporate worship—all are acts of praise. As we engage in these tasks cooperatively, God's kingdom is among us, and God's purposes are accomplished on earth.

Proclamation

The Scriptures are opened to the people through readings, preaching, witnessing, music, and other arts. Interspersed may be psalms, anthems, hymns, and songs.

The Word is central, and as such has the privilege of being presented in the flesh—again. Experiencing the Scripture and the proclaimed Word is the re-fleshing of our own stories, a unique opportunity for understanding and experiencing a growing faith within a loving community.

A primary challenge of proclamation is to understand the Word in regard to individual and corporate stewardship, and to develop a theology of giving.

If the church is acting out the functions of the Body of Christ, this is news worthy of sharing. In the telling, the work goes on. Present deeds find their roots in the old story, which is renewed and incorporated as the people of God release the truth into the world.

Responses and Offerings

The art and act of involvement, the "amen" which not only wishes it so, but by personal intervention, makes it so—this is response. Response to God's Word includes prayers of concerns for others and our work in the world; acts of commitment and faith, including service to God in the world and acknowledgment of our mutual support in this challenge.

The Sacramental Quality of Money
1. Take out any denomination of paper money.
2. Center your thoughts on "In God We Trust."
3. This "bill" does not represent a commodity of secular exchange. It represents:
   people
   sacrifice
   love
   events
4. Contemplate where this "bill" has been.
5. Think of the good that might yet come from this "bill."
6. Let us pray.

God, working through the Holy Spirit, has played, and continues to play, the seeking role. Until we actually respond, the drama is incomplete. Our response in worship is the same as our response in life. All of life is to be lived in responsiveness to the Spirit's leading.

Celebration of the sacraments of Holy Communion and Baptism may be seen as full thanksgiving for salvation and acknowledgment of God's presence among us.

Sending Forth

The people of God are sent into the world with the Lord's blessing. We have dramatized a gathering, encounter, and response in the name of the Lord. Each one is now free to leave the "mountaintop," enabled to live out a life of prayer and praise, through active stewardship as the scattered Body of Christ. We seek to embody in our daily decision making and actions the mind and spirit of Christ Jesus.

There are tasks to be done and words to be shared, needs to meet and challenges to dare. Out of the people of God, emerges the process of daily stewardship. To God be the glory!

 TEACHING HELP

Things a Pastor Can Do to Encourage Planned Giving
DONALD W. JOINER

1. Preach on biblical themes pertaining to being good stewards of one's accumulated assets.
2. Teach on the subject of responsible Christian stewardship in matters of personal financial planning and estate planning, in adult education settings.

3. Counsel with persons as a part of your pastoral ministry, on the importance of wills and estate planning, especially in conjunction with premarital counseling, preparation for baptism of children, death of a spouse, health crisis, and funeral planning.

4. Encourage the formation of an Endowment/Permanent Funds Committee to educate and promote bequests and life income gifts in the congregation.

5. Educate yourself within the area of Planned Giving, drawing upon basic information available through the Annual Conference Foundation or Office of Development, or through the Planned Giving Resource Center of the General Board of Discipleship (P.O. Box 840, Nashville, TN 37202).

6. Communicate with church members, through the various church media channels, about wills and life-income gifts.

7. Promote, as a service to the church membership and community, a Wills Clinic and/or Estate Planning Workshop.

8. Develop with the congregation a long-range planning process, culminating in a mission statement for which major funding will be required to minister to future generations.

9. Create an Endowment/Permanent Fund committee with carefully drawn guidelines to encourage bequests in support of future ministries of the whole church.

10. Acknowledge, personally and publicly, the receiving of bequests and life-income gifts, to encourage others, as well as to thank the donor.

11. Celebrate with gratitude the "fruits" that faithful friends have made possible through gifts that support the ministry and mission of the church today.

12. Evaluate your own estate plan. Have you included the church or other charitable institutions in your will?

13. Minister patiently and faithfully, as this crucial aspect of Christian stewardship takes time to bear fruit.

 TEACHING HELP

Stewardship and Holy Communion

PATRICIA WILSON-KASTNER

When I was a child at St. Edward's in Dallas, the collection of the offering was one of the most interesting moments in Sunday worship. Perhaps that was because sometimes people would drop money on the floor, and we would have some noise and activity closer to my pew; perhaps because the ushers were fathers of other children I knew; and perhaps because the offering was an action in which I had a part. When the congregation's offering was taken to the altar, in the basket was the nickel (what a long time ago!) I had been given to place there. Even if the coin was given specially to me for that purpose by my mother, I still had something tangible to offer, which God wanted and would receive from me.

> "I believe talking about money in the church is holy talk, deeply theological, and as sacred as prayer. I believe using money in the church is both terribly serious and lots of fun. The only thing more exciting than raising money for the Kingdom is spending it for the Kingdom."
>
> —*JOE WALKER*

Stewardship and Eucharistic Offering

The basic pattern of Christian worship is: Entrance, Proclamation and Response, Thanksgiving and Communion, and Sending Forth. This pattern is classic, reaching into the very biblical roots of the church's worship. When we proclaim the Word in worship, and when we participate in the Communion, these acts contain three essential aspects: God's grace calling us together in the Word or Communion actions and elements; our response by offering prayers, gifts (including money) of our whole selves (which in many denominations is signified by rising and going up to the communion rail); and in that offering, God's grace received by us transforms ourselves, our offerings, and our world.

We can explore from many different perspectives the connections between worship and stewardship. My focus is on stewardship and sacrifice. Not sacrifice in the sense of giving up candy, as in a Lenten sacrifice. Rather, I mean sacrifice in the sense of a sacrifice in worship, an "oblation." How is our stewardship during Sunday worship an oblation before God, an essential part of our worship of God?

During the Reformation, the Reformers fought against calling the Mass a "sacrifice," because that word expressed a popular belief that every celebration of the Eucharist offers Jesus on the cross again and again to God, in a reenactment of the sacrifice of Calvary. More merit was reportedly gained each time a "fresh" sacrifice of the Mass was made. The Reformers rejected the language of sacrifice for the Eucharist, and reserved it for Calvary alone. The striving in that era was important, and the point they strove to maintain was good and true, but today we have different contentious issues to contend with.

Presently, we are uncomfortable with use of the language of sacrifice in connection with worship or stewardship, except perhaps to suggest that we should give until it hurts.

Some of our reluctance is even expressed in the desire to avoid the term *Eucharist,* which is an explicit way of naming Jesus' sacrifice. But the language of sacrifice and oblation, with respect to both stewardship and worship, is deep in the Scriptures and vital in the formation of Christian belief and practice. Exploring the idea of sacrifice can enrich and strengthen our theology of worship and our commitment to stewardship.

At the root of the issue is our effort to recover the biblical truth which was the "official" teaching of the Church universal, that "at the Lamb's high feast" we share in Jesus' self-offering made at Calvary. The language of the Holy Communion/Eucharist (and in a very real sense of all our prayers) is present tense: Jesus offers his life to God, and to us. Jesus' self-offering is made once and for all, and at the same time, we continually share and become ourselves a part of the offering, as we are joined by grace into Jesus' own life.

In baptism, the whole Body of Christ is reminded that "we are initiated into Christ's holy church. We are incorporated into God's mighty acts of salvation and given new birth through water and the Spirit. All this is God's gift, offered to us without price."[1] Through our baptism, and our sharing in the Eucharist/Holy Communion, we are accepted into God's love and empowered to be what we are created to be, God's stewards. Our stewardship involves sacrifice—a sacrifice as real in our lives as Jesus' was in his.

The most graphic and dramatic representation in the regular worship of our Christian life as stewards is in the offering of gifts at the Holy Communion. The offering of bread and wine, the stuff of ordinary life, and of gifts of money, the valuing of our everyday work, is the sign of our total self-dedication, accepted and transformed by God through the sacrificial and life-giving death and resurrection of Jesus. One well-known introductory prayer at the offering summarizes well our theology: "As forgiven and reconciled people, let us offer ourselves and our gifts to God."

Oblation is often described as "an offering of ourselves, our lives and labors, in union with Christ, for the purposes of God" (*Book of Common Prayer,* The Episcopal Church). Oblation is, thus, our willing response to God's creative and redeeming love for us by giving ourselves back to God. Oblation is a response we offer to God because we are God's creatures, and this gift is an appropriate creaturely offering. It is also, and perhaps more important, our free gift, not a tribute exacted. An oblation, a sacrificial offering, is an expression of human freedom, a gift from the heart. Oblation is the scriptural notion which most overtly connects our worship and prayer, and our practice of stewardship.

Scriptural Roots: Old Testament

Oblation, or sacrifice, was an essential element of ancient Near Eastern religions. According to the creation account of a Mesopotamian epic, humans are created to sacrifice to the gods and goddesses. Utnapishtim, a Noahlike figure, recounts that after the flood waters that covered the earth had receded, the deities surrounded his animal sacrifices like flies, because they needed the sacrificial lifeblood of the victims.

For the earliest Hebrews, sacrificing to God was so basic that it was not questioned. As Israel matured, and during conflicts between prophets and kings, a distinction emerged: God did not need sacrifices for survival or well-being; God wanted our sacrifices as an acknowledgment of divine sovereignty. In the exacting descriptions of required sacrifices in the Torah, no implication is ever made that God requires that humans sacrifice for divine well-being or satisfaction. Through the prophets, God's challenge rings: "I do not delight in the blood of bulls, or of lambs, or of goats" (Isa. 1:11).

Sacrifices of animals or material goods are required, according to the Law, but, the real requirement of the individual and the nation is an offering of "a sacrifice of thanksgiving" (Ps. 50:14). "The sacrifice acceptable to God is a broken spirit; a broken and contrite heart, O God, you will not despise" (Ps. 51:17). The physical sacrificial system of Temple worship was affirmed as an expression of worship of God, but the essential element was the sacrifice of the whole self to God.

Thus for the people of God, the religious question was not *whether* to sacrifice to God, but *how* to sacrifice to God. Because God is the ruler of life and death, the source of all and the deliverer of all, we cannot "give" anything to God except praise and thanksgiving for all God has given us, creatures of the earth. "What shall I return to the LORD for all his bounty to me? I will lift up the cup of salvation and call on the name of the LORD . . . . I will offer to you a sacrifice of thanksgiving and call upon the name of the LORD" (Ps. 116:12-13, 17).

Sacrifices are important because they are offered "in the presence of God" (Exod. 18:12), and thus link humans with God, offering them an opportunity to rejoice "in all the undertakings in which the LORD your God has blessed you" (Deut. 12:7). The sacrifices are an expression of the communion God offers the worshiper through accepting the offering.

Because sacrifices are accepted by God, the external act must be congruent with the disposition of the worshiper's heart and the person's actions. In the Scriptures, worship and behavior are integrally connected, so that, for instance, sacrifices in the Temple are to be accompanied by acts of justice, especially giving alms to the poor and protecting the interests of the weak (see Isa. 1:11-17; Amos 5:21-22).

A true oblation is offered through a life characterized by moral as well as worship purity. God does not accept one without the other. Particularly in the prophets, interior purity and obedience to God's laws were essential components in God's acceptance of the sacrifice offered (eg., Jer.7:1-20). Offering sacrifices, offering one's life in prayer, and doing good—all are, in the Scriptures, essential aspects in the same offering of the "sacrifice of thanksgiving."

Scriptural Roots: New Testament

Jesus is the sacrifice for humanity, fully acceptable to God. This central theme in the life and teaching of Jesus develops the connection between the life of internal obedience to God and true worship (eg., Matt. 23:1-39). But his death and resurrection also embody the discontinuity with Judaism, the acknowledgment that Jesus is the one true sacrifice acceptable to God (Matt. 26:20-29; 27:45-54).

The letter to the Hebrews develops the theme of Jesus' life and death as the unique sacrifice; no more sacrifices are needed. "But as it is, [Jesus] has appeared once for all at the end of the age to remove sin by the sacrifice of himself" (Heb. 26b; also see Heb. 9:9-12). Jesus is the unique high priest, who atones for human sin and restores humans to relationship with God.

Directly connected to the notion of the unique sacrifice of Jesus is the belief that our life is a life in Christ, that in and through Jesus, we are joined to his unique sacrifice. "Therefore be imitators of God, as beloved children, and live in love, as Christ loved us and gave himself up for us, a fragrant offering and sacrifice to God" (Eph. 5:1-2). "Through him, then, let us continually offer a sacrifice of praise to God, that is, the fruit of lips that confess his name" (Heb. 13:15).

Through Jesus Christ, God's people are made into a spiritual house, a "holy priesthood, to offer spiritual sacrifices acceptable to God through Jesus Christ" (I Pet. 2:5b). The baptized are exhorted to present themselves to God as a "sacrifice, holy and acceptable to God" (Rom. 12:1b). Jesus' unique sacrifice and human sacrifices are not opposed to each other or mutually exclusive; human oblations of self are received by God if they are in communion with Jesus. God accepts our sacrifices and oblations because we offer them joined with Jesus' self-giving love. The sacrifice is Jesus; God's gracious love extended to us allows us to offer ourselves to God through Jesus. Our moral life marks us as Jesus' followers, who have offered ourselves to God through Jesus.

In this New Testament perspective, stewardship is the giving of our whole lives to God, as Jesus gave himself completely to God. In Christ, all the baptized are an oblation to God. All of our words and deeds, gifts and goods, are oblations which partake of the one unique offering of Jesus. Through "conforming ourselves to the pattern of Jesus' life," we show our-

> "If we are enjoying an item, whether or not we own it, we're being frugal. For many of life's pleasures, it may be far better to 'use' than to 'possess' it."
> —*DOMINQUEZ AND ROBIN*
> *Your Money or Your Life*

selves to be people who offer themselves to God through and in Jesus.

Christian Worship and Oblation

From a biblical perspective, Christian worship is interconnected with the idea of oblation and offering—Jesus' self-offering to God, and our response to God through our self-offering. Baptism is compared to the Exodus and deliverance of the Israelites (I Cor. 10:1-4) or to Noah's ark (I Pet. 3:21). The deliverance from danger and slavery into the safety and freedom of life with God is not just an external journey; it is an internal change. Romans 6 explores in depth the theme of death and resurrection in Christ. By dying and rising in Christ, the believer's life and fate is joined to Christ's. Such change is so radical that it can be compared to being born anew (John 3:4-5).

All these themes point to the believer's becoming one of God's people, joined as one with Christ, and living in the Holy Spirit, not in the spirit of the world. Through baptism, the believer becomes one in communion with other believers, through Christ being made one body (Eph. 4:1-6). An essential part of this baptismal commitment to God through Christ is being a part of the world, but not "owned" by it. The baptized are commissioned in Christ to transform the world (Rom. 8:9-25).

The Eucharist is the food of God's people, the meal in which Jesus is both remembered and becomes present as the food of eternal life (I Cor. 11-12). The institution narratives are replete with sacrificial language: my body given, my blood outpoured. This sacrificial language clearly continues the Hebrew tradition of communion with God through sacrifice. The sacrifice of Jesus is acceptable to God and gives life to believers through the communion they have with Jesus, the sacrificial lamb.

This communion with God which the believer experiences is not simply an assurance of everlasting life with God, in some sense divorced from behavior on earth. As Paul insists in I Corinthians 11, the Lord's Supper has specific ethical consequences. Luke, in Acts 2:43-47 and 4:32-34, connects the various aspects of the life of the Jerusalem community, from corporate prayer to the sharing of economic resources.

Luke offered the most radical interconnection between Christian worship and the stewardship of all goods and resources. The Christian community, in Luke's perspective, is one in prayer and community of goods. All pray together and all work for one another's good. Probably very few, even of the Jerusalem community, actually followed this way of life; but it presented a clear and cogent picture of a united community. In reality, most of the early church seems to have understood its stewardship as involving sharing of goods, but not community of property.

One's worship and one's self and goods are no longer one's own, because in baptism and the Eucharist, the believer's self and goods are now God's through Christ. Stewardship is a direct consequence of we ourselves being an oblation to God, through Jesus.

Our Offering in the Eucharist

The New Testament directly connects oblation, worship, and the stewardship of ourselves and our time, our goods, and our gifts. Because Holy Communion is the great center of our community's worship life, it is important that all Christians understand the link between God's gift, our communion, and our offering.

This vision of our self-offering as an essential component of Jesus' self-offering, for the healing and redeeming of the world is acted out in the liturgy of the Eucharist itself. These actions of offering have, from the very beginning of Christian worship, explicitly included offerings of the money and goods of everyday life to be used in the redeeming work of God's people in the world.

In the early second century, Clement reproaches those who come to the eucharistic sacrifice without their gifts ("sacrifices") for the poor as well. His language connects the people's offerings of money and goods with the sacrificial giving of Jesus. In the eucharistic theology of the early church, much emphasis was placed on the necessity and justice of giving to the poor, and in most liturgies, that aspect of stewardship was explicitly acted out by the believers.

Many preachers and bishops of the early church, such as Augustine of Hippo and John Chrysostom, fought against the notion of absolute property rights of ownership. They taught that in Christ, all property belonged to God and to God's people. Christians could not, in any real sense, own property. They could only use it in trust for the good of the whole people of God. The offering at the Eucharist symbolized God's ownership of all property, and the Christian's radical obligation actually to return gifts to God as a part of their use of goods in God's service.

The early liturgies affirm that the Holy Communion is sacrifice, and that in Christ through the Eucharist, we offer ourselves and our goods as an expression of God's acceptance, which already has been offered in Jesus. This is the origin of the offertory, in which bread and wine, as well as goods for the poor and for support of the church, are offered. The way in which this offertory takes place differs in different liturgies, but all share the same holistic vision of our total self-offering to God through Christ.

Worship begins with a calling of the community together, our hearing and responding to the Word of God in prayer and offerings, the great thanksgiving and the communion, and the sending forth of the community into the world in mission. For our theology of stewardship and self-offering, we note the movement of the liturgy as it calls us out of the world in order to send us back into it. Our eucharistic action, between the two acts of gathering and sending out, is a process of feeding and nurturing our unity in Christ. Our transformation in worship is the strengthening of our identity as God's people, who exist to serve God and join in Jesus' healing and redeeming work of love in the world.

Action Possibilities

Here are a few specific suggestions for keeping the offering and stewardship connection clear and obvious in worship. (These suggestions can be adapted for use in a Sunday worship that does not include Holy Communion.)

Preaching. Every sermon can and should make some connection with daily life and our gift of ourselves and our lives to God in Jesus. Our stewardship is our service to God, joining ourselves with Jesus in the sanctification/transformation of the world. Preaching stewardship is an every-Sunday event, and every sermon can be a stewardship sermon, in this wider sense. John Chrysostom, that great and provocative fourth-century preacher, is a good model. He never failed to connect the gospel with contemporary life, including the economy and the social order.

Offertory. The English Reformation vitally restored the early church's insistence on our offering of ourselves to God. It made direct and concrete connections between our offering of our alms for the poor, our other gifts for the church's life and mission, the bread and wine for the communion, and the sacrifice of Christ. The offertory is essential in the Eucharist. Collection triumphalism is to be avoided, when we act as though the baskets or basins of money are the center of the liturgy. However, everything should be done in worship to emphasize that gifts, which are symbolic of our life and labor (including money), are brought to the altar as a sign of our self-offering, our sharing in the self-offering, and God's acceptance of our world in Jesus.

The practice of placing the collection (and other token gifts) on the altar and leaving them there can be very symbolic. The theological implication is that the money and other gifts are also blessed by God as sacramental instruments of grace in the world. Through sharing in the blessed bread and wine, we are nourished by God's life to be sacraments, signs of Christ's love in the world. By extension, our money and other gifts can share in this sacramental activity of Christ in the world. Our stewardship is a sacramental act, a visible sign of God's invisible grace, a bearer of grace and redemption to the world. A faith centered in the incarnation believed in making visible God's love through the holy use of money.

Communion. Through the bread and wine, we share the body and blood, the life of Jesus, and are made one in Christ. This oneness is a mutual community, implying the same interconnection among communicants as among members of a family, God's household. The stewardship aspects of this belief can be very productively explored by believers, and perhaps acted out in the liturgy. What does it mean that we are brothers and sisters? What kind of sharing of goods and time, for instance, is implicit by our taking communion together?

In The Episcopal Church, we send out eucharistic ministers to bring communion to the homebound after Sunday liturgy. May we not wish to find some way to symbolize our being sent out to transform the world with gifts of money and use of talents? Might we symbolically send forth a stockbroker, a merchant, or a farmer, as a sign of our mission to transform the life of the world through economic stewardship?

Dismissal. The dismissal in Holy Communion is not just a signal to fall back into ordinary life after a sacred interlude. It is a renewal of our baptismal commissioning, and needs to be emphasized, rather than lost in the rush to conclude the service. We are going forth to share in Jesus' redemptive transformation of the world. Perhaps a blessing, from time to time, might give some direction to the stewardship dimension of our going forth. Announcements might be made before the blessing and dismissal (as they are in some churches). This placing of the announcements could remind people of the varied aspects of living out their self-offering.

The preacher or the person making the announcements may want to make the connection explicit for the congregation from time to time: "You are invited to offer God your time and talents on Saturday, June 5, from 9 to 12, at a churchwide work day." Or, when announcing a study group: "Through our baptism, we are called to offer ourselves and all we are to God. Beginning next Sunday, our 10:00 study group will explore good stewardship and the referendum to legalize gambling in the city."

Stewardship is an essential aspect of the Christian life. Our Sunday worship, especially Holy Communion, expresses a radical biblical theology of stewardship, connecting the Christian's offering of self and possessions with Jesus' self-offering. Through baptism and Eucharist, we can preach and lead worship in ways that strengthen this cornerstone of the Christian faith. Thus our worship can better express the integrity of the connection of daily life with the creative, redeeming, and sanctifying alive and active God among us.

Note

1. *The United Methodist Book of Worship* (Nashville: The United Methodist Publishing House, 1992).

 NEWSLETTER

Committed to the Challenge

Three Open Letters from the Pastor

FIRST UNITED METHODIST CHURCH, HENDERSONVILLE, TENN.

1. Philippians 3:13-14

Today we begin a three-week time of preparation toward lifting up our stewardship commitment on Sunday, November_____. Stewardship is mistakenly seen only in terms of giving money through the church for the work of ministry and mission. Although our stewardship includes supporting the work of the church through our giving, it is also much more than that.

Stewardship is what we do with all we have, all we are, and all we can become. It is a spiritual journey in life, responding to what God has done for us in Jesus Christ. It begins with the affirmation that we are children of God. "God so loved us," we are told in the Gospel of John, that God gave. That's where our stewardship begins. Do you believe that you are a child of God? Do you believe that God loves you? Your answer to those questions will guide your stewardship in all of life!

The theme of our stewardship this fall is "_____." How you live your life, how you respond to God's call in your life, and how you are growing in your faith are this week's stewardship issues. Join with me this week, in a journey of stewardship as a faith issue.

How will you grow in your faith this next year? Will you be part of a Sunday school class each Sunday? Will you begin a daily journey through the Bible? Will you join a study class? How many Sundays each month will you be in church this next year? How often will you be in prayer each day? As you prayerfully consider your stewardship response, I invite you to join me in including these covenants as well.

2. II Corinthians 9:6

One of the areas on this year's commitment card is about "Time and Talents." Stewardship is about giving! It is about responding to God's love. That response includes money, but it also includes much more than that.

Stewardship is about who you are and what is important to you. Stewardship has been defined as "everything you do after you say YES to God." Have you said YES to God in your life? What will you do because of that yes?

One way to respond to the YES is in your work. The theological term is *vocation:* incorporating our response to God in our daily work. We invite you to look at what you do each day. How can your faith touch each day in a special way?

A second response to your stewardship is in the community. How can you touch this community in a special way through your faith? A third area of your stewardship response is your family. How does your family show its faithful response? Is going to Sunday school and worship a regular part of your family's faith? Do you include God in your meal plans?

This year we are asking you, as part of the _____ campaign, to decide how you might be part of the church's life. Each person has special gifts that God has given them. The Apostle Paul says that for some, it is teaching; for others, witnessing, serving, and giving. Other gifts might include ushering, serving as a greeter, or even on a community service organization. What are your gifts? How can the ministry of God be enhanced because of those gifts? Will you covenant this week to share those gifts this next year?

3. II Corinthians 9:7

IT IS A JOY TO GIVE! This next Sunday is Commitment Sunday. Now don't let that scare you away! It is also Holy Communion Sunday. Is that a coincidence?

In II Corinthians 8:2, the Apostle Paul talks about the "joy of generosity." In II Corinthians 9:7, he talks

> "Frugality
> is learning to share,
> to see the world as 'ours.'
> Frugality is balance.
> Frugality is right use.
> Frugality is enough."
> —*DOMINQUEZ AND ROBIN*
> *Your Money or Your Life*

about "the cheerful giver." I enjoy giving. I often wish I had more to give. I give because I believe that all I have and all I am is a gift from God. My wealth, my family, my gifts and abilities, even my thoughts, are from God. In communion, we celebrate what God has done for us in Jesus Christ, the greatest gift. I give, because God gave first.

I give because I enjoy seeing the results of my giving. Joe Walker wrote: "There is only one thing better than raising funds for the Kingdom of God, and that is spending money for the Kingdom of God."

I give through the church because I know that my giving makes a difference. I give because I see children singing, playing, and growing in the church. I give because worship touches me in a special way. I give because I see youth serving others, especially in their mission work. I give because I see how the church, working together, serves the world.

On a trip in central Illinois, I saw the place where more than 100 semi-truckloads of cleaning supplies came to a central warehouse from churches all across the United States. One of those trucks came from our city. Our church had provisions on that truck. Those supplies made a difference in cleaning up after a flood.

When I bring my commitment card to church this Sunday, I expect to increase my commitment. I know that my giving makes a difference. What will you do this Sunday?

 DRAMA

An Interactive Worship Benediction

FRAN CRADDOCK

LEADER: Standing together in this circle, we are part of the family of God. Each of us has been created by God in the image of God, called by name, and given distinctive features and unique gifts.

Look at one another. Each of us is different. We have different physical characteristics, different likes and dislikes, different faith journeys, and different

gifts. Yet, each of us is a part of the family of God, and we bring these unique and special gifts into the life of this congregation.

The Apostle Paul emphasized the value of differing gifts within a congregation when he wrote to the church at Ephesus: "The gifts [Christ] gave were that some would be apostles, some prophets, some evangelists, some pastors and teachers, to equip the saints for the work of the ministry" (Eph. 4:11-12*a*).

In the life and ministry of this congregation, every gift is important!

May we use these gifts to be creative forces in this congregation and in the world in which we live. For Paul has reminded us that "the whole creation is on tiptoe to see the wonderful sight of the sons [and daughters] of God coming into their own" (Rom. 8:19 Phillips).

PRAYER: Thank you O God, our creator and sustainer, for the gifts you have given to each of us. May we be faithful stewards in using these gifts to help build up the kingdom of God in our time and in this place. Amen.

 TEACHING HELP

The Pastor As Financial Counselor

WAYNE BARRETT

The Signals of Spiritual Health

Few opportunities occur for clergy to touch the lives of persons on so profound a level as in counseling regarding financial matters. In today's world, money is a powerful symbol of values and a component of nearly every dilemma or opportunity in life. In fact, this is not a modern phenomenon. Jesus said it best: "Where your treasure is, there will your heart be also" (Luke 12:34 RSV).

The pastoral ministry presents a wide variety of situations where a capable (and willing) pastor may render a meaningful service to persons struggling with money issues. We will examine several "contact points" for financial counseling from a pastoral perspective. It is our view that this role is a fundamental part of authentic pastoral ministry.

At the root of the pastoral relationship is the biblical image of the pastor as one who "knows the sheep." Clergy who pursue this role are making a commitment to acquire and exploit an intimate level of knowledge regarding the financial lives of parishioners. This will require a high level of maturity and utmost professional standards.

Perhaps the fundamental point of the pastoral relationship is awareness of the giving level of each family in the congregation. There is no better indicator of a variety of faith/financial issues than the amount of money contributed. This information is a "signal," a catalyst for pastoral intervention. Among the messages signaled by the giving pattern may be:•

● A Faith Crisis—Low giving may be a measurable expression of a vague spiritual disease. Intervention triggered by this may not even require the pastor to mention what prompted the visit; the faith issue may surface spontaneously, with no need to announce the financial signal that enabled its diagnosis.

● A Family Crisis—Among the symptoms frequently exhibited by families in turmoil is a lowered giving level. We have observed this often enough to understand a reduced pledge to be a call for help.

● A Financial Crisis—One of the first expressions of a financial reversal is often a dramatic reduction in giving. Pastors on the lookout for this phenomenon can often render an important service of counsel and support.

● A Medical Crisis—Occasionally a desperate person will use stewardship as a bargaining chip with God. Faced with a life-threatening illness, a person may

"Psychologists call money the 'last taboo.' It is easier to tell a therapist about our sex life than it is to tell our accountant (or our pastor) about our finances. Money—not necessarily how much we have, but how we feel about it—governs our lives as much or more than any other factor. Why?"

—*JOE WALKER*

dramatically *increase* the level of giving. This is a true cry for pastoral care, and yet, clergy who do not know the giving pattern of their people will never be able to offer the necessary intervention.

The Pastor and New-Member Orientation

Much of the fear of intervention that many pastors feel will be removed if an active program of new-member orientation is practiced. During this process, the pastor can create a "climate for giving." Prospective members are searching, and they often exhibit a much higher level of openness regarding stewardship and other financial concepts.

Among the issues to be explored during a new member orientation process:

Biblical/Theological Basis of Stewardship. Until we know what we believe about stewardship, it is unlikely that we will find much satisfaction in our practice of stewardship.

Explanation of the Liturgy of the Offering. What is the function of "the offering"? How does this differ from a "collection"? Many persons know little about the symbolism of the act of giving in worship. (Some churches, to their regret, seem to give the impression that the only purpose of the offering is to finance the church budget!) The pastor who substantiates the relationship between the Holy Communion and the offering (based on the biblical link between worship and sacrifice) will have built "staying power" into the giving experience of new members.

Values Clarification Strategies. Social scientists Milton Rokeach and Seymour Parker have developed an exercise of ranking one's values from a list of eighteen common value issues. Participants are asked to select five of these values as being more important, and then rank them, one through five. Additionally, participants are asked to place dollar signs ($) beside those values that require money or influence the use of money. The Rokeach/Parker list appears below.[1]

- A comfortable life
- An exciting life
- A sense of accomplishment
- A world of peace
- Equality
- Family security
- Freedom
- Happiness
- Inner harmony
- Mature love
- National security
- Pleasure
- Self-respect
- Social recognition
- True friendship
- Wisdom

> "Learn to choose quality of life over standard of living."
> —DOMINQUEZ AND ROBIN
> *Your Money or Your Life*

Tithing and Proportionate Giving. A fundamental question on the minds of inquiring new members is, "How much should I give?" Until we give assistance with this question, it is unlikely that our members will experience much satisfaction from their giving or that giving will climb much beyond its current level.

The Pastor and the Newly Widowed

A significant opportunity for meaningful pastoral intervention is found with those who have lost a spouse. Particularly among the generation of "traditional" women, a common phenomenon is the woman whose deceased husband "handled the

> "Giving away one's wealth without having one's heart in it brings euphoria—but not joy. And what comes is ultimately manipulation and vengeance."
> —PAUL TILLICH

money." In some cases, it is the sheer novelty of the new responsibility that is intimidating. In other situations, there is powerful new information that can be absolutely overwhelming. We have encountered widows who were devastated to discover that they had virtually no money; we also have worked with widows shaken by the unexpected discovery of significant wealth. Each can be a fertile field for pastoral care and support.

Widowers are not immune to this syndrome. In today's world, a substantial percentage of couples have developed the tradition of the wife as bill-payer/financial manager. A newly widowed man may be intimidated by the new responsibilities facing him. A pastor who indicates an interest and the ability to help can be a godsend.

The Pastor, Marriage Counseling, and Divorce

Among the primary sources of marital tension and conflict is money. Pastoral counselor Paul Schurman points out that "9 out of 10 persons who divorce suffer conflict with money."[2] Can you offer helpful intervention to such a couple?

When a money problem surfaces in pastoral counseling, it is sometimes adequate to provide a book or other resource for the couple's use. Pastors should discover what financial counseling resources are available in their community. Credit counseling may be appropriate for severe financial stress. Some agencies may be able to offer low cost services. Financial planners may be able to assist, but be careful about automatic referral here. If the planner can be compensated only by commission, it may not be fair to either planner or client when the issue is *lack* of money, rather than its investment.

The Pastor and Premarital Counseling

When I entered the ministry, it was a common part of premarital counseling for the pastor to inquire if the couple needed sex education. How quaint this seems today! Yet there does exist today a profound need for economic education—particularly among those who are marrying for a second time or later in life. These persons have already existing spending patterns in place, patterns that may be absolutely "out of sinc" with those of their new mate. Discovering who is a spender and who is a saver is often a surprising experience for couples.

Varieties of values-clarification exercises as presented above can be enormously useful in the context of premarital counseling. Identifying one's own and one's partner's orientation can be a source of tension but also a substantial confirmation of the relationship.

The world is ready for pastors who exhibit interest in the total lives of their parishioners. This requires active involvement in the economic, as well as the spiritual dimensions of our members' lives. The challenge is substantial, but how great the satisfaction of touching lives at this most profound level. The pastor who can provide a faith and economic perspective out of which persons can grow as disciples, will have performed important work indeed.

Notes

1. See "Values as Social Indicators of Poverty and Race in America," *The Angels of the American Academy of Politcal and Social Science,* Vol. 388 (March 1970), pp. 97-111.
2. Paul Schurman, *Money Problems and Pastoral Care* (Minneapolis: Fortress Press, 1982), p. ix.

PART THREE

MONEY MANAGEMENT IN THE CHURCH

For Pastors and Finance Teams

Introduction

DONALD W. JOINER

The role of the pastor in financial stewardship is to bring together the vision of the congregation in ministry, and to ground that financial ministry with a spiritual focus. The role of laity, or more specifically, the financial officers of the congregation is to design and manage the financial-management process.

"Help us with our finances" is the frequent cry of congregations today. Many churches are experiencing "tight money," and the same cry is heard locally, regionally, and nationally: "Help! The same old ways are no longer working!"

Many church leaders think about financial stewardship the same way they have for the past forty years. Financial stewardship is not a new issue. It has merely caught up with us in an environment where the competition for financial support is enormous! Symptoms of "tight money" began showing up in the early 1980s. Many churches solved the problem by cutting programs and pinching pennies. The current problem is that perhaps we have cut as much as we can, and we have pinched as many pennies as we can. Where do we go from here?

Over the previous 25 years, many corporations, and some denominational offices, have been heavily involved in a movement known as Total Quality Management. One phrase that keeps ringing in the ears of church leaders: "The system produces the results that it is designed to produce." Are you satisfied with the results your church is getting—in membership, in attendance, in participation, in giving? If not, look at your church's system.

The goal of this section of the *Abingdon Guide* is to provide insight into the financial management system of the congregation. Laura Wright begins by challenging the concept that people are giving all they can or want to give to the church. There are enough financial resources in each congregation to do what God wants that congregation to do in ministry. The question is not, "Is there enough money?" but "Do you believe enough in the ministry and mission of Jesus Christ?" Mary Boyd tells the story of one church in which the system was broken, with advice to get back to the basics.

When you read everything in this book, the normal response is "Where do I begin?" Hilbert Berger lists 14 clear and concise steps that will focus any church's financial system on the basics.

Congregational budgets are confusing subjects in funding ministry. Finance leaders develop a budget and then try to raise money by pushing that budget on the members. In reality, there are two budgets in every church. There is a management budget and there is a promotional budget. One is needed to operate the church. The other is needed to raise funds for min-

istry. Richard Kelly shows a way to create and use a budget.

One of the barriers that needs to be lifted is the perceived conflict of Unified Budgets versus Designated Giving. James P. Johnson points to both. Back in the 1950s, churches of all denominations accepted a unified-budget concept. It was probably viable for the church in 1950. And it may still be correct for some budget items today. Jim points to a larger issue: "Do we need an institution-based or a donor-based system?"

 MEDITATION

Give the Givers a Voice!

LAURA E. WRIGHT

High commitment Christians want to support their church. The people of God continually show love for the church and their belief in the gospel, when tithes and offerings are poured out without question. Gifts of money and time stream into congregations, and out into the world, with rarely an inquiry about financial reports or profit-and-loss statements. Other secular charities face more careful screenings.

Clearly, there are more than enough funds available to ensure God's work all over the world. One need only look at the amounts of money contributed and distributed during major disasters and crises to realize the potential. Yet, in spite of their financial capabilities, church structures in most major denominations are striving to carry on their work with less funding every year. This may be because many people in congregations feel that decisions for the use of their money are being made without their input.

It is therefore necessary for national and judicatory branches throughout the church to help the people of God become more aware of continuing needs in the world—to advise often, and in detail, where money has gone, what effect it has had, and how it has changed lives. If the financial support given to the church at any level is not seen as nurturing and life-changing to the recipients, it also is not seen as supporting and spreading the gospel of Jesus Christ.

The mission and ministry of the church at large, and throughout the world, often can be done most effectively at a different level than through the local congregation. After years of experience through ecumenical relationships, there are structures, programs, and organizations in place at national and global levels. These enable appropriate communication of needs and distribution of goods and funds.

Almost every person or congregation has a particular interest or concern that appeals to them more than others. Many congregations have food pantries or shelters for the homeless. There are Christians everywhere who minister to AIDS victims or conduct prison ministries. Churches, dioceses, and conferences all over the United States and Canada sponsor refugee families who seek asylum or have been displaced during wars or disasters. There are opportunities for individuals and churches to support a wide variety of ministries.

> "It's always worthwhile
> to make others aware
> of their worth."
> —MALCOLM S. FORBES

Those who provide support must also be allowed to be part of the decision-making process.

Denominational churches have become aware in recent years that when the church does not involve itself in addressing the basic needs and concerns of God's people—food, shelter, work, and health care—people will give their support to agencies outside the church where they see these economic essentials being given the attention they deserve.

In addition to supporting the global work of the church, lay people can fully participate in the mission of Jesus Christ and see the results personally through the ministry of the congregation. It is here, the place where they feel closest to God, that they experience the greatest satisfaction in their giving. It is in the community church that individual Christians are able to participate more fully in decisions about what will be funded and which local ministries are required. It is here, too, that they determine how much they will give personally to the projects and programs offered.

With appropriate and cooperative congregational leadership, they can also sometimes participate in the decisions about how much money the congregation will expend. It is not a question of control. It is that the giver must feel that he or she is a part of the process.

There is much talk today, in and out of the church, about paradigm shifts. But there has been no shift regarding the expectation of God's people as to where their gifts are spent. The mission of Jesus Christ and the ministries of God's church have always been ardently supported by committed lay people. We will continue to do so, as well as increase our giving, as long as we are asked, given the opportunity to give, and kept informed of what our gifts are accomplishing.

 MEDITATION

City Repossesses Church Piano!

MARY BOYD

One evening two weeks before Christmas, the TV newscaster was heard to announce: "The city has repossessed a piano from a church in this city, due to nonpayment of penalties." He went on to explain that a total of seventeen false fire alarms had resulted in charges against the church, and officials of the church had neglected to pay the fines.

Included on the telecast was a church member, who replied, "The Christmas pageant will not be affected. We still have an organ." What a shame. What a sorry story just prior to Christmas.

The following morning, on the front page of the daily newspaper (lower right column): "Judge calls city Mr. Scrooge; admonishes authorities to exemplify true 'spirit of Christmas' by returning the church's piano."

It is puzzling how a church of more than 250 members can get into such a financial bind. That church had existed for at least fifteen years. The pastor was well respected by the community, held several degrees, and was esteemed as a coordinator in the national work of the church. He was relatively young

as a leader (mid-forties). His wife also was well educated and respected for her business expertise. How could a church (seemingly in good standing in other areas), stay in financial trouble? Something definitely was amiss.

The pastor apparently addressed the subject of "money" in an apologetic manner. Several members of the Finance Committee were considered professionals. However, an attitude of reluctance to approach the subject of money was obvious within this group.

In many instances, leaders fail (by precepts and example) to teach giving as being a response to God. Since there is joy in giving, why do so many worshipers "live below their privilege"? They don't experience this joy. The leaders of these financially ailing congregations apparently do not have adequate know-how in this phase of the ministry. It takes money to provide shelter, food, and clothing. It takes money to send our kids to college. It takes money to travel. Let's go back to the basics!

 HANDOUT

Back to the Basics: 14 Commandments

HILBERT BERGER

1. Begin by affirming that a theology, a church lifestyle, does not insist that a personal response and an effective witness must be held suspect. Without a call for generous response and effective witness, we "play" church.

2. Preach the essence of Christian stewardship in every sermon. (Every sermon should call for a personal response.)

3. Make many stewardship tools available to the total church.

4. Study carefully all the options for funding a congregation, in order to educate and lead people to a generous response.

5. Supervise the teaching of the principles of stewardship at every level in the church school.

6. Keep a careful accounting of the church's corporate stewardship. (Is money being spent as it was appropriated?)

7. Develop a program worthy of generous support. It must be seen as a good investment by potential givers. (How will lives be changed?)

8. Teach giving as a spiritual act, as a response to God's grace, at every opportunity.

9. Select carefully all stewardship program leaders.

(Even God cannot build a church out of uncommitted leaders.)

10. Study carefully the giving patterns of all the members of the church, especially its leadership.

11. Focus a new kind of attention on the core givers. Understand the Rule of 3 and the Rule of 7. Be aware of the 80-20 concept: 20 percent of the givers contribute 80 percent of the funds.

12. Understand and act on the fact that there is an increasing demand for our charitable dollars, but an increasing desire to spend the budget at home. (Our people need help in deciding.)

13. Plan an annual celebration, during which the total church can reflect on its present and future. Do not ask for commitments at this event. This is a party!

14. Remember always that leadership sets the style and quality of the stewardship response. Total staff involvement is compulsory.

"A dead church doesn't ask
for money."
—*CLARA BESS EIKNER*

BUDGET TOOL

Back to the Basics: 12 Stewardship Sins

WAYNE BARRETT

How do we learn effective stewardship skills? For most of us, it comes from experience—our own or vicarious experience. And how are these experiential skills achieved? Commonly, by making many mistakes! These mistakes, our "stewardship sins," may be the "flip side" of powerful stewardship strategies. When we repent of these sins, we begin to practice positive stewardship techniques that can build the church.

What we offer here are not presented as scientific formulae, but as basic components of the stewardship mosaic. Stewardship is, after all, much more an art form than a science. What works in one congregation

will not necessarily work in the same way in another. Common to each, however, are these "fundamentals" which we now present.

Sin #1. Confusing Fund-raising with Stewardship

Note a critical difference between stewardship and fund-raising. This does not imply that one is qualitatively better than the other. They are simply *different.* Each may be appropriate at some time in the life of every congregation, but the fundamental "sin" is to miss the distinction between them. Congregations in trouble are frequently churches that practice nothing but fund-raising.

What's the matter with this approach? Among the practical implications is the matter of competition. When the church becomes a fund-raising organization, it is competing in a much larger universe. Check your community, and you will find that it is filled with fund-raising organizations. In addition to the obvious nonprofit competitors—United Way, colleges, and hospitals—don't overlook a much bigger source of competition from the for-profit sector. As a fund-raising organization, you will be competing with Wal-mart, Ford, and L. L. Bean.

The auto dealer in town is in business to sell and service cars. Such products and services also are part of a much larger goal, a goal that makes business enterprise possible—raising money for shareholders! The church that presents itself as merely another fund-raiser will compete head-to-head with marketing powerhouses that often possess superior locations, marketing budgets, and sales staff. Under these circumstances, is it really any surprise that the church frequently experiences failure and frustration?

The church that practices *stewardship,* however, will have this market all to itself. Nobody else in town is in the stewardship business. Stewardship is one motivation that is uniquely religious, or spiritual. And yet, our "sin" is that we frequently forfeit this edge by practicing fund-raising instead of stewardship. It's like having the best athletes in the state and keeping them on the bench. You may still win a few games that way, but why would you *want* to? Stewardship is our "star"; put it in the game!

Sin #2. Begging Instead of Motivating

Many of the procedural mistakes we make in the finances of the church are rooted in this fundamental error. We couch the language of giving in the context of the church's plans to spend, rather than the donor's motivation to give.

A quick test to see whether your church is in the begging business: Do you distribute a "Proposed Budget"? When we ask for funds in the context of our proposed budget, we are *begging*.

Ask yourself, "Is this budget really a motivational tool?" Probably not. In fact, the budget often contains information that serves to depress motivation for giving. On the one hand, it may contain items the donor doesn't understand or support or, on the other hand,

the "bare bones" budget contains so little real ministry that it elicits no response at all. Even worse are the "bait and switch" budgets which include a wide array of exciting new projects in the "proposed" version, only to remove all the new items when the "real" budget is finally prepared.

We have much to learn about motivation in our churches. If the budget doesn't motivate (and it doesn't), what will? Look at two common strategies—one not likely to work, and the other, a proven "winner."

A common, if unsuccessful, strategy is called "The Pharaoh's Method." As the name suggests, this is an ancient device developed by the pharaohs of Egypt. When building the pyramids, the workers were divided into crews of ten. Occasionally, however, the stone to be moved proved impossible to budge. At this point, the pharaohs would send out an archer, who would shoot one of the ten. Invariably, the surviving nine could move what ten had been unable to budge.

Can this method be used in the church? Of course not. Even if we had the right to shoot our underperforming donors, it still would not be appropriate. Yet countless churches practice a form of the Pharaoh's Method by haranguing their members with guilt-laden diatribes. We must always remember that the church is a *voluntary* institution. Negative motivations seldom work in such an environment.

A positive motivational technique that does work, however, is the "Salt Block Method." This method, learned by countless farm kids, recognizes the truth of the aphorism, "You can lead a horse to water but you can't make it drink." It is pointless to lead a horse directly to the water. Rather, take the horse by the salt block first. Then, when arriving at the water, the animal is thirsty. This is the soul of motivational theory. Create a thirst, a hunger, a demand. Then people (and horses) will respond.

Before we give in to the temptation to beg for funds, let's take some time to create interest in what the funds are needed for.

Sin #3. Lowering the River
Instead of Raising the Drawbridge

A time of financial crisis in the church is a classic example of the need to make a distinction between the *symptom* and the real *problem*. Most important, this requires us to be clear about strategies meant to solve the problem.

When a boat won't fit under a drawbridge, there are two possible solutions. Efforts can be directed toward lowering the water level of the river itself, or the drawbridge may be raised. It should be no surprise that in most such situations, the response is to raise the bridge.

In the church, we usually do just the opposite. When confronted with a proposed budget that won't fit under the current level of giving, many churches give in to the solution of lowering the budget, instead of raising the giving.

A common proposal in such an environment is the suggestion that we should "run the church like a business." This proposal is frequent, plausible, and wrong. It is ill-suited to most churches because of a failure to make a critical distinction between the church and a for-profit enterprise.

Two generic methods are available for improving profitability in a business: One could, on the one hand, increase revenue (usually by raising prices or increasing sales), or one could cut costs (usually by reducing payroll). Either of these strategies could increase profitability, if everything else remained equal.

The problem comes when we attempt to introduce these proven strategies into the voluntary arena of the church. In the church, we seldom have cost-cutting alternatives fully available to us. While some churches have "fat" that could be removed from their budgets, most churches really don't. In these situations, when the finance leadership attempts to address a budget shortfall solely on the cost side, the result is a reduction in what, in business terms, would be called "inventory." There is simply less "ministry" to offer to our donors. Donors often then respond with reductions in giving, and the shortfall is never eliminated.

For the vast majority of our churches, the only meaningful solution is to be found on the reverse side of the equation. Only increased giving will result in a stronger congregation.

Sin #4. Focusing on the Product Instead of the Person

Many churches behave like "sales" organizations. Their emphasis is always on selling their product, whether it is a ministry or the entire budget. Sooner or later, however, you will come face-to-face with something you can't "sell." A new parsonage, for example, is not something that can be promoted easily to donors as a good deal. Ultimately, these items are funded by gifts, not purchases.

Successful churches focus on their people and become oriented toward marketing, rather than sales. Marketing organizations try to respond to the market, rather than attempting to make the market respond to them. If your church is experiencing difficulty in increasing its income, perhaps you are "selling" when you should be "marketing."

Sin #5. Assuming Everybody Is Alike

If there is one major error that finance teams make, it is to presume that everyone in the congregation will be responsive in the same way to the same stimuli. Team members often believe that everyone feels just as they do. When they don't like special second-mile offerings, they may suppose that nobody likes them.

Often a well-meaning member will propose that everyone be asked to pledge a "fair share," or increase giving by $5.00 per week. No matter how rational this may seem, such efforts always fail, because *all people are not alike.*

I once thought that I had discovered the exception to the rule—a church where everybody was alike. When I arrived at the church, I couldn't help noticing that all the people there were couples and all in their twenties. Moreover, all the women were pregnant. Just as I was marveling at the homogeneity of the church, a leader arrived and announced, "Welcome to our Lamaze Class!" The Finance Committee was down the hall.

You will unlock tremendous potential when you recognize that a wide variety of motives and preferences exist in every congregation. Look for the untapped resources. Be alert for those who respond in new ways. Work at expanding the horizons of your congregation's giving.

Sin #6. No Target for Giving

The longer I am involved in stewardship, the more I become convinced that people need targets and goals for giving. Underlying virtually every gift solicitation is the donor's question, "What is it you want me to do?" Providing a clear answer to this question is not only helpful, it promotes additional giving.

The best targets are clear and specific—the equivalent of a "Bull's Eye." Ask yourself this question: "If we had to, could we express our expectation from our donors in a single sentence?" What would that sentence say?

The great labor leader Samuel Gompers was once asked, "What does labor want?" He replied with one word—"More!" Such messages, while direct, are much too vague to serve as motivational tools. Yet many a church routinely sends out such signals. "More" is not an adequate target for increased giving.

Perhaps the best learning experience I ever had about targets occurred long before I became involved professionally in fund-raising. While conducting a neighborhood canvas for the March of Dimes, I came to the last house on my block. All I knew about this person was that he was a funeral director who had recently sold the funeral parlor and now, for the first time in his life, was living in a residential neighborhood.

When I asked for a contribution, he queried, "What's the usual gift?"

I swallowed hard and replied, "The usual gift is $25.00," whereupon he took out his checkbook and wrote a check for $25.00.

As I accepted his gift, I responded, "Thank you, Max. In the entire neighborhood, you're the only one who gave the 'usual' gift. Everyone else gave a dollar."

Sin #7. Selling a Dead Horse

While it should be obvious to everyone that it is more fun to buy something new than to pay for something old, finance teams often behave just the opposite. Appeals for additional giving are just as likely to occur after funds have already been spent. In fact, it is often when the church has a serious deficit that we start to ask for giving.

Extra giving to "bale out" the deficit is no fun and usually grows solely out of loyalty. As loyalty becomes in shorter supply, the ability to "sell a dead horse" becomes extremely limited. But enabling something new is fun and exciting. (And more likely to generate the largest amount of extra cash.)

Two little churches had nearly identical problems— cash deficits of about $2,000 (two weeks worth of usual giving). The first church chose to have a "Catch Up Sunday," when members were urged to give extra to help the church finances catch up with expenditures. Each member who made a second-mile gift would receive a bottle of ketchup as an incentive. Sure enough, "Catch Up Sunday" brought in an extra $1,800 (after deducting the cost of ketchup).

The other church, however, emphasized funding for several popular future projects, ministries that could not be assured, given the congregation's precarious finances. Donors were challenged to give a second-mile gift designated for one of these future ministries. On the next Sunday, an additional $7,700 was received. Freed of the obligation of these now fully funded ministries, the deficit was easily financed out of future offerings. Everyone was happy, and a burden had become an opportunity.

Sin #8. Protecting the People

Clergy are guilty of this sin above all others. If there is one heresy heard more frequently than any other, it is, "Our people are already giving all they can."

A young boy was once fiteen minutes late for school. When he walked in tardy, the teacher asked, "Why are you late, Johnny?"

Johnny replied, "Well, teacher, I'm a Boy Scout, and we are taught to help people. I'm late because I've been helping a little old lady across the street."

The skeptical teacher remarked, "That shouldn't have taken fifteen minutes."

Whereupon, Johnny rejoined, "It wasn't easy. She didn't want to go across the street."

Stewardship Myths
1. People are giving all they can.
2. When people sign an annual pledge, that is all they intend to give.
3. People think through each act of giving before they give.
4. When times are tough, giving can be expected to decline.
5. There is never enough time, or money, or . . . .
6. Pastors should not know what members give.
7. Charity begins at home.
8. If you ask people to give, they will get mad and leave.

Presumably, many Scouts have grown up to become clergy and possess a powerful instinct to offer "help" that is neither appropriate nor desired. Laity regularly express the thought, "Why didn't somebody tell me about this need/opportunity/crisis?"

A critical role of leadership in finance is the obligation to share opportunities and challenges for giving. The rank and file may not always respond with an outpouring of money, but they are infinitely more likely to give than if they are kept in the dark.

Sin #9. Allowing "Lost" People to Be Leaders

Moses may have been the first, but certainly not the last person in a leadership role who had no clue as to how to get to the promised land. We regularly encounter congregations in financial crises, when a significant contribution to the problem is the lack of leadership from finance leaders. In nearly every case, the source of this dilemma is the fact that these "leaders" are lousy givers. This is the financial equivalent of lost people being asked to serve as navigators.

If there is one fundamental technique that can improve the financial health of nearly any church, it is to recruit finance leaders solely from a pool of dedicated givers. This does not imply recruiting only the wealthy. In fact, persons of means who are contributing large but statistically insignificant gifts would set a miserable example. Look for people who are contributing amounts that demonstrate commitment. These will be the true leaders of the financial ministry of your church.

Sin #10. Too Much Emphasis on Donor Income

After 2,000 years of stewardship campaigns, I believe it is fair to say that our members are now aware that we wish them to give a portion of their incomes to the ministry of the church. Unfortunately, this is not an adequate standard—either for many donors as a giving guideline, or for the adequate funding of our churches.

A true revelation can occur when donors are reminded that income alone is but one source of giving. We frequently present this by using the metaphor of two "pockets." Each "pocket" represents a source from which gifts may be made.

The first pocket represents income. It is the "change" pocket because, comparatively speaking, income is small change. The positive side of the income pocket is that it is replenished regularly. It does not matter when the paycheck arrives—weekly, bi-monthly, monthly—the fact is that regular income makes an excellent source from which to make regular gifts.

The second pocket, however, corresponds to the wallet, where bills, rather than change, are kept. The second pocket represents not income, but assets. While the first pocket is what we *earn*, the second pocket is what we *own*. As we grow older, the relative balance between the pockets shifts heavily in favor of the second pocket. Donors age 50 and older usually find that the asset pocket will be 100 times or more larger than the income pocket.

Whenever the church needs extra funds—a capital project, endowment, or anything beyond the regular budget—look beyond the income pocket and you will find what successful congregations have known for years. The second pocket is where the real money for funding ministry can be found.

Sin #11. Failure to Emphasize Commitment

What we believe intuitively can now be substantiated as a fact: People who give out of a sense of commitment not only enjoy a richer relationship with the church, they also *give* considerably more money!

The Rockefeller Foundation study of giving patterns in America established these striking details. The average annual giving to the church of American Protestants in a recent year:

Nonpledgers	$440
$ Pledgers	$880
% Pledgers	$1,220

Why Do Contributors Give?
What Do They Get in Exchange?

- *Pride of association, prestige relationships*
- *Need for personal power, control*
- *To demonstrate gratitude*
- *Guilt*
- *To be liked or appreciated*
- *Recognition*
- *To meet a responsibility*
- *Sense of spiritual elevation, satisfaction*
- *Feeling of moral obligation*
- *"Enlightened" self-interest*
- *Interest in helping others*
- *Peer pressure*
- *To build self-esteem*
- *To set an example of leadership*
- *Sympathy*
- *To improve quality of life*
- *To honor a loved one*
- *Sense of "equity" in an organization*
- *To feel wanted or needed*
- *Because they were asked*
- *To end the solicitation*

People willing to make a financial commitment and express it in terms of dollars gave twice the amount nonpledgers gave. Furthermore, those willing to express their commitment as a percentage of household income gave nearly *three times* the amount nonpledgers gave.

Don't claim that it doesn't matter whether people pledge or not. The numbers make it clear that it makes a great difference indeed. When people tell me, "I'll give, but I won't pledge," I make a mental note that what they are actually saying is, "but I won't give very much."

Sin #12. Failure to Understand Where Money Comes From

As one who has seen both success and failure in congregational funding campaigns, I observe that a common cause of the failures was a profound ambiguity regarding where church money comes from. Many persons are absolutely convinced that the funds will come from "somebody else." Consider this myth that has an all-too-true ring to it:

WHO DID THE JOB?

Did you hear the story about four people: Everybody, Somebody, Anybody, and Nobody?

There was an important job to be done, and Everybody was sure that Somebody would do it. Anybody could have done it, but Nobody did it.

So Everybody blamed Somebody, when Nobody did what Anybody could have done!

Ultimately, the members of our congregations must become aware that they are the source of the church's resources. *Their* pockets, both income and capital, become the ultimate source of financial resources for today's church.

The best days for the church lie ahead of us. There are more than adequate resources for all our ministries—if only we would learn from and repent of our financial "sins." Perhaps the French theologian Teilhard de Chardin has put it best: "Someday, after we have mastered the winds, the waves, the tides, and gravity, mankind will learn to harness for God the energy of human love; then, for the second time in history, we truly will have discovered *fire*."

 BUDGET TOOL

Making the Vision Visible

The Program/Budget Building Process

RICHARD KELLY

A compelling vision is required if the church is to have a dynamic, growing life. The people must look into their hearts and see what their church can become. How can we develop the vision into a visible vehicle that will involve many people?

This vision is not directly related to growth in numbers. It is concerned with self-image. The knowledge that we are working in the image of Christ and doing our part toward the building of God's kingdom must be known and owned. Without this awareness, some programs of great value are merely exercises in staying busy.

Here is one way to assimilate your annual program. It has been refined many times. Each church is different and may find it more convenient to alter this process. But no matter what revisions are made, the plan should include the following:

1. Involvement, for increased ownership.
2. Visibility, for enhanced communication.
3. Realistic goal, to insure success.

This process is not without obstacles. It will take a significant amount of time and energy, particularly in the first few years. But you already knew that hard work is crucial to any plan that yields results.

A friend of mine, who enjoyed sleeping very late, once said, "I really love the early morning. It's so calm and peaceful. I just wish it didn't start so early!" Many churches will experience a similar emotion with this planning process. But like the farmer who knows that you cannot cram in the planting just before the harvest, finance leaders in the church who plant early will achieve a bumper yield.

Step I

In July, the program council or committee conducts a serious evaluation of all programs. Every area must be considered: nursery, maintenance, worship, janitorial, education, cost control. The questions must be searching, and asked by persons other than those directly responsible for the program:

- What is working well?
- What isn't working?
- What is working okay but needs refinement?
- What does each ministry cost?
- Could these same dollars be better used elsewhere?
- What new ministry needs to be started?
- What existing ministry has outlived its need?
- Are the ministries consistent with this particular church's mission and vision?

A large number of people—both leaders and participants—must be involved in this process. Each work group is to develop a method of gathering data from persons involved in their program. Face-to-face interviews work best, but written surveys that need not be signed are sometimes helpful. Every church, every area, every department, will need to find the way that best suits the character of the people. In the middle of the summer, it may be difficult to gather this level of interest and energy, but it is vital to do this. If people are not given a chance to be heard and let the leadership know their real needs, they will not participate in the results. Our ability to listen and understand the needs is critical to this step.

Step II

Once you have completed the evaluation, begin to sketch plans for the next year. This is the time to determine the reasons for each program. What needs are you attempting to satisfy? Establish a specific time for special events. If you are planning a church-wide event in April, care must be taken to avoid conflict with other energy-consuming programs. Each program should be documented. We are not always clear about what to document, so a sample worksheet is provided to assist you (see p. 70).

PROGRAM WORKSHEET FOR 199___   WORK GROUP _____

Describe your program as specifically as possible. Objectives should be realistic, attainable, and compatible with the congregation's overall goals and priorities. Establish time frames and estimate expense as closely as you can. Priorities should be marked: (1) a must; (2) highly desirable; (3) desirable, but can be deferred. Anything not marked will be considered a (3). NOTE: The estimated cost for 199___ must be a realistic estimate of what you think the program will cost—please don't just use the budgeted cost.

PROGRAM MINISTRY	OBJECTIVE	WHO DOES WHAT, WHEN, HOW	ACCT. CODE	ESTIMATED COST IN 199___	ESTIMATED COST IN 199___	PRIORITY

Each work group or ministry area is urged to write down all plans and programs on the worksheet. This documentation is extremely important if you expect funding for the coming year. When you make these programs and events visible for yourself, you begin to understand the impact. However, it will take a number of people, committing a number of hours.

You also will want to calculate and write down the costs. There is a space on the form that allows you to put down the cost of the same or similar program that took place in the current year. Remember that in the evaluation process, we were asked to determine the cost of current programs. This will be an *estimated* cost, since the year is not complete. Make sure you enter the estimated cost, not the budgeted amount! These are often very different. These figures will be a basis for estimating the actual increase or decrease in the need for funds. They also become important for the finance committee to do a better job of cash-flow management in the current year.

On the worksheets, list the programs for the current year that are not to be continued. Others will want to know about such changes. This will also alter the total picture for funds needed in the current year and in order to compare that with the coming year's expenses.

Note that areas should record the various programs that do not have a direct expense connected to them! This is not just *budget* building, it is *program* building. This helps us to understand that some of the most important ministries that take place do not cost a lot of money. Ministries accomplished by caring and committed volunteers have great impact on the life of a church.

When each work area completes the program worksheets, the leadership group can review the total program of ministry. Priorities should be established. Some programs are a "must"; others fall into a second place group, which can be called "highly desirable." The third ranking is "desirable" but could be "deferred." When all is said and done, we need to accept the fact that we probably can't carry out every program and event we dream up. Organizing priorities at this point gives us a more rational system of dealing with the total church priorities at a later date. An example of a completed page follows, based on the program for the commitment campaign at a fictitious church.

PROGRAM WORKSHEET FOR 199__   STEWARDSHIP WORK GROUP_____

Spell out your program as specifically as possible. Objectives should be realistic, attainable, and compatible with the overall goals and priorities. Establish time frames and estimate expense as closely as you can. Priorities should be marked: (1) a must; (2) highly desirable; (3) desirable, but can be deferred. Anything not marked will be considered a (3). NOTE: The estimated cost for 199__ must be a realistic estimate of what you think the program will cost—please don't merely use the budgeted cost.

PROGRAM MINISTRY	OBJECTIVE	WHO DOES WHAT, WHEN, HOW	ACCT. CODE	ESTIMATED COST IN 199__	ESTIMATED COST IN 199__	PRIORITY
COMMIT-MENT	To challenge every member to grow in service, and financial and spiritual gifts.	This is a specific point of renewal and commitment for the coming year. The Stewardship Committee will select a chairperson, and with that person and any other resource person necessary, design a program, recruit volunteers, coordinate the work, and see that the pledge campaign is complete by early in December.	53021	$1,250	$1,400	

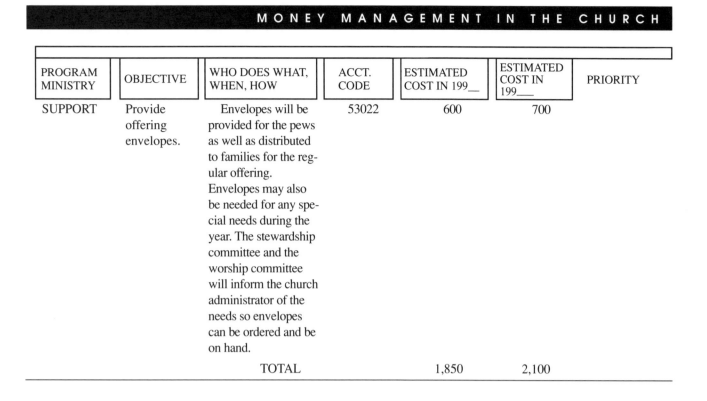

PROGRAM MINISTRY	OBJECTIVE	WHO DOES WHAT, WHEN, HOW	ACCT. CODE	ESTIMATED COST IN 199__	ESTIMATED COST IN 199___	PRIORITY
SUPPORT	Provide offering envelopes.	Envelopes will be provided for the pews as well as distributed to families for the regular offering. Envelopes may also be needed for any special needs during the year. The stewardship committee and the worship committee will inform the church administrator of the needs so envelopes can be ordered and be on hand.	53022	600	700	
		TOTAL		1,850	2,100	

Step III

All worksheets are turned in to the church office and collated into a workbook. A summary of the funds needed by each program area is developed. (An example follows.) The ministry workbook is then given back to the program council or church board in late August. The book may have as many as 40 pages. Size is not important; the content is. Try to include every program and ministry. Do not leave out maintenance, janitorial needs, and all support systems that enable direct ministry to individuals. The tasks of faith development must have strong support if they are to be effective.

Now everyone has a chance to see all the different program plans for the coming year. A few weeks is allowed for everyone to study the plans. Look for events that would conflict on the calendar. Ask questions. Learn what goes on in other areas. In larger churches, few people know what happens in every area!

Step IV

The program council or church board gathers on a Saturday morning in mid-September for a light breakfast snack. Then, work begins on an item-by-item, page-by-page review of all the ministries. This might seem unnecessary in the beginning. However, for most of the people who participate, this will be a time when they learn more about the church and the multitude of programs than at any other time.

Every program area and ministry must be given the opportunity to tell its story. All the leaders should share their dreams and their plans for the coming year. Everyone is free to ask questions and point out ways to improve. Discover how different programs complement each other or compete. Expect differences of opinion when you come to priorities. Those differences should be discussed so that everyone can see the issues involved. We thus learn that we can disagree and still love one another. After all, all of us together are more effective than any one of us! This sense of team participation is valid, whether we are dealing with a large or a small congregation.

Step V

When this process is complete and the total dollars needed to support all the programs are known, a report is needed from the finance group. The finance team should present this report based on patterns of giving and pledging, twelve-month moving totals of all available income, as well as other studies and/or projections that indicate the probable total funds that will be available in the coming year. These projections are measured against the total requested in the program workbook.

YOUR CHURCH BUDGET SUMMARY WORKSHEET

AREA	St. Paul's 199__ BUDGET		Emmanuel Church 199__ BUDGET	
OUTREACH	417,105	428,400	50	23
WORSHIP	1,700	1,800	300	125
STEWARDSHIP	1,200	1,900	500	0
MUSIC	16,380	16,680	750	500
FOOD MINISTRY	4,200	4,600		
EVANGELISM	850	7,000	50	0
LIBRARY	1,200	1,200		
TELEVISION	2,000	1,000		
LEISURE MINISTRY	2,200	2,500		
FAMILY LIFE	2,900	2,950		
OLDER ADULT	6,300	3,800		
ADULT	11,760	9,850		
SINGLES	3,250	3,300		
YOUTH	13,450	13,400	100	100
ELEMENTARY	9,570	10,245		
PRESCHOOL	4,250	5,150		
NURSERY	14,250	15,250		
STAFF	722,869	823,375	31,000	21,500
OPERATIONS	266,583	247,800	12,700	10,000
CAPITAL FUNDS	124,700	81,800		
TOTAL	1,626,717	1,682,000	45,450	32,248

Note: This summary sheet reflects a large congregation with diverse ministries. The same process can be adapted to a smaller congregation, as seen, by limiting or combining the number of line items.

Let us assume that the council or church board is advised by the finance leader or team that the expected income for the next year is $925,000.00, while the workbook projects a program that calls for an expense of $1,250,000.00. The same concern, if not a more immediate one, arises in a smaller congregation that expects $95,000 dollars from income but has a ministry that costs $106,000! A serious consideration of options and priorities is called for.

Options

The council could say, "It isn't our problem. The stewardship and finance committees should come up with a commitment program to influence the giving patterns and enhance the income, making the program possible. Just present the proposal and see how the pledges come in. If it isn't adequate to support the budget, we will make adjustments then."

Another approach is for the council to take the responsibility of determining a realistic goal for their giving. They can examine all factors and reduce the cost of the total program to fall within the envelope of a budget that challenges, and is still one that can be achieved. The vision will often exceed our ability to fund it. (Or what's a vision for unless it is almost unreachable?)

The Debate

This is not an easy call. The stewardship of our resources should be challenging. In order to grow, we need to stretch. The other perspective is that the goal of any church in giving should be one that can be reached. Nothing feeds success more than success; nothing feeds failure more than failure. If the proposed budget is not underwritten with pledges, and the church must reduce its program, a church can have a budget of over a million dollars, providing multiple ministries for hundreds, and still "feel" like a failure.

A New Role for the Council or Church Board

Why should the council assume this responsibility? Isn't that the job of the finance team or stewardship team? That is the case in some churches. When making such a call, ownership by a large number of persons is needed. The ministry workbook, if pursued with high participation, is the product of many people from every area in the church. It's already "theirs." They have already set priorities in every aspect of the program. They are best able to judge what can be deferred and what is urgent. Their ownership makes them principal advocates of the entire process. In their groups, they can "sell" to their constituents. They become the best support system of any commitment program.

The council or board then must have the courage to delete or defer some of the lower priorities from the program and make the goal realistic. If the congregation understands that the program has been given this much attention by this many people and has been positioned for success, support is more attainable.

If the commitment program yields more support than the proposal requires, a celebration can begin! The headlines on the newsletter might read, "Our Budget Is Oversubscribed." That's much better than, "Cutbacks Necessary in Proposed Program."

Step VI

Once the council sets a goal in terms of finances, then they can go back through the workbook to finalize the program budget. It may become apparent that some programs need to be strengthened. Priorities may help defer some items. Question, discuss, compromise, and agree. Area by area, the second program review brings refinement. When the work session is over, there is a sense of ownership. Everyone knows what is being proposed.

The Next Step

From this point, the format is redesigned in a way that will communicate it to the total congregation. It goes out to everyone in printed form. It is carried to Sunday school classes by the members of the program council who helped build it. The elements of ministry must be communicated in terms of what the money does and how it affects people's lives. The process continues into the time of communication and on through the commitment program.

A program/budget building process is critical. When a small group makes decisions for many others, very little happens. When more people make proposals that others can see and understand, there is a real opportunity for growth in stewardship.

The more people participate, the clearer the vision. The more the vision is made visible, the more vital a church becomes in its mission to serve Christ.

 BUDGET TOOL

The Funding of Mission

Designated Giving? or Unified Budget?

JAMES P. JOHNSON

"I think our members should be able to designate their offerings anywhere they want, so that their money is used only for those things that are important to them," said the new church member.

"How could we possibly operate the church like that? We must have a unified budget, so the church will be able to carry out its total mission," responded the pastor.

"But I don't think the church is spending the money for the things that are really important," the new member continued.

"Our board members are the most committed and informed members of the church. They can see the total picture and make sound decisions, based on where funds are most needed," said the pastor.

Should the church have a unified budget? Or should the members be given the opportunity to designate offerings for specific causes? Should the denomination have a unified mission budget? Or should individuals and congregations be given the opportunity and encouraged to designate their offerings for specific causes?

The church has discussed such questions for years. Each method has its advocates. One way to discuss the issues is to identify one end of the continuum as a "donor-based" system; the other end, as a "needs-based" or "mission-based" system.

In a donor-based system, the donors determine where the money goes, based on their understanding of needs and their personal interest. In a mission-based system, the donors contribute to a unified fund that is divided among various causes, based on needs as determined by an informed decision-making body.

Each system has rather easily identified positive and negative aspects. Consider some of the possibilities of these systems in their "pure" form.

Mission-based System

POSITIVE ASPECTS

1. Funding is based on need and identified mission. The most vital and urgent needs, and the ongoing needs of operation are funded, not necessarily the ones that are most attractive or popular.

2. The system provides stability and continuity in funding, so that the mission can be carried out over a long period.

3. Promotion is done, so that donors see and support a broad mission enterprise.

4. The system is unified and serves as an important aspect of community identity.

5. The system is perceived to be more efficient, less competitive, and less costly.

NEGATIVE ASPECTS

1. There is low donor involvement in and control of the ministries that are funded.

2. Promotion and interpretation are difficult. The donors often are not clear as to what their gifts accomplish.

3. A decision-making body of well-informed, committed, unbiased persons is essential and often difficult to maintain by democratic means.

4. Response to new or changing needs is slow. Traditions and structures can be the primary factors in decisions.

5. Particular interests of the donors are secondary.

Donor-based System

POSITIVE ASPECTS

1. There is high donor involvement in and control of the ministries that are funded.

2. Promotion and interpretation are simplified and focused. Donors know what their gifts accomplish.

3. No decision-making body is necessary. The donors control the funding in a direct way.

4. Response to new and changing needs is fast.

5. Particular interests of the donors are primary.

NEGATIVE ASPECTS

1. Only the popular and exciting needs are funded. The urgent and vital needs, and the ongoing needs of operation and mission, especially the unpopular ones, may go unfunded.

2. Instability is inherent in the funding process. As donors change their interests and giving patterns, important mission responses may go unfunded and never be completed.

3. Each project that requires funding needs special promotion. Donors tend to see only isolated aspects of total mission.

4. The system is fragmented and does not build a sense of community.

5. The system is perceived to be less efficient, more competitive, and more costly.

Often, the struggle between mission-based and donor-based systems is seen as a problem to be fixed. Discussions tend to focus on which way is better, without considering the positive and negative aspects of both. A better way to see the situation is that it is a polarity to be managed. By using these same illustrations, the polarity is clear.

Positive	*Positive*
1. vital needs funded	1. high donor involvement
2. stability	2. promotion easy
3. broad mission	3. no decision-making body
4. unified	4. fast response
5. efficient	5. donors primary
MISSION-BASED	**DONOR-BASED**
Negative	*Negative*
1. low donor involvement	1. only popular needs funded
2. promotion difficult	2. instability
3. decision-making body	3. isolated mission projects
4. slow response	4. fragmented
5. donors secondary	5. costly

In such a polarity, the tendency is for those who perceive the negative aspects of the system currently in use to want to move to the positive aspects of the other system. For example, those who are experiencing the negative aspects of the mission-based system, in its slow responsiveness to meeting new needs, favor a donor-based system, which can respond quickly. Those who are experiencing the negative aspects of the donor-based system, with its fragmented and competing appeals for funds for specific causes, favor moving to the more unified approach of the mission-based system.

Such movement, however, is often opposed by those who also see the negative aspects of the system that is being proposed. Thus, the movement within the polarity is established. It is a dynamic process. It is not a problem that can be solved. It is a polarity, a set of attitudes, to be managed.

Neither system exists in the church in its "pure" form. Congregational and denominational church life is somewhere on the continuum between mission-based and donor-based systems. It is clear, however, that our congregational and denominational church life has been built upon the "mission-based" side for decades. It is equally clear that the current times are challenging old assumptions and calling for change.

On Not Giving to the Budget

The church is not under financial strain. There is no serious worry that "We might not make the budget." In fact, the numbers all look very good this year.

That's great. But, it's also of secondary importance. Too often, when we ask people to consider their financial contribution to the church, we have our eyes on the budget. This fosters the misguided notion that our giving is to perpetuate an institution.

But ultimately, the budget is beside the point. Sure, the congregation would not be able to continue without our contributions. But more important, our own faith will not be vital and lively without sacrificial giving. Giving keeps us alive spiritually.

Our Church Visitor
First Christian Church
Louisville, KY

Dissatisfaction is evident among church members. Many perceive current congregational and churchwide mission-funding systems as dysfunctional in today's church. Donor perceptions—that the system cannot respond to new ministries quickly, is funding activities the donors oppose, and is funding too much structure and administration—have led to increasing stress within the entire system and to decreasing support. When donors believe that their money is funding structures and not mission, they will increase their practice of designated giving.

Dissatisfaction is evident also among church leaders. Many believe the system does not distribute the money equitably, is not really responding to current needs or priorities, and is based more on history than mission.

Options for Response

If church leaders and other members perceive the negative and not the positive aspects of our mission-based system, there are two options for response. The first option is to move to a donor-based system. Congregations and denominations have been moving in this direction for the past several years. Consider some of the illustrations.

Annual Funding. When funds are insufficient, specific projects are taken out of the unified budget and funding is sought from individuals or groups. In the congregations, the women or youth or church school classes are asked for support. Beyond the congregation, all manner of individual donor support is developed—donor clubs, direct-mail requests, special fund-raising events, special named funds, and a host of others. Individual congregations may be asked to assume responsibility for a specific (special) project.

Capital Funds. Capital-fund campaigns permit donors to contribute to a very specific project. When the campaign is for more than a building, there is often a feasibility study to determine what the donors will support.

Planned Giving. In the past few years, increasing emphasis has been placed on planned giving, through bequests, annuities, and trusts. Development officers know that their task is to help the donor accomplish what the donor believes is important. In the case of institutional development, the task is to find where the needs of the institution and the interests of the donor coincide.

When funds are inadequate for unified support, or when conflicts arise regarding specific projects or ministries within a unified approach, the tendency is for the unified fund to become the "base" budget. It becomes less "exciting" than the projects funded directly, receives less energy from the leadership, and grows at a slower pace than the other projects.

Will this shift to a more donor-based system continue? The answer seems to be clearly yes, unless action is taken within the congregations and within denominations to choose the second option—to design and implement a mission-based system that has high donor involvement, flexibility, and widespread support of leadership.

Most congregations currently use some form of unified budget. It is nearly impossible to imagine a congregational life if the members had the ability to designate their whole offering. Suppose a member wanted to contribute to the pastor's salary, but not to the part that allows the pastor to participate in anything beyond the congregation. Or suppose a member wanted to contribute to the utilities for the congregation, but not for the

> # "People support institutions they perceive as reinforcing their own values."
> *—JAMES W. FRICK*

utilities when an unpopular group meets in the building. Some form of unified budget is essential for congregational life.

Some form of unified budget is essential also for church life beyond the congregation. Ministries carried out through denominational structures and institutions must have some form of unified giving. Without it, congregations would be besieged with appeals for special offerings and fund-raising events for every cause. This was the situation before Unified Promotion [in the Christian Church (Disciples of Christ)] when many Sundays were designated and promoted as "Special Offering Sundays." Unified Promotion (now Basic Mission Finance) significantly reduced such competing appeals. What was lost in the process, however, is the individual's sense of support to particular mission causes or projects.

Can we imagine a mission-based funding system that would include high donor involvement and participation, flexibility, and widespread support of leadership? Can we imagine a denominational mission-based system with high congregational involvement and participation, designed to function in the climate that exists in today's church?

What would be the role of congregations and their pastors in such a system?

BULLETIN IDEA

Ways to Increase Giving—Without Asking

DONALD W. JOINER

Heart-Warming Tree

One church decided to have such a tree after seeing one in another church decorated with fabric patches to represent blankets. They took a small bare tree, painted it white, trimmed it with miniature white lights, and placed it in the front of the sanctuary.

For Blanket Sunday in February, they placed red cardboard hearts on the tree and announced the theme: "A Heart-Warming Event." For a donation, members of the congregation could have their own or a loved one's name printed on a heart. The money was used to purchase blankets to be distributed by the denomination's missionary ministries.

Because nearly twice as much money was collected that year as in previous years, it was decided to keep the tree and use it for other church fund-raising projects. In March, shamrocks were placed on the tree and the money raised was used to carpet one of the Sunday school rooms.

This is a great idea! In April, crosses can be used; in May and June, praying children and churches; in July, flags; in August, butterflies; in September, churches; and in October, pumpkins. In November, turkeys might be placed on the tree and the money raised could be used to aid the victims of a hurricane, flood, or other disaster.

(Based on accounts from Shirley Alvord, Calvary Church, Wiconisco, Penna., as reported in April 1993)

Tax-Wise Giving

While most giving to the church is not influenced by the possibility of an income tax deduction, at some times in the year, people are naturally thinking about giving, as well as the tax deduction. Here are some paragraphs to include in church bulletins or newsletters:

Giving at Year End

The end of the year is an opportune time to be reminded of commitments we made during the year. Sometimes we forget about a gift we wanted to make: a special gift to the youth ministries of the church; a memorial or honor gift through the church for someone special; or even a completed commitment to the general ministries of the church.

Now is the time to make that gift! The calendar year is rapidly coming to a close. If you want to include that gift in your charitable deduction for tax purposes this year, now is the time!

Tithe Your Tax Refund

Herb generously announced at a stewardship meeting that he had come across a new idea. Every year he received a refund check from the IRS due to an overpayment of his taxes. Since the money was withheld from his pay check each month, he never really had a sense of having that money. He described it as a gift from Uncle Sam. Since this was a gift to him, and he really did not count on it for his budget, he thought, Why not "Tithe the Tax Refund" to the church? He figured that this was one little way the government could help support his church. What about you?

Summer Slump Envelope

The time of the year when most churches experience a decrease in giving is during the summer. We often refer to this as the Summer Slump, and churches accept it as a natural part of the year. But it doesn't need to be that way!

Consider "Barrett's Law" (from Wayne Barrett): "When they park it in the pew, they plop it in the plate." In other words, when people are in church, they give, and when they are not in church, they tend not to give. Why do we accept this as an axiom of church life and not do something about it?

People often do not give because the church does not give them an opportunity to give. Let's give them an opportunity! At the beginning of the summer, give each member (and each friend of the church) a special "summer-giving envelope," so that they can make a gift while they are gone. Along with the envelope, enclose a letter inviting people to use the envelope *before* they go on vacation.

PART FOUR

1995 COMMITMENT CAMPAIGN SAMPLER

For the Finance and Stewardship Teams

Introduction

DONALD W. JOINER

When we consult with the financial leadership for congregations, we are often asked for the "five things" that will cure their financial illness. Here they are:

1. Conduct an All-Church Commitment each year.
2. Create a special task group to design and conduct the All-Church Commitment program.
3. Recruit top leadership to conduct the program.
4. Give this special task group time to do a good job.
5. Do not attempt to sell the budget. Tell the story of ministry and mission.

"Reverend Dole, as the new chairperson of the finance committee, I want to do something new and creative. In the past, we have waited until September to decide what to do, and we have not been all that effective. What are our options?"

Do you wait until early September each year to decide what to do for your church's annual financial campaign? Is there always a rush to decide? Does your finance team struggle for several meetings to decide what program to use? Do you then turn to the same people and to the same ways you have done it in the past, just to get through it?

Until the early 1970s, the EMV (Every Member Visitation) was one of the few options for many of our churches. It was a good option, but it was well worn, and churches looked for something else. That something else has consisted of a number of options that might be called "packet circulation" programs. These are good programs, whereby packets of pledge cards are circulated. Each home receives a packet, fills out a pledge card, or an estimate-of-giving card, and delivers it to the next house on the circuit. After several years, the horse died from overuse. But in many of our churches, we have simply dragged that dead horse around a few more years. Dead horses smell!

Then churches again decided to do something new. Finance teams determined that "everyone knows what is going on anyway. Let's just send them one letter and a commitment card." Even the members of the committee did not all respond.

A recent study in Kentucky confirms the apathy. Over 61 percent of the churches are now doing nothing. The reason they are not doing anything is because they do not know what to do.

Most annual-fund programs can fit in one of the following styles:

1. All-Church Visitation—This can be done on the phone or through visiting people in their homes.

2. Commitment-Sunday Programs—These may be organized in several ways, but all lead up to one particular Sunday when commitments are made.

3. Group Meetings—This is a variation of All-Church Visitation, but done in groups (in people's homes; in group meetings at the church; or at a rally or dinner).

4. Circulation Packet—In this program, commitment packets are circulated among homes.

Several years ago, we discovered that after giving churches a suggestion regarding what to do that year, the next year they would call again with the same question: "What should we do this year?" At that time, we responded with the "Cycle Theory" for local church finance campaigns. The Cycle Theory alternates the four most successful programs in successive years. Using the Cycle Theory, you can plan the next four years, then repeat the cycle again for another four years.

The annual commitment program is the one program of the church that has major influence on how people feel about the church. More important, it determines the bulk of income for the next year. Care in the design and conduct of this program are of extreme importance to the entire ministry of the congregation. Each year in this Guide, we will be presenting a miniprogram to fit into this cycle. In addition to the many good programs available from a variety of sources, with

several issues of this Guide, you will be able to complete the cycle.

The goal of this section of The Abingdon Guide is to invite you to evaluate your church's annual financial campaign. Herb Mather suggests that the campaign focus on the joy of giving, not on the obligation of membership or the need of the church to pay bills (secure the budget). Don Joiner's steps for success will fit any style of campaign. We define a successful campaign as one in which worship attendance increases, members feel good about their giving, more people are excited by the ministries of the church, and, of course, increased income becomes available.

A signed commitment card is not the end of responsibility for either the church leaders or the givers. The Cycle Theory begins in receiving. "You cannot be a giver until you are first a receiver" is the first principle in funding ministry. Giving is the first act, but the church also acts in the giving cycle through management and distribution (spending). Donors need to be involved in all parts of this cycle.

Phil Williams presents our first program in the Cycle Theory, a model that can be completed by any size church, and with a great deal of fun. This fits year three in the Cycle Theory, and does an excellent job of presenting and celebrating the ministries of the church.

To have "fun" while funding ministries is a very desirable benefit. Gil Miller, through a miniplay, does just that. He gets the message across. This miniplay can be used in worship, in a special program, or even at the "Stewardship Fair."

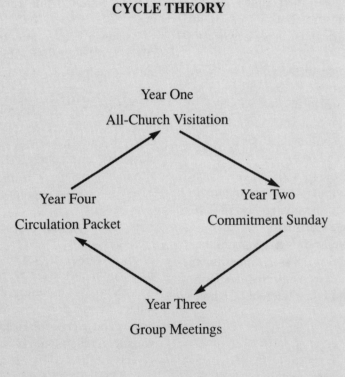

CYCLE THEORY

Year One
All-Church Visitation

Year Four
Circulation Packet

Year Two
Commitment Sunday

Year Three
Group Meetings

MEETING MEDITATION

Give for the Joy of It!

HERBERT MATHER

The financial stewardship program of any congregation need not be a "downer." It can be an exciting and spiritually refreshing part of a congregation's life. The secret is to provide constructive attention to all three dimensions of a giving program: the giver, the channel, and the receiver.

For too long, we have emphasized the church as the channel and have neglected the giver and the receiver. A move to vigorously proclaim the people's need to give, but without ignoring the church's needs for funds to support its ministries can make a world of difference.

Our need to give is rooted in the Christian faith. God gives. Creation is a gift. Faith and salvation are gifts. "God so loved the world that he gave . . . " (John 3:16). "My peace I give to you" (John 14:27). "Not as an exaction, but as a willing gift" (II Cor. 9:5c RSV). The list could go on and on.

We are created in the image of a giving God. Generosity is far more than an attractive ornament for Christians. It is a response to the giving God of love. It is part of the definition of a Christian.

Christian giving has more to do with worship than with education. It has more to do with commitment than with calculation. Giving as a spiritual discipline leads toward wholeness, and is a reflection of wholeness.

The Joy of Giving

Loyal members respond to appeals to "pay the bills" because they care about the church. Year after year, many of them give far more than the tithe. Unfortunately, many of them miss the joy of giving.

Critical problems often distract church leaders from important issues. Budgets require approval. Bills demand a payoff. It is tempting to dwell on the immediate needs of buildings while ignoring the needs of people, and a basic need of all people is to give.

Tithers often speak with satisfaction of the pure joy of giving. When they speak of rewards, they do not mean that tithing makes them rich. Instead, they experience tithing as a discipline that leads toward freedom. Their decision to tithe developed out of

their need to give, rather than the church's need to receive.

Jesus asked a rich young ruler to sell all his possessions and give the proceeds away, promising him "riches in heaven."

Many Christians swallow hard when talking about "riches in heaven." It sounds like pie-in-the-sky escapism. The temptation is to scoff at heavenly "rewards" while concentrating on the here and now.

Whatever heaven may have meant to Jesus, it certainly involved relationships that transcend the present. Limitations of time and space cannot contain the mystery of heavenly relationships.

God created us for community. We were made to love our neighbor as ourselves. God created us to love. "If God thus loved us, my dear friends, we also must love one another"(I John 4:11 REB). Loving, responding people will look for ways to express that love. Giving is an appropriate response.

Intentionality Is Required

The chairperson of a finance committee listened to these comments and remarked, "All that sounds fine, but reality is something else. We have to meet the budget. People don't give simply because it is the religious thing to do. We need a bang-up financial campaign to get the money!"

Why Many Fund-Raising Programs Fail

1. Unclear expectations
2. Not knowing the target market
3. Not planning far enough into the future
4. Not having an adequate budget
5. Think you can do it yourself
6. Lack of patience
7. Energy diverted elsewhere
8. Too few staff
9. Lack of marketing

The chairperson is correct about the need for intentionality. Because other factors are not in place, most congregations need to conduct an annual campaign. The question is: "What kind of a campaign will we conduct in this church?"

What would be different if a financial stewardship campaign focused on my need to give, rather than on the church's need for money? Here are some ways:

Write campaign letters that emphasize giving and the blessings that come to the giver. Include a brief testimonial from a joyful giver in each letter.

Don't send a copy of the line-item church budget. It's boring, and few people will read it. It communicates the message that giving should be based on the church's need.

In place of the budget, send an attractive brochure. Organize the budget items in three to seven broad categories. Write a brief narrative describing each category. Include pictures. At the bottom of the brochure, offer to send a copy of the line-item budget to anyone who asks for it.

Urge your pastor to preach on giving. Excellent passages for sermons on giving include II Corinthians 8:9; Philippians 2:5-11; Luke 19:1-10; and Luke 21:1-4.

Ask speakers to tell the stories of their personal pilgrimages as giving Christians. Invite people for whom giving has become an important part of their discipleship to tell their stories. Do not ask them to tell *how much* they give, but something of their journey toward becoming giving Christians.

These suggestions demonstrate that our interest is in making disciples more than in "making" a budget.

Dare to Challenge

Jesus dared to challenge. He asked people to stretch. He pointed to a poor widow who gave "all that she had." We are not told what Jesus said to Zacchaeus. But when they concluded their conversation, Zacchaeus announced that he was giving away half of everything he had.

Jesus asked fishermen to leave their nets and follow him. Don't shrink from the challenge of asking people to share what is valuable to them. For most people in this society, money is a major symbol of value. It is not evil, but there is more to life than more money.

At each meeting with your campaign team, don't ask, "How many dollars will the program bring in?" Instead, ask, "Does the plan we are using bring out the best in people?" "Are we challenging people in ways that encourage their growth as disciples?"

When these questions are raised honestly and prayerfully, you are on your way to having joyful, giving people—trusted channels—who know that Christ has ministered to their needs.

Once people are challenged to become givers, address the issue of where they can give funds to make a difference in the world, in the name of Jesus Christ.

 # MEETING HANDOUT

Six Steps to a Successful Financial Effort

DONALD W. JOINER

A finance program is most appropriately begun as soon as the previous year's drive is completed! Too many times, we try to short-cut both time and effort, just to "get it over with."

The best effects are in those churches that work at stewardship education and commitment year-round, rather than just during the September-November finance drive.

I. Work at It All Year

Begin early to help members understand the biblical, theological, and historical tradition of being a steward.

Build on your church's understanding of tithing and proportionate giving. Discuss the importance of time and talents, and of covenanting those gifts as a steward. Sermons, articles in newsletters, stewardship moments before the offering, special small-group study, and stewardship inserts as part of a quarterly financial statement—all assist to keep giving a year-round concern and help us to grow in commitment.

II. Develop the Church Program Ministry

The second step is perhaps the most important, and generally gets the least amount of effort. In many churches, five or six "men" in a back room decide the budget and ministry of the church for the next year. It is no wonder that the budget is seldom underwritten! It's not the members' budget or a clear approximation of the church's ministry. All the members need to feel that the program of the church, which the budget reflects, reflects their desire and concern for ministry. The second step, therefore, in successful funding and church management is the development of a church program. Four considerations help in accomplishing this goal:

1. Involve all members in determining your church's ministry for the next year. This must be a conscious decision by the leaders of the church. For the average church member, increased involvement in making decisions about the congregation's ministry will result in increased commitment to, and participation in, that ministry.

2. Go to the members. Through home meetings, a questionnaire, or congregational meeting, learn the members' desires for the future and upcoming ministry.

3. Discuss the results. When the information has been gathered, have the membership help you interpret those results into activity. Who will help you do what? What special financial commitments will they give to the church to accomplish these goals? What are their priorities?

4. Channel those priorities and commitments to the appropriate committee, or set up a new task force. Don't just go about business as usual! Asking for congregational input and response does more harm than good, unless you actually intend to carry through their desires, with their involvement.

III. Communication

Reach out in as many ways as possible to positively interpret the direction you are going in ministry. Tell the church's story. This step cannot be underestimated. One or two communications (i.e., one letter and a short pulpit announcement) are not enough! Use posters, three- or four-minute messages from the pulpit by lay persons, three or four letters, brochures, and a congregational meeting to discuss and communicate your story.

IV. Response

Unfortunately, this is where we usually center our time and effort. The gathering of pledges, of estimate of giving or commitment cards, is fruitless without the previous steps. Several excellent programs are available. The best response usually comes from person-to-person, house-to-house visitation. This is also the most difficult. Yearly house-to-house visitation is probably not needed. A variety of programs, over a cycle of three to five years usually produces the healthiest response.

The Rhyme of the Ancient Canvasser

He was an ancient canvasser
Who served his parish well,
And he could hold you by the hour
With stories he could tell.
With stories of good parish folk
Whose doorbells he had rung;
Many gladly welcomed him;
Others wished him hung.
There's Mrs. Perch who loves her church,
But cannot pledge this fall.
"I always give when I come," she says,
But rarely comes at all.
Now Tommy Twig gives nothing big,
His wife gives nothing small;
And so between them both, you see,
They never give at all.
Yes, Charlie Slup was quite fed up
With churches needing money,
And to his saintly wife he said,
"We can't afford it, honey."
Chubby Chin, he grins you in,
Spends half an hour in chat;
"I'll send my pledge by mail," he says.
And that's the end of that.
And Hoddy Huff was pretty tough,
But on the dotted line
He pledged to God a handsome sum,
But never paid a dime.
If this was all our sinful fall,
Our little church would close;
But many folks gave much to us,
Our balanced budget shows.
It is no joke, my goodly folk,
There really is good reason
For asking you to do your share
This annual canvass season.
—Farley Wheelwright

V. Budget Preparation

An appeals presentation, or goals budget, is developed prior to the appeal, as a result of Step II. The actual, or operating, budget must wait until the response is in before it is completed. In the operating budget, income must equal expenditures.

VI. Follow-up

Once the campaign is completed, the work is just beginning. An immediate report of the campaign results should be given from the pulpit by the chairperson of the campaign. A follow-up letter of appreciation, giving the results of the campaign and an acknowledgment of their pledge, should be sent to everyone two to three weeks, or as soon as possible, after the conclusion of the campaign. Monthly, or minimally quarterly, reports of progress in attaining the church's program and financial goals should be reported to everyone.

Next year's plans should be started as soon as this year's campaign is completed. Some forward-looking congregations suggest that every financial campaign team should have three coleaders: last year's chairperson, this year's chairperson, and next year's chairperson, plus the rest of the team. I suggest that the committee be separate from either the finance or stewardship committees, but certainly should have representatives from each. Finally, after follow-up, return to Step I and begin making stewardship a year-round effort.

Funding the ministry of your congregation has never been an easy task. In the unpredictable future, the task will not get any easier. These few steps, followed each year, can maximize your results in program ministry and spiritual growth.

COMMITMENT CAMPAIGN

The Stewardship Fair

A Method for Enlisting the Annual Financial Pledge

PHIL WILLIAMS

Many methods are available for enlisting the annual financial pledge (sometimes called "enlistment," "commitment," "intention," and so on). Numerous congregations find that a three-year cycle is helpful. That is, a very intensive method is used the first year (say, the every-member visitation), while the second and third years are less intensive (e.g., telephone, direct mail, personal delivery, etc.). The Stewardship Fair is useful for a less intensive campaign (year two or three of a cycle).

In the following pages, you will find the organization, timeline, and supporting materials needed to implement The Stewardship Fair.

Please note that when you see an asterisk (*), supporting suggestions will be found in Part Nine.

Purpose

On the Sunday prior to Commitment Sunday, a Stewardship Fair is presented to highlight each ministry area of the congregation's life (i.e., worship, education, stewardship, property, etc.), to share the goals of each area and distribute pledge cards.

Method

A carnival-like atmosphere is developed through the work of the leadership team and the ministry area committees. The Stewardship Fair takes place in a large open area, such as a social hall or multipurpose room. Booths are designed and decorated by the ministry area teams, with the help of the leadership team. Information about the total program and outreach ministries of the congregation, including plans for the future, are presented. Commitment cards are distributed to members as they leave the Fair. Other support materials and information have been mailed and announced in the months prior to the event.

Leadership

Six months prior to Commitment Sunday, the leadership team is selected and meets.

81

- Coordinator   (one person). The overall chair for the program calls the leadership group together, makes sure everyone understands their tasks, supports the team with materials, keeps tabs on the timeline, and reports progress to the congregation's leadership.

- Reservations   (one person). Responsible for organizing the contacting of all members of the congregation to secure reservations* for Fair day. Reservations are sought in order to plan the amount of food needed. Also responsible for making a Reservation Card* for each person or family in the congregation, and to have commitment cards ready in addressed envelopes, to be handed out as people leave the Fair.

- Communications   (one person). Begins two months before the Fair to publicize the event in the congregation, using the newsletter or special mailings.* Other persons are recruited to make announcements* on Sunday during church school and worship. At least one announcement and article/picture about the event is submitted to the newspaper. Two weeks prior to the Fair, eye-catching posters (ask children's classes to make the posters!) are placed around the church building. Another is developed and mailed to each family or person to be put on a home bulletin board or refrigerator door.

- Task Group I   (two persons). Work with the various work areas (called functional committees, commissions, etc., by different denominations/congregations) to design and organize their booth* at the Fair, including what food/beverage is to be offered at each booth. These creative persons should be able to work with the ministry areas and assist them to develop attractive and decorative booths for presenting their work.

- Task Group II   (two persons). Develop the "entertainment" program* to be presented during the Fair. Skits, songs, magic acts, etc., with messages about various facets of stewardship and/or ministry areas. Because most congregations will probably hold this event in the social hall, it is suggested these presentations be "in the round," using portable risers (as opposed to a stage and/or one end of the room). The entertainment should be in about 30-minute short segments, spaced through an hour and a half or so.

- Worship   (one person). Works with the worship committee to arrange for stewardship emphasis on the four Sundays prior to and including Commitment Sunday (i.e., opening sentences, collects, introits, special hymns, anthems, etc.), and/or other pertinent changes in the order of worship.*

- Pastor   In addition to keeping the various implications of stewardship highlighted in the usual sermons, the pastor is requested to have four "stewardship sermons,"* beginning three weeks prior to the Fair, and on Commitment Sunday.

Timeline

- Six Months

The Leadership Team is selected and meets. In addition to reviewing the various responsibilities, the group may want to consider a particular theme around which the booths would be decorated and the entertainment developed.

Task Group I meets and organizes for meeting with the various ministry areas. The whole team meets with each work team the first time, in order to help generate ideas of ways to organize their booths.

- Five Months

Task Group I meets with the work areas to explore ideas for the booths. This needs to clearly include what the work areas do, the amount of money they spend, and how, as well as goals and costs for the coming year in their specific ministry areas.

Task Group II meets to begin to make decisions about the subjects to be organized for special emphasis (i.e., motivation to give/pledge; outreach ministries beyond the congregation, both in the community and worldwide; special music by individuals, quartets [barbershop maybe], and choirs [handbells, youth, etc.]; or puppets). Assign each member specific responsibilities.

- Four Months

Task Group I assigns one team member to meet with each work area to follow through on the decisions made in the team meeting in month five. Each person arranges to be present for about 30 minutes at each monthly meeting of each work area. These persons are assist-

ing the work areas in their planning; they maintain liaison to avoid duplication. In the meeting this month, decide on the food to be offered and who will prepare it.

Task Group II makes final decisions about what acts are to be included in the entertainment and begins planning for any props or other needs.

- Three Months

The Reservations Chair recruits other persons to work with him/her. Insofar as possible, contacts to request and receive reservations need to be face-to-face (phone only as a last resort). If the congregation has a "deacon" group, these persons (or one or more adult church school classes) might be willing to make the contacts. Whatever group agrees to make the contacts, the names need to be organized—distribute them evenly, and try to hold each person to 3 to 5 contacts.

The Communications Chair recruits people to make the announcements in church school classes and/or during worship (this could be done by the usual announcements, or, for example, play a cassette tape of a small group singing the information). Plans for publicity in the community and newspaper needs to begin.

- Two Months

The coordinator calls a team to organize the procedure from now until the Sunday of the Fair.

The communication group is working on the content of the various announcements, in both the congregation and the community. Six weeks prior to Commitment Sunday, mail Letter #1—the general announcement letter.

The persons in charge of worship begins working with the worship committee and/or choir director to plan the orders of worship.

Begin the preparation of the pledge cards, either through the church office and/or a small committee of two additional persons (depending on the size of the congregation). The envelopes are to be addressed with the pledge card letter and number of pledge cards needed for that giving unit enclosed (this information is gathered from a family's practices in previous annual emphases). Putting names and addresses on each pledge card is strongly encouraged (this ensures being able to read the names). This can be done using address labels or may be carefully hand-written.

- Four Weeks

Begin announcements in Sunday school classes and worship.

- Three Weeks

The pastor begins a four-week series of sermons on stewardship and financial commitment.

- Two Weeks

The communication committee mails the poster with the words, "Please Post on Your Bulletin Board or Refrigerator," next to the address label.

Everyone in the congregation is contacted to make a reservation for attending the Stewardship Fair. This needs to be completed a week before the Fair, in order that food preparations can take into account the number of persons expected.

- One Week

Each committee/work area of the congregation sets up and decorate its booth in a pre-assigned area of the fellowship hall or some other large area.

The "entertainment" persons/groups rehearse to familiarize themselves with staging "in the round."

- Stewardship Fair

All participants arrive early enough to complete last minute preparations. Avoid, unless there is an absolute emergency, anyone working during worship!

- Commitment Sunday

Mail all envelopes that were not picked up at the Fair. (Ask all persons to come forward at the close of worship to place their pledge cards on the altar or on a special table.)

Have available additional pledge cards in envelopes for those who may have left them at home or for some reason did not receive one.

- One Week After

Mail the "Follow-up Letter" on the Monday following Commitment Sunday.

- Two Weeks After

Mail the "Thank-You Letter" to all persons or families who have made a pledge. Mail this letter immediately to all who get their pledge cards in late or during the follow-up process.

COMMUNICATION MATERIALS

LETTER #1--GENERAL ANNOUNCEMENT LETTER

Aldersgate United Methodist Church
23 West Crescent Blvd., Denton, Any State 77443
Phone: (173) 555-4323

Dear Friends,

Our congregation will celebrate Commitment Sunday on _____(date)_____. Our theme for this year is "_____(theme)_____."

An integral part of out financial stewardship emphasis this year is "The Stewardship Fair," on the Sunday prior to Commitment Sunday, _____(date).

In a light and fun-filled atmosphere, we will have the opportunity to examine all the ministries in which we are engaged, as well as plans for the future. In addition to displaying, in various ways, their particular ministries, our ministry groups (or functional committees, or whatever you may call them) will also provide finger food.

Come prepared for a light luncheon and the fun fellowship of sharing and receiving information about the ministries of our congregation.

Please begin to support our financial stewardship emphasis with your prayers. We are accomplishing much for which to be thankful. Consequently, there is much God is calling us to undertake in our journey of faithfulness.

In the near future, you will receive a call requesting reservations for The Stewardship Fair, so that we will know how much food to prepare.

We look forward to seeing you there!

(This letter should be signed by the coordinator, moderator/board--congregation chair, and the pastor, as a sign of solidarity.)

LETTER #2--FINANCIAL STEWARDSHIP REFLECTION

TRINITY CHURCH
9005 WEST PARK AVENUE   POUGHKEEPSIE, ANY STATE 00225
PHONE: (102) 555-6744

Dear (personal to every previous pledger and all others--i.e., Bob and Sue, Sarah, James, and Mary)

We are deeply appreciative of the financial stewardship commitment exhibited by our congregation in years past.

We realize that, while giving of our financial resources is an important part of our stewardship, it is also part of our spiritual development as persons "growing into the fullness of the stature of Christ Jesus our Lord."

In this spirit, we encourage you to continue your journey toward, and beyond, a tithe.

The enclosed materials are intended to be "food for thought" and instruments to assist us in our personal decision-making about our pledge for the coming year.

Remember The Stewardship Fair and Commitment Sunday, on _____ _____(dates)_____.

We are excited about the unique learning and sharing opportunity of The Stewardship Fair.

Plan on your family calendars to attend both congregational worship and the Fair on these Sundays. Please continue to undergird our planning with your prayers.

(This is to be signed by both the coordinator and the pastor.)

(Note: This letter incorporates instruments found in Part Nine. Similar materials may be provided by your denomination.)

LETTER #4--THANK YOU TO PLEDGERS

Calvary Church of Christ

One Windsor Commons,   Green Hills, Any State   23118   (178) 555-9999

Dear (personalize),

This letter is to express our gratitude for your commitment to undergirding the ministries of our congregation during the next year.

As you are aware, our financial stewardship is part of our spiritual growth. We are particularly grateful for the increase in this year's pledging. At this moment, we have pledged $____ for the coming year. This is ____ percent increase over last year's pledging. A most sincere THANK YOU! for your part in this effort.

We are deeply aware of what the participation of all our members means to our life together. Thank you for all you mean to the life and ministries of our congreagation and the mission of Christ's church in the world.

We look forward to another year of faithfulness and growth as we seek to serve God's calling for us and the whole church.

(To be signed by the coordnator Board/Congregation Chair, and the pastor.)

LETTER #3--THE FOLLOW-UP

Faith Brethren Church

**776 Willowbrook Road   Cumberland, Any State
34567   (165) 555-5643**

Dear (again personalize),

We are pleased to announce that on Commitment Sunday, we received $____ in commitments toward undergirding our ministries for the next year.

This is higher (or "about the same," whichever is appropriate) than at the same time last year. We are excited by this opportunity to greatly strenghten the financial foundation of our mission and ministries.

As your pledge was not among those recieved this past Sunday, we hope that you will submit it by mail in the enclosed envelope, or in the offering plate next Sunday.

Thank you for your faithful support in the past, and for your immediate response to this request.

(This is to be signed by both the coordnator and the pastor.)

(To be mailed on Monday or Tuesday following Commitment Sunday.)

SAMPLE ANNOUNCEMENTS FOR THE NEWSLETTER

1.

Coming Soon in Our Congregational Life
The Stewardship Fair
Date—Time—Place

This year we will distribute our Commitment Cards
on this day, as people leave
The Stewardship Fair.
Commitment Sunday will be following Sunday.

2.

* Good Food * Clowns * Fun * Skits * Displays * Learning *

Under the "Big Top" of the Community Hall
Everything You Ever Wanted to Know
About the Ministries of Our Church
and More
at

The Stewardship Fair
Date — Time

3.
On _____(date)_____, come to The Stewardship Fair, immediately following worship. All people of the congregation are invited. There will be booths presenting the various ministries in which our congregation is involved. Entertainment in various forms will be presented during our time together. A light lunch will be offered. This is a way we can learn about all the involvements, work, and ministries of our congregation, as well as a way to distribute our commitment cards. Commitment Sunday will be the following Sunday.

Motivational Humor

"The mustard-color pledge cards you were mailed were treated with a coated substance that will begin to emit smoke fumes within 10 days. Cards not returned by ___(date)___ will begin to self-destruct, releasing an unpleasant odor. The Stewardship Committee hopes you will protect yourself from these hazards by returning the card immediately to the church office."

BOOTH FORMATION

Booth is a generic term to denote a designated area for the display of the information/materials/equipment/pictures of a particular mission/ministry of the congregation (i.e., the stewardship committee might want to develop a booth about the subject of tithing—see "Preaching Resources" for suggested materials).

A "booth" can be anything from a simple table display to a more elaborate "model" (life-size or miniature) of the ministry location/work.

The "booths" may incorporate any number of ways to communicate the information. In addition to those above, there also could be slides, filmstrips, or videos.

ENTERTAINMENT SUGGESTIONS

Entertainment for The Stewardship Fair could take many forms. Some, undoubtedly, will use the talent already present in their congregation.

Personal Witness—A personal sharing about tithing or a particular experience while being involved in some mission/ministry project (i.e., overseas volunteer, "meals on wheels" worker, children/youth visitors to nursing home, flood relief worker, etc.).

Two-Person Dialogues—These can take place around a variety of subjects: some community/national/global mission project/ministry supported by the congregation, identification and use of some talent/skill/interest.

Short Drama—See several short dramas in Ann Weems book *Multiply the Gift* [Presbyterian Church (U.S.A.) Distribution Center, PDS 918-01-086, Tel. 800-524-2612], as well as the theme materials produced ecumenically, available through your denominational stewardship office. (If not, contact the Ecumenical Center for Stewardship Studies, 1100 W. 42nd St., Suite 225, Indianapolis IN 46208; Tel. 317-926-3525).

Music—Handbell choirs; solos/duets/trios/quartets from the chancel choir/youth choir; group singing; puppet ministry presentation; junior choir; brass ensemble.

WORSHIP RESOURCES

Many sources of stewardship worship resources are now available. One place to check is your denominational stewardship office and the mailings received from them. See Part Nine of this *Guide* and below for other stewardship resources.

Ann Weems, *Multiply the Gift*, Presbyterian Church (U.S.A.) Distribution Center, PDS 918-01-086; Tel. 800-524-2612.

Theme materials produced by the Ecumenical Center for Stewardship Studies, 1100 W. 42nd St., Suite 225, Indianapolis IN 46208; Tel. 317-926-3525, if they are not available through your denomination's stewardship office.

The Gifts We Bring: Worship Resources for Stewardship and Mission, Volumes 1-4, Church Finance Council, Christian Church (Disciples of Christ) in the United States and Canada, P.O. Box 1986, Indianapolis IN 46206; Tel. 317-353-1491.

Following is a sample section of the Order of Worship for Commitment Sunday, when people come forward to place their pledge cards on the communion table/altar.

WORSHIP INSTRUCTIONS BY THE LEADER

Moments for Preparation of Pledge Cards

Dedicatory Prayer: "O Gracious and Holy God, we approach the Table with the offering of our planned financial stewardship for this coming year. Accept also the consecration of ourselves to be more effective instruments of your will and way, both in the church and in our daily living. In the name and for the sake of the continuing ministry and mission of Christ Jesus our Lord, we pray. Amen."

Placing of Pledge Cards on the Communion Table

HYMN OF DEDICATION

BENEDICTION

PREACHING RESOURCES

In addition to the specific suggestions in *The Gifts We Bring,* Ann Weems' *Multiply the Gift,* and the theme materials, there are:

Timothy J. Bagwell, *Preaching for Giving,* Discipleship Resources, P.O. Box 6996, Alpharetta GA 30239-6996; Tel. 800-685-4370.

Brian K. Bauknight, *Right on the Money,* Discipleship Resources, P.O. Box 6996, Alpharetta GA 30239-6996; Tel. 800-685-4370.

Edward W. Bauman, *Where Your Treasure Is,* Bauman Bible Telecasts, 3436 Lee Highway, Arlington VA 22207.

Patricia Wilson-Kastner, *Preaching Stewardship: An Every-Sunday Theme,* The Ecumenical Center for Stewardship Studies, 1100 W. 42nd St., Suite 225, Indianapolis IN 46208; Tel. 317-926-3525. (This may be available through your denominational bookstore or stewardship office.)

SPECIAL TITHING RESOURCES

John K. Brackett, *On the Pilgrim's Way: Christian Stewardship and the Tithe,* Office of Stewardship, The Episcopal Church, 815 Second Ave., New York NY 10017; Tel. 212-922-5141.

Norma Wimberly, *Putting God First: The Tithe,* Dis-cipleship Resources, P.O. Box 6996, Alpharetta GA 30239-6996; Tel. 800-685-4370.

The author acknowledges and expresses appreciation to Central Christian Church, Elkhart, Indiana, where the basic idea of "The Stewardship Fair" was developed in the fall of 1993.

Sample Commitment Cards and Letter

BUSINESS ENVELOPE SIZE

Theme or Congregation Name
Congregation Address
Logo
City/town/state/providence/zip

In __(year)__ I prayerfully intend to give $_____ for all the ministries of the congregation:

(check only one)   _____ Weekly

     _____ Monthly

     _____ Quarterly

     _____ Semiannually

     _____ Annually

I understand that this commitment may be increased or decreased as circumstances change during the year.

---

6 X 3 5/8 ENVELOPE SIZE

Congregation Name
Address
City/town   state/providence   zip

In __(year)__ I prayerfully intend to give $_____ for all the ministries of this congregation:

(check only one)   _____ Weekly

     _____ Monthly

     _____ Quarterly

     _____ Semiannually

     _____ Annually

I understand that this commitment may be increased or decreased as circumstances change during the year.

COMMITMENT CARD LETTER

Theme Logo or Congregational Letterhead

Date _____

Name _____

Address _____

City/Town,   State/Province   Zip _____

RESERVATION CARD

Reservation Card

Name _____

Address _____

Phone _____

Name of Contacting person _____

Date of contact _____

Support Materials for Letter

"GROW ONE STEP" STAIRCASE

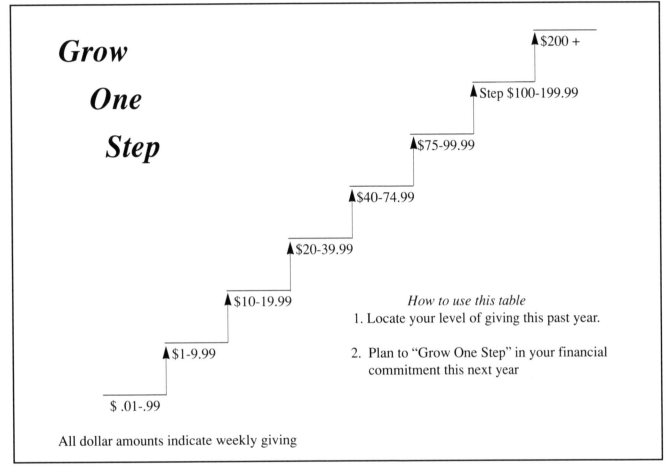

Grow

One

Step

▲$200 +

▲Step $100-199.99

▲$75-99.99

▲$40-74.99

▲$20-39.99

▲$10-19.99

How to use this table
1. Locate your level of giving this past year.

2. Plan to "Grow One Step" in your financial commitment this next year

▲$1-9.99

$ .01-.99

All dollar amounts indicate weekly giving

Instructions and information for the Planning Group:

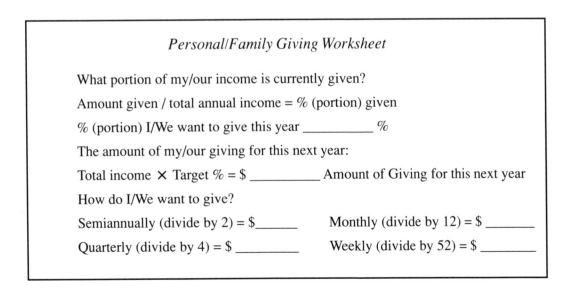

Personal/Family Giving Worksheet

What portion of my/our income is currently given?

Amount given / total annual income = % (portion) given

% (portion) I/We want to give this year _____ %

The amount of my/our giving for this next year:

Total income ✕ Target % = $ _____ Amount of Giving for this next year

How do I/We want to give?

Semiannually (divide by 2) = $_____   Monthly (divide by 12) = $ _____

Quarterly (divide by 4) = $ _____   Weekly (divide by 52) = $ _____

 **DRAMA**

THE APPEAL

GILSON MILLER

CAST OF CHARACTERS

Larry Lazylap
Carla Fromfelter
Herb *(a neighbor)*
Player #1
Player #2
Solicitor
Caller #1
Caller #2

Costumes....?

Props........?

Larry: Knock 'em unconscious! Disable 'em! Dismember 'em! Boy, do I have it made! A Saturday afternoon with nooooo responsibilities. My favorite team on the tube; my favorite junk food; the family's gone; and best of all—nooooo interruptions!

Carla: *(knocks—speaks as Larry opens door)* Hi, I'm Carla Fromfelter and I'm collecting for the aardvark extinction fund.

Larry: I had no idea such a fund existed. Well, I guess I can help out. By the way, what is an aardvark?

Carla: Don't you know that the aardvark is vital to our survival? It is an integral part of our food chain. If the aardvark goes, can civilization be far behind?

Larry: That's a good point.

Carla: Thanks, and the aardvark says thanks too. *(walking away)*

Larry: By the way, you never told me what an aardvark looks like. *(still standing in doorway)*

Herb: *(walks over from next door)* Larry, I hope I didn't interrupt anything, but I've got a problem. You see, my blades are so dull that you could stand on them barefoot and not cut yourself. *(laughs)* So could I borrow yours?

Larry: Herb, I'm not sure whether you want to shave or cut your grass.

Herb: Larry, you're such a kidder. I want to trim the grass. You see, I was referring to the blades on my mower. Why, anyone knows you could never walk on the edge of a razor, even if it was dull. But that's a good one, Larry. *(laughs)*

Larry: Sure, help yourself. It's in the garage in the same corner you borrowed it from the last time. *(goes back inside)*

Player #1: *(knocks—speaks as Larry opens door)* Hey mister, we're selling candy bars for the league.

Player #2: Buy a dozen today, and we'll see that your windows don't get waxed on Halloween.

Larry: This kid obviously has a future in sales! *(contributes, goes inside)*

Herb: *(knocks—speaks as Larry opens door)* Larry, I hate to bother you, but your mower, not my razor, is out of gas. I don't suppose you'd have some petrol available?

Larry: It's on the same shelf where you found it the last time you borrowed gas. *(goes back inside)*

Solicitor: *(knocks—speaks as Larry opens door)* Kind sir, would you give to a worthy cause? I am collecting for the widow of the unknown soldier.

Larry: That's nice. I'm a veteran myself. Hey, wait a minute. How do we know who the widow of the unknown soldier is, if we don't know who the soldier is?

Solicitor: Well, how should I know? It worked on your neighbors!

Larry: Well, it won't work on Larry Lazylap! *(goes inside, slams door)*

Herb: *(knocks—speaks when Larry opens door)* Say Larry, I hate to bother you again, but now that I've finished cutting the grass, I'd like to attack that hedge, you know the one . . .

Larry: Yes, the one that blocks your view of your neighbor's pool! Here are the clippers, and you might as well take the binoculars, because I know you'll want them as soon as you improve the view. Now go away and don't bother me any more! *(goes inside, slams door)*

Herb: Larry, you are one of the most generous people I know. Gee, what a guy—lawn mower, gas, clippers, and even binoculars, although I can't imagine why I would want them, ha ha. Oh-oh, there's one more thing. I hope he doesn't mind. *(yells, knocks)* Larry, are you in there?

Larry: What is it this time? You've borrowed the entire contents of my garage. You've completely ruined the best game of the year. I know, you want my car. Well, here's the key. And here's my wallet, in case you need to buy gas. And here—take my pretzels and chips and Coke! And why don't you help yourself to my shoes. And maybe you'd even like my shirt! Now, just LEAVE ME ALONE! *(slams door again, goes back inside)*

Herb: I guess he's a little upset. But what a guy! He gave me all these things, and all I wanted was a little extension cord to run the clippers!

Caller #1: *(standing at Larry's door)* I'm a little nervous about this. I've never made a call asking for money for the church before. I sure hope this first call goes OK. I hope we get a warm reception.

Caller #2:: They said at church that this would be an easy call to begin with. The pastor assured me that all you had to do is get Larry Lazylap talking about football, and the rest would be simple.

Caller #1: It says on this card that Larry is a very generous person. The pastor also noted that he's the kind of person who would give you the shirt off his back!

THE END

PART FIVE

AFTER THE CAMPAIGN—
YEAR-ROUND STEWARDSHIP

Long-Range Planning, Education, Calendars, Planned Giving, Endowments

The Stewardship of Enjoyment

* Money possibilizes the imagination. Positive imagination enhances your world; negative imagination detracts from it by projecting onto it. Growing can be negative; maturity is positive growth.
* Money potentiates the soul to resource (spend, give away) a need. A resource meeting a need is an occasion for love. (Remember that Monika Hellwig defined vocation as the place where a resource and a need meet.) Money cannot buy love.
* Money is the second most powerful thing. Imagination is first. Soul is almost equivalent to imagination. Soul is God's knowledge of me, always a mystery. Self is that knowledge I have about myself, this organism.
*Money touches hope and fear. What do you fear? What gives you security also reveals what you fear. What do you most hope for? Where there is no hope on earth, there is hell.

Robert Cooper
Ministry of Money

Introduction

NORMA WIMBERLY

Pastors, stewardship leaders, the finance committee, a missions task group, Christian educators, and church planners can benefit from a closer look at ways to practice faithful stewardship all year long. The annual financial emphasis may be over, but the love of giving goes on, especially as we think about giving in terms of global mission.

Jim Tarr's "Profile of a Model Church" should be your guide for approaching Part Five. If you prefer to quantify your relationship to the ideal church, try this:

Count the number of A's and
multiply by 2   = _ _ _ _ _ _
Count the number of P's and add   + _ _ _ _ _ _
to give a total of   = _ _ _ _ _ _

The above-average church gets a score of 24 or more.

"The ABCs of Giving" by Greg Ingram is rich food for spiritual thought as the congregation continues to practice year-round stewardship in meetings, in mission, in Christian education settings for all ages, and in planning for the future.

Paula Ritchie's "Year-Round Approach to Stewardship Education" offers a list of how-tos for a variety of settings within the life of the congregation, such as those that follow, and Don Joiner suggests that we look seriously at a simple three-year plan for programming.

"Deciding to Make a Difference" by John and Sylvia Ronsvalle confronts us with the continuing suffering and need that exists both in North America and around the world. When emphasizing mission giving during an annual commitment program, we do not go far enough!

As you read, study, and reflect on these articles, carry with you this story: Betty Lee Nyhus, a stewardship staff officer with the Evangelical Lutheran Church of America says that her father gave her a perspective on giving that continues to shape her whole life—not just what she does with her money. Betty

---

Profile of a Model Church

JIM TARR

(circle one)

	Always // Partially // Seldom		
1. The full meaning of stewardship and the way a Christian responds is emphasized throughout the year.	A	P	S
2. Every new member receives orientation about stewardship and is given an opportunity during the first 30 days to make specific commitments in service, attendance, and resources.	A	P	S
3. The church budget reflects special concerns for others in ministry, missions, and giving.	A	P	S
4. There is an approved endowment fund, and an active volunteer team works year round to help people understand and practice the stewardship of accumulated assets through bequests and planned gifts.	A	P	S
5. An educational stewardship program is developed and used annually for Sunday school classes (adults, youth, and children) and all operating units in the church. Information on stewardship resources in the church is shared through literature, videos, and training opportunities.	A	P	S
6. Stewardship is preached throughout the year.	A	P	S
7. Stewardship success is reflected in the willingness of members to serve and to use their talents in a Christian manner. Actions in the church show that people are learning the joys of giving.	A	P	S
8. Funds are available to accomplish the mission and ministries of the church.	A	P	S
9. A model stewardship church will have educational programs that help people understand and make appropriate choices in relation to issues of our natural resources, economic lifestyle, and visions of mission and ministry. There is recognition of the fact that stewardship is a result of spiritual formation and growth.	A	P	S
10. The challenge to tithe is a part of the educational program.	A	P	S

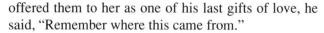

Lee was born into a farming family in rural Minnesota. The church offerings she remembers as a child were fruits of their labor—eggs, cream, potatoes, and other farm products. Her father always said to the children, "Remember where this came from."

Just before he died, Betty Lee went back home for a visit. Although her father was frail and elderly, he insisted on going out to the garden to dig some new potatoes (Betty Lee's favorite) for their supper. As he offered them to her as one of his last gifts of love, he said, "Remember where this came from."

As you engage in life after the campaign, "remember where this came from." All that we are, all that we have, all that we are gifted to do, all that we give, comes from God. Faithful stewardship as response to a loving, creating, giving God is much, much more than a financial program in the fall. It is year-round; it is all of life; it is a life of giving.

 MEETING MEDITATION

The ABCs of Giving

GREGORY G. M. INGRAM

The period through which the church is passing at the present moment is witnessing a widespread revival of interest in stewardship and tithing. We are not surprised, in light of this renewed interest, that various debates are underway on the subject. While historically, we have statements that interpret the biblical rules for giving, and though we can refer to our traditional position on tithing and stewardship, we still perceive discord within our ranks on the standard of giving.

When we view tithing and Christian stewardship as fulfillment of our covenant with God, we also view giving as a lifetime pattern. A life of giving ultimately leads us into a life of faith, excitement, and commitment to the Lord. When we develop a pattern of freely giving of ourselves, we are no longer the same. We make a commitment to God, which in turn results in a commitment from God.

When we are in covenant with God, new life takes place. Our lives are no longer the same. Because of the covenant, a life of giving becomes a pledge, a compact, a contract with God, which results in our lives mirroring God's willingness to give God's most precious gift to others. A life committed to God becomes a life in which a person is pledged to radiate a new spirit, a new feeling, and a new vision—according to both Jesus and the Apostle Paul.

When God has us, God has our property. For example, when Jesus had Peter, he also had Peter's boat. He had the lad's lunch, with which to feed the multitude, because he had the lad. When God has a person with a car, God also has a car to be used in holy service. When God has a man or woman of tal-ent, God has talent to be employed in the interest of God's kingdom. When God has a person with wealth, God has wealth to be used in furthering the kingdom of God. We become Christ's stewards when God becomes our Lord, the authority in and ruler of our lives. To acknowledge the Lordship of Christ means that we willingly accept the principle of stewardship, as the hallmark of our commitment to a life of giving.

A Christian who has not adopted a life of giving is a contradiction. An individual who has said that he or she is committed to Christ, but has not demonstrated a giving pattern indicative of a lifetime commitment, is not being true to self or Savior. An individual who says, "Christ is my guide," and then refuses to develop a life of giving, denies—as did Peter when Jesus needed him the most—that God is most important in his or her life.

What perceptions, attitudes, and behaviors are manifested by individual members, when it comes to giving in the church? Many social, psychological, and spiritual behaviors are exhibited during the Sunday morning worship service, particularly during collection time. These behaviors indicate churchgoers' motives and reasons for giving, which range from a sincere desire to do God's will and aid in Kingdom-building, to a self-centered hope that the giving will result in some form of receiving, to a spiritless, weekly exercise done by rote, often with reluctance, if not outright hostility.

The implementation of a tithing and stewardship program always will be difficult, until pastors and parishioners alike clearly understand the dynamics and effects of the antecedents, behavior, and consequences (the ABCs) of giving.

A. The *antecedents* are the conditions, events, or causes that precede a subsequent action and response (e.g., the pastor's appeal to the congregation to become tithers).

B. The *behavior* is the way an individual or group responds to the antecedents (e.g., the congregation wholeheartedly accepts or strongly rejects the pastor's tithing appeal).

C. The *consequences* are the effects or results of the behavior (e.g., the church's financial health either improves, remains the same, or declines, depending upon the membership's reaction to the pastor's tithing appeal).

Let's take a closer look at these ABCs of giving:

A. *Antecedents* are the stimuli or conditions that set the stage for the occurrence of the behavior, in this case, tithing. It is at this pre-tithing stage that a persuasive presentation that promotes a life of giving and stewardship must be made to the congregation, to increase the probability of a favorable response to the impending tithing appeal.

B. The *behavior* is tithing. To properly manage a tithing program, it is necessary to maintain records on the number of tithers, the amount of their tithes, and the impact of tithing on the church's total collections, expressed as a percentage. Data should be collected at prescribed intervals (e.g., weekly, monthly, or quarterly). A tithing campaign is the ideal time to begin the process.

C. The *consequences*, both positive and negative, are the outcomes of any behavior. They can be influenced through positive reinforcement. The key to understanding and controlling what happens during a tithing campaign is in making sure that the tithing and stewardship promotion is properly planned and executed, and that the principles and guidelines for implementing the program are followed.

To effectively promote the ABCs of giving, tithing and stewardship appeals must be reinforced consistently. Monthly, quarterly, and annual appeals alone will not do. To make it work, stewardship and tithing education must be emphasized weekly in the church bulletin and articulated by the pastor. I believe that part of my success in the stewardship of giving has been precisely in this area. Each week, emphasis is placed on the stewardship of giving by challenging members to review their convenantal

relationship with God, exercise their faith, and come to grips with the fact that tithing and the stewardship of giving is not a human scheme; it is God's plan. To do this is not easy, because, as stated earlier, people have different motives and reasons for giving.

Here, then, are people's eight motives for giving to the church:

1. *To avoid guilt feelings.* The rationale behind this motive is, "I ought to share in the support of the church; if I fail to do so, for whatever reason, I will feel guilty." The question for those who fall into this category ought to be, "Is the quest for a guilt-free conscience sufficient motivation for giving to the church?" Giving to the church should not be dependent upon feelings of guilt, but upon feelings of duty and obligation that come from a loving heart. Giving to the church should always be a response to the goodness and grace of the God who loves us.

8 Positive Motivations for Giving

1. Gratitude to God.
2. People really want to be giving persons.
3. People want to be a part of something that positively affects the lives of others.
4. Awareness of a particular need (different needs for different people).
5. People give to a cause that interests them.
6. Desire to be recognized as a person who wants to count for something significant.
7. Some persons give to lessen their taxes and help a charitable cause.
8. Some give out of a deep sense of loyalty.

2. *Fear of retribution.* This motive emanates from the fact that some people feel that not giving to the church is risky business, that God might punish them for the oversight. To them, God, like the bogeyman, is a terrifying figure who will get them if they don't give. Giving may be generous in dollars, but if the heart is not right and the giving is not motivated by love, then the gift is unacceptable.

3. *To keep up with the Joneses.* Those who fall into this category are persons who give according to what other folk are doing. Those who try to keep up with the Joneses are people who want to be a part of the "in" crowd. Giving to the church based on what

other people give completely dismisses what God has done for us. The scripture says, "Freely you have received, freely give" (Matt. 10:8 NKJ).

4. *To avoid excommunication.* There are those who are motivated to give as little as possible to the church, just as long as they can maintain some self-respect, keep their name on the church roll, and claim that they are part of the household of faith. Giving that is deceptive, mechanical, and joyless makes the church weak, lethargic, and ineffective. Members who give to the church fraudulently, with shallow commitment, are not dependable or reliable.

5. *To seek God's favor through coercion, force, or intimidation.* Many people try to relegate God to the position of a cosmic bellhop. Some even try to reduce God to the likes of Monte Hall of the television game show, "Let's Make a Deal." In other words, some people try to bribe God. "If you scratch my back, God, I'll scratch yours. If you do this for me, God, I'll do that for you. After all, one favor deserves another, right, God?" Jesus did not suggest that if you give enough, you will pressure God into giving you what you want. What he did say was, "Seek first the kingdom of God and his righteousness, and [a whole lot of things] shall be added to you" (Matt. 6:33 NKJ). The Apostle Paul further stated, "My God shall supply all your need according to his riches in glory" (Phil. 4:19 NKJ).

6. *Whether the pastor is liked.* Some givers would

withhold God's money, refusing to give to God's work, and in the process restrict their blessings, simply because they don't like the preacher. Since we are the recipients of God's divine grace, and since God looks beyond all our faults and sees our needs, we should feel so morally obligated to respond to the grace of God that we give to the church, whether or not we like the preacher. We must remember that the preacher is human and subject to err, just like anyone else. In our giving, we must look beyond the imperfections of the person and see the perfection in the goodness of the Lord.

7. *Out of habit.* Some people are motivated to give but don't know why. These are people who give out of habit and have never really taken the time to understand the biblical and theological rationales for giving. While giving in this manner assists the church in meeting its obligations, the givers miss out on the joy of knowing why they give. Church members who fall into this category should be educated in tithing and stewardship, if they are to be converted into knowledgeable, cheerful, generous givers.

8. *Due to a thankful heart and love for the Lord.* Obviously, these givers are the people who make the difference in the church. They are the ones who give to the Lord off the top, not from the leftovers, which means that they have made God the head of their lives, not the tail.

 PLANNING TOOL

A Year-Round Approach to Stewardship Education

PAULA K. RITCHIE

No two congregations have exactly the same calendar of events, although some aspects of congregational life will be in the same time frame, no matter which church you visit—the children's Christmas program will be in December, vacation church school will be held during the summer, church school will begin anew in late August or early September.

But stewardship programming does not have the same uniformity from congregation to congregation. A congregation may do its annual enlistment program any time of the year, as it fits with its own history and schedule.

The information that follows is designed to be used according to the calendar of your congregation. There is

no compulsory calendar for doing the work of stewardship; the guidelines will help to provide a framework within which any congregation can build its program.

A stewardship education program deserves the same kind of planning. By looking ahead, you can select the topics that best fit the needs of the congregation at a given time. Planning a program over a two- to three-year time period will help the committee in implementing the programs it wants.

Scheduling Enlistment and Education

In many congregations, the programmatic church year is composed of three blocks of time: September to Thanksgiving, January through May, and the summer. It is helpful to think of these blocks as units of time for accomplishing specific tasks. By breaking up the year, we are more likely to carry out specific tasks for that block of time. For example, in one block, you might carry out the enlistment program; in another, some element of stewardship education; and in still another, a special program related to some aspect of stewardship.

Most congregations carry out their stewardship enlistment (pledge) program in the fall or the spring. That program will require time and energy from the team, so it is a good time to plan education specifically related to the congregation's budget and the mission and ministry made possible by offerings. Depending upon the size of the congregation, the size of the stewardship team, and the importance of the program in a given year in the congregation, it may be wise not to carry out other stewardship education at this time.

Many congregations find it more helpful (and sustainable) to present other aspects of the stewardship education program in the season of the year when the annual enlistment program is *not* taking place. It provides a more even pace for the stewardship team, and it keeps stewardship before the congregation over a longer period of time.

Steps to Implementation

1. Determine the amount of time and energy in the congregation that is available to spend on stewardship education this year. Coordinate, through the pastor or staff, with other ministry teams. The congregation may have an established annual focus, such as education, evangelism, spiritual renewal, and so on. For example, if the annual theme for your congregation is "Building God's Kingdom," you do not want to compete with the established focus. Work *with* it. Stewardship would be a vital ingredient for this theme. You also will want to work toward having the congregation identify stewardship as a focus for a future year.

2. Determine those whom you most want to reach. Few congregations can do every aspect of stewardship education for every age range every year.

Many congregations find it helpful to begin with the leadership, or with various segments of the leaders. This intentionality will produce much more fruit than would a random approach.

3. Decide on your topic for education. You need not—indeed cannot—cover all aspects of stewardship

in one year. For example, you might choose personal/family finance as your topic, but for what age group? Retirees? Young married couples? Youth? Children? All of the above? Or you might choose environmental responsibility, but what topic? General environmental issues? How the congregation can be a better environmental steward? A specific topic of concern in your community?

Wisdom at Age 5

On Religion: Prayer is about God, rabbits, dogs, and fairies and deer and Santa Claus and turkeys and Jesus and Mary and Mary's little baby.
On Birth: You go to the store and buy one.
On Money: The government gets money from God and gives it to the churches. You can get money from church—if you go. My mom does.

By planning together as a department/committee/team and as a congregation, you can ensure that stewardship education is carried out over a three- to five-year period.

The term *stewardship* is not necessarily the name of the theme you will select as a focus to be emphasized for any given year. Try to come up with relevant positive metaphors that evoke the desired emphasis. (See suggested topics below.)

4. Look first at existing structures and meetings that might be suitable for stewardship education. For example, if you want to reach the leadership of the congregation, you need to find ways of reaching the elders, members of the diaconate, board, and cabinet. In some congregations, the elders and/or the diaconate meet monthly for a special study. Make stewardship the topic of study for one year. Many congregations open their general board or cabinet meetings with meditations or brief studies; stewardship could be the topic for a year.

Other existing structures include: Christian Women's Fellowship, Christian Men's Fellowship, youth fellowships, church school classes, fellowship dinners, Lenten series, annual retreats, newsletters, mailings. In addition, worship can be an important place to integrate stewardship education. The worship bulletin, sermon, offering meditation, or presentations during worship—all are possible means of continuing stewardship education. It is not always necessary to create a new event to carry out effective stewardship programming.

5. Decide whether your topic needs a special time frame or event. If it does not fit into an existing structure, create one that works. For example, the topic of wills and estate planning may not fit easily into most congregations' existing structure. You may need to set up a seminar held at a convenient time for the members.

The following charts give some ideas for topics and avenues of implementing stewardship education with adults, youth, and children. You will have additional ideas—use them, and send them in to the editors of this *Guide*.

Stewardship Education

Topics for Study

CHILDREN

	General Stewardship Education	Financial (allowances) Spending/Saving	Environment	Knowing & Using Our Talents	Sharing	Giving to the Church	Tithing
Church School							
Extended Session							
Junior Youth Fellowship							
Special Activities							
Camp							
Vacation Church School							
Field Trips							
Children's Sermons							

YOUTH

	General Stewardship Education	Financial Goals Saving/Spending	Time	Vocation Career	Environment	Lifestyle Issues	Giving to the Church	Tithing
Church School								
Youth Group								
Retreat								
Lock-in								
Camp								
Conference								
Work Camps								
Field Trips								
Projects								
Youth Sunday								

ADULT

	General Stewardship Education	Giving to the Church	Personal/Family Financial Stewardship	Wills and Estate Planning	Environment	Lifestyle Issues	Parenting/Tithing for Stewardship
Newsletter							
Special Mailing							
Offering Meditation							
Sermon							
Worship Presentation							
Brochures							
Seminars							
Special Events							
Meetings							
Fellowship Dinners							
Retreats							
Worship Bulletin							

CALENDAR

A Three-Year Stewardship Program

DONALD W. JOINER

Year One

January — Begin Program Planning Process
    What is our philosophy of ministry?
    Who are we as a church?
    Where is God calling us in ministry?

May — Recruit Every Member Commitment Committee
    (Fall Funding Program—
    Every Member Visitation)

Quarterly:
    1. Stewardship mailing to all members
    2. Stewardship Sermons
       (building on commitment and convenant)

Year Two

March — Stewardship Festival

May — Organize for Fall Funding Program
    Recruit committee
    Program: Congregational meetings

September — Conduct Time/Talent/Gifts for Ministry survey

Quarterly:
    1. Stewardship mailing to all members
    2. Stewardship sermons
       (building on commitment and covenant)

Year Three

January — Emphasis on Wills and Bequests

March — Emphasis on Proportionate Giving and Tithing

May — Organize for Fall Funding Program
    Recruit committee

November — Christian Financial Management Seminar

Year Four — Begin with Year One

 CALENDAR

A Planned-Giving Promotional Calendar

DONALD W. JOINER

January— Send a letter to your congregation, or through a church newsletter article, suggesting that members make a New Year's resolution to write or bring their wills up to date. Reinforce the letter/article with a brochure distributed with a Sunday morning bulletin.

February— Follow up the January letter/article with a presentation during a church service. A brochure may be distributed.

March— Send a letter to your congregation outlining the uses and management policies of your church's endowment fund. Enclose a brochure on Christian philanthropy and planned giving.

April— Follow up the March letter with a presentation during a church service. A brochure on planned giving may be distributed.

April/May— Give a presentation on wills or planned giving to church groups.

June–August— If you have identified them, call on prospective donors.

August /
September— Work with your church's annual fund-raising campaign team to "hitchhike" will and planned-giving information with the annual campaign promotional materials. This can be done by suggesting that appreciated assets may be used to fulfill one's annual pledge, or also can be effectively used through wills and planned giving.

October— Send a letter to your congregation suggesting that now is the time to do final tax planning for the current year. Include in the letter an invitation to the November seminar on financial and estate planning. Enclose a brochure on tax planning.

November— Follow up the October letter with a presentation during a Sunday church service. A brochure on tax planning may be distributed that Sunday. Hold the financial and estate-planning seminar.

December— Follow up on the November seminar by sending thank-you notes to those who attended and by calling on those who wish additional counseling. If you have time, you might telephone your thanks instead of writing.

SMALL GROUP STUDY

Deciding to Make a Difference

JOHN AND SYLVIA RONSVALLE

What are we to think?

Two people reacted very differently to the information contained in Figure 2 below, which compares potential church-member giving with world need. These statistics suggest that church members in America could make a major impact on their neighbors' suffering by giving more of their incomes to their churches.

A high school senior, with the straightforwardness of youth, asked, "If we can end most of the child deaths in the world, why haven't we?"

A middle-aged woman looked at the same statistics and concluded they were not true. Her reasoning? "If we could end all this global suffering, why haven't we?"

The same statistics produce the same verbal response, with exactly the opposite effect. The student wonders why we haven't gotten organized and done it. The woman finds it hard to believe, because surely, if it were possible, we would not be guilty of letting this suffering go on; therefore it must not be true.

In fact, James Grant, executive director of UNICEF, suggested that the only reason 35,000 children die daily around the globe from preventable poverty conditions is because nobody has decided they shouldn't. Nobody has decided to make these children enough of a priority to change the conditions that are killing them.

Ralph Winter of the U.S. Center for World Missions is convinced that we could evangelize the globe by the year 2000—if we don't, it will be because we did not decide to do it.

> Lord, help us remember that giving does not empty or drain our resources, but provides a space for You to refill.
>
> —DOMINQUEZ AND ROBIN

On the next few pages are some illustrated facts, accompanied by discussion questions. The graphics consider how current U.S. per-capita income compares to the past. These facts present information on how Americans, including church members, spend money. Information about the difficult situations faced by both our local and global neighbors is also included.

These facts and the related questions are designed to help you think through some of these issues. It might be helpful to talk about them in a small group, perhaps in a Sunday school class or another gathering of your friends from church.

The facts on the following pages should be considered in light of relevant Bible verses. Some examples might be Matthew 22:39, where Jesus said, "Love your neighbor as yourself." Or Jesus' statement in Matthew 6:21 that where our treasure is, there our hearts will be, too. Or the challenge in Matthew 28:19-20 to be faithful in word and deed, to go into all the world to preach the gospel, teaching others to obey all he taught them. Or the promise in Ephesians 3:20 and 21, that God is able to do more than we ask or imagine.

Some of the information on the following pages may surprise you. Some of it may disturb you.

Most of all, we hope it will help you make up your mind as to how you find your answer to the question—if we can make a major impact on domestic and global need in Jesus' name, why don't we?

Fact 2: Church member giving in the U.S. is about 2.5% of income. If church members decided to increase their incomes to the classic tithe (10%), there could be billions of dollars to apply to world need. The best estimates are that $2.5 billion could end most of the 35,000 daily child deaths, and $30 to $50 billion could impact the worst of physical poverty. There would still be billions of dollars available for Word mission.

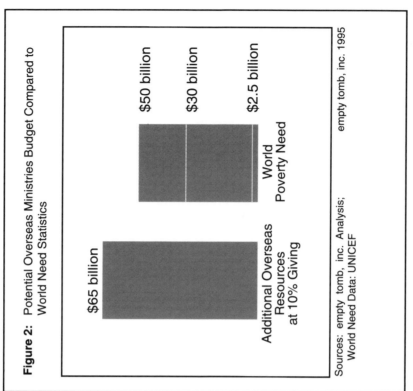

Figure 2: Potential Overseas Ministries Budget Compared to World Need Statistics

Sources: empty tomb, inc. Analysis;   empty tomb, inc. 1995
World Need Data: UNICEF

Question 2: Do you feel encouraged when you find out that Christians in the U.S. could make a bigger difference in world need if we decided to?

Fact 1: Since about 1950, a new situation has existed in the U.S. Instead of the majority of people being poor, the majority of people had more than needed for basic needs and still had money to spend. In 1993, per capita income in the U.S. was over 200% greater, after taxes and after inflation, than in 1933, the depth of the Great Depression.

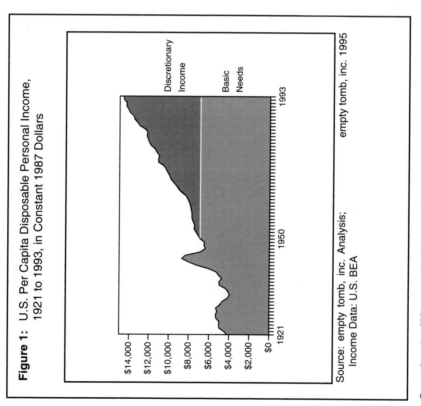

Figure 1: U.S. Per Capita Disposable Personal Income, 1921 to 1993, in Constant 1987 Dollars

Source: empty tomb, inc. Analysis;   empty tomb, inc. 1995
Income Data: U.S. BEA

Question 1: What are the biggest changes in life-styles that have taken place since your grandparents were young?

Fact 4: Church members have been giving a smaller percentage of their incomes to their churches. In 1968, on average people gave 3.1%; in 1991, 2.5%. At the same time, people have been buying more on credit. In 1991, it's estimated that Americans paid $33 billion in credit card interest, not fees or purchases. By converting the figures to constant 1987 dollars, we can compare credit card interest payments from 1975 to 1991.

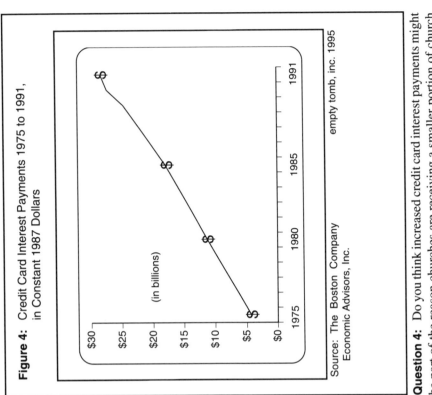

Figure 4: Credit Card Interest Payments 1975 to 1991, in Constant 1987 Dollars

Source: The Boston Company   empty tomb, inc. 1995
Economic Advisors, Inc.

Question 4: Do you think increased credit card interest payments might be part of the reason churches are receiving a smaller portion of church member incomes?

Fact 3: Many people are unaware that progress can be made in global need. There are still too many children dying around the world from preventable poverty conditions, but there were fewer dying in 1990 than in 1950. Progress has also been made in global life expectancy and literacy. In addition, there are fewer people groups who do not have access to a church than ever before.

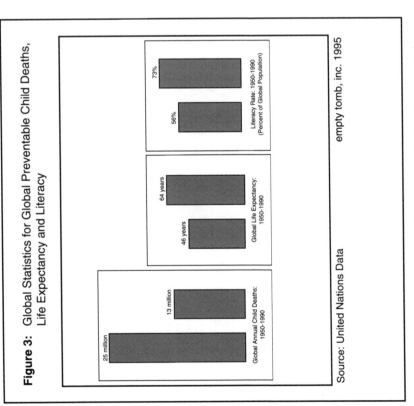

Figure 3: Global Statistics for Global Preventable Child Deaths, Life Expectancy and Literacy

Source: United Nations Data   empty tomb, inc. 1995

Question 3: Were you aware of the progress that has been made in our global neighbors' living conditions, many times as a result of the work through our denominational church agencies? How does it make you feel to know these facts?

107

Fact 5: Many children in the U.S. receive money from a variety of sources. A recent study found that children in the U.S. aged 4 to 12 have an estimated $12.6 billion a year to spend. They receive allowances, earn money by doing household tasks or other jobs, and receive money as gifts. Some children in the U.S. have larger annual incomes than some Third World adults.

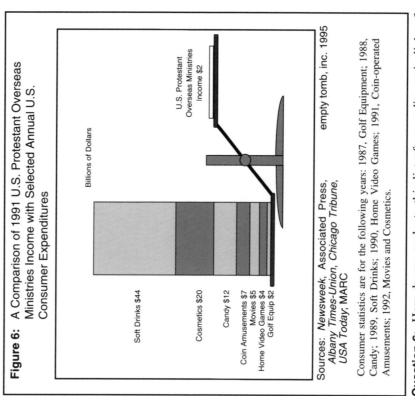

Figure 5: Aggregate Annual Income of Children in the United States, Four to Twelve Year Olds, 1991

Sources: James U. McNeal, Texas A&M University; U.S. Census Bureau   empty tomb, inc. 1995

Question 5: How does your church help children understand what the Bible says about the responsible use of money?

Fact 6: Protestant denominational offices and missions organizations in the U.S. received $2 billion for overseas ministries in 1991. This amount was about half of what Americans spent on home video games.

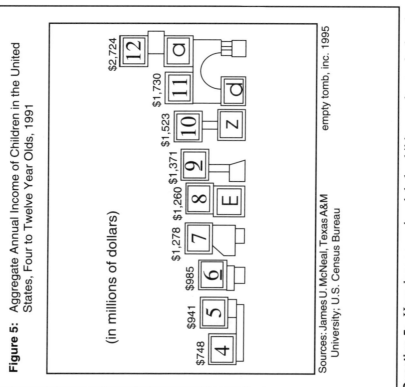
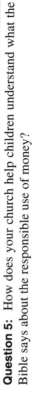

Figure 6: A Comparison of 1991 U.S. Protestant Overseas Ministries Income with Selected Annual U.S. Consumer Expenditures

Sources: *Newsweek*, Associated Press, *Albany Times-Union, Chicago Tribune, USA Today*, MARC   empty tomb, inc. 1995

Consumer statistics are for the following years: 1987, Golf Equipment; 1988, Candy; 1989, Soft Drinks; 1990, Home Video Games; 1991, Coin-operated Amusements; 1992, Movies and Cosmetics.

Question 6: How do we evaluate this list of expenditures in light of Jesus' comment that where our treasure is there our hearts will be (Matt. 6:21)?

Fact 8: Domestic poverty continues to be a problem in the U.S. The Infant Mortality rate in a country indicates how many babies die by the age of one per each 1,000 born alive. Finland has the lowest infant mortality rate. There are 21 countries that have lower infant mortality rates than the U.S.

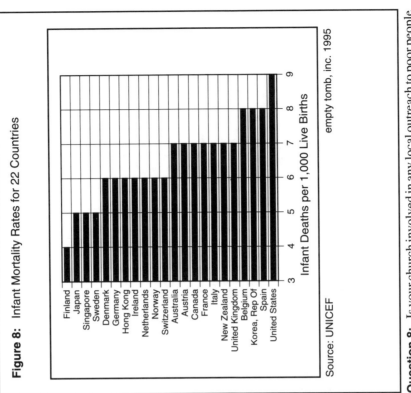

Figure 8: Infant Mortality Rates for 22 Countries

Source: UNICEF   empty tomb, inc. 1995

Question 8: Is your church involved in any local outreach to poor people in your area?

Fact 7: The U.S. Social Health Index includes 16 categories like poverty, highway deaths due to alcohol, and teenage suicides. The Index suggests that U.S. social health declined 45% from 1970 to 1992. During the same period, the portion of income church members were directing to Benevolences— the budget category beyond local church operations—declined by 27%.

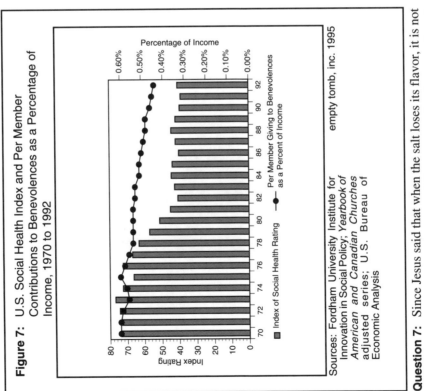

Figure 7: U.S. Social Health Index and Per Member Contributions to Benevolences as a Percentage of Income, 1970 to 1992

Sources: Fordham University Institute for Innovation in Social Policy; *Yearbook of American and Canadian Churches* adjusted series; U.S. Bureau of Economic Analysis   empty tomb, inc. 1995

Question 7: Since Jesus said that when the salt loses its flavor, it is not good for much, do you think there could be a connection between church members investing less beyond their own congregations and a decline in the general condition of society?

Fact 10: Studies show that when the child death rate in a country declines, the birth rates begin to go down faster. However, many children continue to die from preventable poverty conditions. More children under five died from preventable poverty conditions in one recent fifteen-year period than all the people killed in the wars between 1500 and 1990.

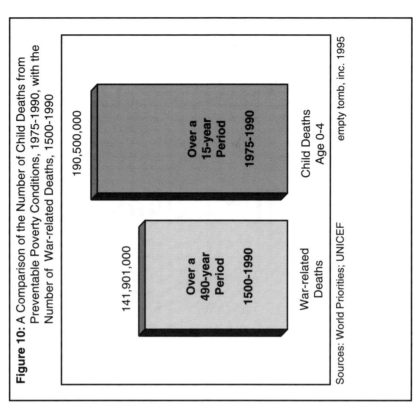

Figure 10: A Comparison of the Number of Child Deaths from Preventable Poverty Conditions, 1975-1990, with the Number of War-related Deaths, 1500-1990

190,500,000

141,901,000

Over a 490-year Period 1500-1990

Over a 15-year Period 1975-1990

War-related Deaths

Child Deaths Age 0-4

Sources: World Priorities; UNICEF

empty tomb, inc. 1995

Question 10: What verses give us guidance regarding our response to parents facing the death of their children from poverty conditions around the globe? What specific actions can you take through your congregation to help stop children from dying in at least one area of the world?

Fact 9: The demand for Bibles worldwide is great. It costs $4.18 dollars, on average, for a Bible to be printed and distributed anywhere around the globe. Yet projections indicate that the combined efforts of the world's United Bible Societies can only meet two-thirds of the 51.5 million requests they receive.

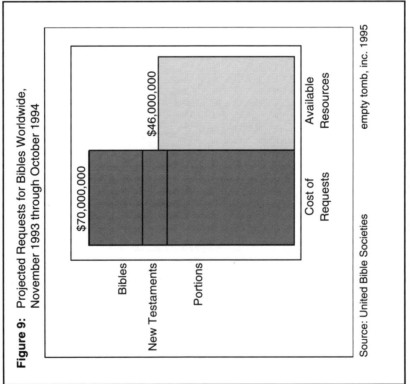

Figure 9: Projected Requests for Bibles Worldwide, November 1993 through October 1994

$70,000,000

$46,000,000

Bibles

New Testaments

Portions

Cost of Requests

Available Resources

Source: United Bible Societies

empty tomb, inc. 1995

Question 9: Do you know if the mission activities supported by your congregation include the distribution and printing of Bibles somewhere in the world?

PLANNED GIVING

Church Endowments?

DONALD G. STONER

"Old First," known as the "church of the open mind, the open heart and the open door," ministers in a deteriorated area of the city, where it has served for more than 150 years. The surrounding community is ethnically diverse and economically deprived. The membership of "Old First" has ebbed and flowed as immigrant groups arrived in the city and eventually made their way to the suburbs. Presently, under vital pastoral and lay leadership, the congregation is experiencing a renewal, attracting new members and reaching out again to the neighborhood. The ability of the congregation to be so engaged is due in no small measure to their endowment. For instance, it provides additional funds for an associate pastor to serve the community and engage in a youth ministry.

St. John's, located nearby, is of similar age to Old First. It is known as an "ethnic" church, given its historic roots. It is served by a part-time pastor who gathers the elderly few in a cavernous Gothic sanctuary for worship on Sunday, which basically constitutes St. John's ministry. The outlook of this declining congregation is one of survival. A small endowment, whose principle is dwindling, maintains the congregation. The members are determined to "keep the doors open" as long as they live, or "until the money runs out." Lacking is a sense of mission, an openness to the community, and a vision for tomorrow.

A Biblical Perspective

Some congregations question why we have endowments. Some church officers would even say that it is not wise Christian stewardship, perhaps even unbiblical. Some leaders feel that endowments are a deadly influence on the life and giving of a congregation, in the same way that too much capital reserve can lull a business into complacency.

Yet Jesus offers a perspective that does not condemn money, nor the accumulation of wealth, as long as it serves a worthy purpose and does not become the object of worship. Money, especially when invested, can tempt individuals and congregations to place undue reliance and trust in it, as with the rich young ruler (Mark 10:17-31) or the builder of bigger barns (Luke 12:16-21). In these Scriptures, we hear the legitimate warnings and harsh judgments of Jesus. In contrast, the parable of the talents (Matt. 25:14-30) has Jesus commending the servant who multiplied what he had been given, that it might serve an even greater usefulness.

When monies are placed in endowments and prudently managed by faithful stewards on behalf of God's mission, endowments can indeed be a blessing.

> "Each of us will one day be judged by our standard of life—not by our standard of living; by our measure of giving—not by our measure of wealth; by our simple goodness—not by our seeming greatness."
>
> —*WILLIAM ARTHUR WARD*

When so understood, an endowment need not become a "crutch" to be dependent upon or a "curse" that exerts a deadly influence. An endowed congregation can avoid having a "survival mentality" and be enlivened to engage in mission. In addition, endowments can serve to encourage the giving of present members for the sake of their own spiritual health and well-being. "Bigger barns" are not necessary, nor need they be maintained in perpetuity, unless they are utilized to serve the ministry and mission of the church in a fuller and more faithful way.

Endowments Related to Stewardship and Mission

The encouragement of endowment giving is not to be seen solely as a means for undergirding the future mission and ministry of the church. Giving to endowment funds must be conceived and offered as part of a theologically sound, holistic approach to stewardship education. This is part of the varied means of responding with one's gifts to God's call. The church, through its teaching, preaching, counseling, and administration, enables its members to become better stewards of their assets for the sake of themselves and their families. For instance, the drawing of a will and the preparation of an estate plan are to be considered acts of stewardship. As the church addresses these matters and serves its membership, people's desire to make long-term financial commitments to the church's mission will be greatly enhanced.

The need for endowments becomes even more clear and persuasive when seen in relation to a congregation's plan for its present and future mission. Development of a mission statement and engagement in strategic planning is a key to learning why endowments will be necessary and how the income will provide for the congregation's mission in years to come. Such endeavors also will serve to build confidence and encourage members to consider making bequests, life-income gifts, and outright gifts to the endowment fund.

Having a Plan

Prior to the active encouragement of endowment giving, the leadership should review any existing endowment policies and guidelines, or establish new ones. This will serve to educate the congregation regarding endowments and their particular role in its life. This can also help avoid misunderstanding and confusion, once gifts are received. Legal counsel should be engaged to assure that all requirements of state and federal law are met. Once developed, all guidelines and bylaw provisions should be adopted by the congregation or its governing body. Management of the funds can be maintained under the general oversight of the official corporate structure of the congregation. Except under unusual circumstances, it is neither advisable nor necessary for the congregation to create a separately incorporated body.

An essential part of any plan should be a statement of purpose which clearly defines how endowed gifts will be used by the congregation to further its total mission. The plan should provide for the purposes of the gifts to be carried forward, in case the congregation changes its identity through merger or otherwise ceases to exist.

Once a plan is approved, it should be interpreted and promoted regularly by an officially constituted committee, in order to make it a visible and vital part of the congregation's life. This will serve to encourage giving to the endowment fund, as well as keep the congregation informed.

Managing Endowments

The management of endowment funds usually calls for a proper balance between income and growth of invested principle, utilizing professional investment management. Most national church bodies provide asset management for their congregations. Clear lines of authority with respect to all management decisions are necessary, along with the proper bonding of responsible treasurers of the funds. Regular third-party auditing is needed to protect the interest of donors, managers, and the congregation. Conflict of interest must be avoided on the part of the managers. The interest of the church as to where and how dollars are invested must be the guiding concern. A provision that prohibits borrowing against the principle is a matter of good business practice and sound stewardship that will maintain the funds for their intended use. Also, consideration should be given to any investment policies or social-investment guidelines that pertain to the congregation and the denomination.

Guidelines for Distribution of Income

For what purposes should income be distributed? It is important to have a consensus around the distribution of income that will enhance and extend the mission and ministry of the church and not deter individuals from increasing their annual giving. A sample set of guidelines for inclusion in a congregation's bylaws might appear as follows:

*One-fourth for capital improvements, debt reduction, or building program of (name of congregation).

*One-fourth for scholarships or grants to members of the congregation for the purpose of attending college or seminary; for church-related camping or leadership conference; or such other training to enable the congregation to grow in Christian faith and service to God's people.

*One-fourth for outreach into the community, including, but not limited to, grants to colleges, seminaries, social service agencies; institutions to which this congregation is related; and special programs designed for those in the parish area who are in spiritual or economic need.

*One-fourth for the wider mission of the denomination at home and abroad, including, but not limited to, grants for new church development, ministerial leadership, educational ministries, world hunger, redevelopment, evangelism, and various ecumenical ministries.

The Endowment Committee shall receive and consider all proposals for distribution of income under this plan, and make its recommendations for distribution to the congregation's governing body for approval.

Role of Leadership

For those who claim that "the best way to kill a congregation is to endow it," I would suggest that it is not endowments per se that kill churches, but rather the weak, ineffectual leadership in charge of available assets. When a congregation simply exists by "living off its endowments," it has lost its spiritual nerve and ability to serve. The words concerning living monuments from the movie *Grand Hotel* come to mind: "People come, people go. Nothing ever happens." Lay and pastoral leadership frequently become secure and complacent in the face of endowments. Leadership begins to function like the biblical servant who, once given the talent, proceeds to bury it rather than faithfully multiplying it. I observe, however, that more churches have failed in their mission because of the lack of an endowment than those who have one. Strong, committed, creative leadership is essential if a congregation is to remain faithful to the purposes of an endowment.

The commitment of pastoral leadership to endowment giving is critical. The pastor plays an exceedingly key role in the membership's openness to understanding and advocating the stewardship of assets in the life of the congregation. This entails the persistent teaching and preaching of stewardship. It involves offering counsel through pastoral care. It is undergirded through skills in administration for securing and managing gifts. Above all, it necessitates the practice and witness of stewardship in their personal lives. The approach and tone set by the pastor is, at best, an act of gratitude and an expression of hope. Endowment giving is a response to what God has so abundantly bestowed upon us. This is part of the mystery and joy of giving, which so often seems to be missing when considering endowments solely from a business or investment point of view.

A crucial role of leadership is communication with the church membership on a regular basis. Information on the purposes of the endowment, status of the funds, and utilization of income are critically important. When consistently and creatively done, this will serve to keep the endowments in perspective and before the people in a positive manner. Too often, endowment funds are held in secret, which serves to breed misunderstanding and suspicion. Full disclosure regarding the management of funds and the purposes being served lend credibility and invite support for the endowment.

Further, where members are familiar with endowments and how the church's mission is being fostered, congregations invariably experience increases in their regular giving. They invariably become churches with an "open heart, open mind, and open door," as well as the church of "the open purse." Individuals come to share in the true joy and love of giving, of all kinds. As the late Warren H. Denison wrote, "It is not loving that empties the heart nor giving that empties the purse."[1]

Pastors have a special relationship with parishioners, given their unique status as trusted counselors. The pastor has the special privilege of exploring with parishioners their deepest meanings and desires concerning wealth and possessions. The pastor needs to be open and sensitive to the parishioners' dreams and desires for the church through their giving. The pastor needs to be equipped to enable the parishioners to make appropriate gifts, working with their advisors. The pastor can provide the counsel and spiritual direction that can help fulfill the stewardship aspirations of a parishioner's life.

For instance, at "Old First," Miss Z is one of the longest and oldest members. She has been most faithful in the stewardship of her time, talent, and treasure over the years. Recently, she has made major outright gifts to provide for building renovations, especially the historic organ. She has shared with the pastor her desire to sustain the church's ministry of music for years to come. She is motivated to do so because of her gratitude for the nurture the church has provided her and her family over many years. She is also grateful for the church's outreach in the community. She feels confident about the church's leadership, especially in regard to the endowment fund. As the pastor works with her and her advisors on a gift to the

> "If I were building an organization, I would hire the best 'praise and appreciation' expert I could afford. It is critical to show gratitude continuously and systematically. Philanthropy is a people-to-people emotionally based activity, and often there is a tremendous imbalance between the gifts and the recognition of these gifts."
>
> —*DOUGLAS M. LAWSON*

endowment fund, the pastor realizes that this is an important and valued part of her ministry. She is enabling this gift to be truly her "last will and testament," an everlasting act of stewardship that will shape the future of Old First.

In the last analysis, the developing and encouraging of endowments in the life of a congregation is akin to the line of the old hymn: "They builded better than they know, they trusted where they could not see." A positive response to the question Why Church Endowments? is ultimately an act of faith in the future of the church and its mission in the world.

1. From the *Stewardship Notebook* of Warren H. Denison, Missions Council, Congregational Christian Churches, New York City, N.Y.

PLANNED GIVING HANDOUT

Options for Funding the Future

NORMAN J. TELLIER

Most church members are accustomed to giving to the church. Many of us were brought up to do so. When we were children, our parents gave us money to put in the offering every Sunday. We were trained well to give, but we were trained in only one method of giving. Therefore, when we think of giving, we usually think of the amount of money we will put in the offering plate next Sunday.

A story is told about the great composer Rossini. When on tour, he would go from town to town, incorporating the local talent into his concerts. In one town, there was only one singer, and the only note she could sing was B flat. People were sure that at last, Rossini's great genius had met its match. The time for his concert came at last, and nearly everyone in town was there to see what he could do with this pitiful one-note woman.

When the curtain rose, the woman sang her one note, pure and strong. Then Rossini's music floated in, intertwining and swelling, surrounding her note with beauty and perfection, enveloping it in a glorious symphony!

This is what God does with us. We need only offer the gifts we have been given, no matter how small. God will do the rest, turning it into the very music of the spheres.

Mark 14:8—"She has done what she could."

—*BETSY SCHWARZENTRAUB*

Certainly there is nothing wrong with putting money in the offering plate! But when we think that is the only way we can give, or the only way the church expects us to give, we are missing a large part of stewardship.

Sometimes we do think of giving in different ways, but those ways usually are connected with our Sunday morning giving. Maybe our congregation is going to build a new building and is having a capital-fund drive. Someone probably will visit us and ask for a pledge for that building. We'll make it, and fulfill it by dropping into the offering plate every Sunday a certain amount designated for the building fund. The only thing we really have done differently is to make a multiyear pledge. We still give in the same way.

Some people of means are very aware of tax laws and see an advantage to increasing or doubling their giving in one year. They know that it is advantageous to itemize on their income tax, but they may not have enough deductions in one year to take advantage of itemizing. However, if they give their contribution to the church for next year now, they will have the advantage of a larger deduction this year, and still get the standard deduction next year. That may help reduce their taxes.

Others know that there can be an advantage in giving stocks or other assets that have increased in value. Instead of selling the stocks, they give them to their church and receive a full tax deduction of the trading value of the stock. In addition, they avoid all capital-gains taxes.

We also give in a different way when we give a one-time gift to a special fund. This often happens when someone dies and a memorial fund is established. Our gift is pooled with that of others, and a suitable memorial is purchased for the person who has died.

All these are methods of giving with which we are

familiar. They all involve a gift that, once made, is ended.

There are many other ways in which we may give, but we don't know about most of them because the church often fails to mention them to us. In most cases, they have to do with gifts of $1,000 or more and are part of our estate plan- ning. Some of them offer income to us even after we have given the money or other asset.

These other options may be arranged or completed now, but the church receives the gift in the future. Some of these gifts, usually called life-income gifts, also provide income for the donor. A few of these are listed below.

"We must give not only what we have; we must give also what we are."

—DESIRE MERCIER

Gift Annuities. Since the rate of return on a gift annuity is based on age, older is better. A gift annuity provides income for one or two people, with the remainder going to the church upon the death of the last annuitant. A tax deduction for a portion of the principal placed in a gift annuity is deductible as a charitable contribution in the year in which the gift- annuity agreement is signed. Also, a portion of the income received annually is not taxed for the life expectancy of the donor.

Deferred Charitable-Gift Annuity. This one is for younger folks. Some people look at the gift annuity rates and know that because of their age, they are not going to get a high return. However, they have some assets which they would like ultimately to go to the church, but they would like to have income from them when they retire. They can put their assets in a deferred charitable gift annuity. They make the gift now, but don't begin to receive income from it until a later time, which they specify. Because the receipt of income is deferred, the income will be relatively high when pay- ments begin. A tax deduction also is allowed in the year in which the assets are placed in the deferred annuity.

Pooled-Income Fund. The pooled-income fund "pools" the small gifts of many people into one larger fund. These monies are then invested, and the earn- ings are paid to the participants in the fund. Upon the death of the participants, their share is separated from the fund and paid to the church. Because the gift to the pooled-income fund is irrevocable, a charitable deduction is allowed for a portion of the gift in the year in which it is placed in the fund. The interest received each year is taxable income.

Revocable-Gift Agreement. This agreement is for those who know they would like to make a gift to the church, but are concerned that they might need some of that money for their own needs. The revocable gift agreement pro- vides a way for donors to make a gift now and receive all or part of that gift back, should the need arise. Interest is paid on the gift while it is placed with the church. Upon the death of the donor, the funds left with the church become a gift to the church. Because the donor maintains control of the funds, no tax deduction is allowed.

Charitable-Remainder Trusts. Several types of charitable remainder trusts are possible. Each is cre- ated by legal documents which place the property in trust, naming charitable organizations to receive the distribution of the property at the trust's end. Because of the charitable intent, a tax deduction is allowed for a portion of the assets placed in the trust. Income is paid to the donor or someone designated by the donor, based upon the terms in the trust agreement. Since trusts are legal documents, the donor must work with an attorney to establish the trust.

Charitable Lead Trust. This trust provides a way the earnings on a sum of money may be given to the church for a term of years, and the principal then given back to the donor or someone designated by the donor. It is a legal trust document, which provides that the interest earned on certain property be paid to the designated church (denomination or congregation) for a certain number of years. At that time, the property goes to the person designated by the donor. Tax deductions are allowed at the creation of the trust, and also for each year the income is paid out to the church. Since a trust document is needed, the donor must work with an attorney to establish the trust.

In addition to "life income gifts," a gift may be made to the church in still other ways. Some offer income-tax deductions, others offer estate tax deduc- tions. Listed below are these methods.

Life Insurance. Life insurance policies make excellent gifts to the church and often provide a means of making a larger gift than one ever expected would be possible. An existing policy that may no longer be needed to provide protection for the donor's family may be donated to the church by making the church the owner and beneficiary. A tax deduction roughly equivalent to the cash value of the policy is allowed. If premiums continue to be paid, these also may be allowed as tax deductions. A new policy may also be purchased and assigned to the church. Again, tax deductions are available.

Life-Estate Contract. In a life-estate contract, the donor gives a home or farm (the donor must live in or on it) to the church, while continuing to live in it for life. The donor must continue to maintain the property and pay the real-estate taxes, but a tax deduction is given because the title has been irrevocably transferred.

Pension Fund. Some pension funds allow the naming of a charitable beneficiary. If that is the case with your fund, you can name the church to receive your funds upon your death. Doing so should provide a charitable deduction for estate-tax purposes. Individual retirement accounts (IRAs) allow the naming of beneficiaries. There may be an estate-tax advantage in using an IRA as a charitable gift, since upon the death of the owner of the IRA, the principal amount is brought back into the estate. If the IRA is given to the church, an equivalent charitable estate-tax deduction is given, and no assets need to be taken from the rest of the estate in order to make the gift.

Bequests Through Wills and Trusts. A will is a vitally important document for every person. It provides for the distribution of your property upon your death. Without a will, your property will be passed on to others, according to the state or province in which you live. You should check the laws of your state or province to see whether the distribution required by law is what you really want. If not, you must write a will. The easiest way to provide a gift to your church is to put a provision in your will. By providing an outright gift to the church, you can be assured of making the gift you wish to make in gratitude to God.

Why would you consider using some of these options? One reason is simply that they offer a way to make a gift to the church—often a larger gift than you thought possible.

A second reason is that these gifts often provide a way to receive maximum benefit from an asset. Perhaps you have a stock that pays low dividends. By putting it into one of these gift vehicles, your income could actually go up.

A third reason is that these gift vehicles also offer a way to reduce capital-gains tax. An asset that has increased in value may be contributed to many of these gift vehicles. When such assets are contributed, all or a part of the capital-gains tax attributable to them may be avoided. In some cases, taxes are partially avoided and the rest spread out over the life expectancy of the donor.

These methods of giving are not as easy as simply dropping money in the offering plate. But dropping money in the offering plate doesn't offer some of the benefits of these ways. In order to take advantage of some of these methods of giving, you will need the help of someone who has knowledge of them. Where do you get that help?

The first place to begin is your church's office. Most denominations have someone who works with these kinds of gifts every day. The office usually has a name like "planned giving," "gift planning," "foundation," or something similar. Someone there will be glad to explain any of the methods of giving more fully, and will be willing to give you a detailed proposal for your specific gift, based on your age, size of gift, and type of gift. These services are provided at no cost to you and will help you make a decision as to the best way to make your gift.

You also may need some other help. While gift annuities and pooled-income fund gifts usually can be handled by the gift-planning office, others will need the help of an attorney. It is usually best to use your own attorney, who will work with the denomination's attorney to complete the gift in a timely fashion, and in the way that is best for you. You also may want to consult your accountant or tax attorney, if you already have a relationship with either or both.

The important thing is to feel good about your gift. That will happen when you know what you are doing and have confidence in those who are helping you. Don't be afraid to ask questions, to be sure you know what you are doing. These gifts can be exceedingly gratifying, and will be for you, if done correctly. Don't be afraid because they seem complicated—that's what you and your denomination's advisors are for—to help you make the gift you want to make.

Making a "planned gift," may give you a sense of gratification you never before have known.

BULLETIN COPY

Planned Giving One-Liners

RENARD KOLASA

> "Insecurity causes some people to insist on being the giver rather than the receiver. When we let others give to us, and when we accept their gifts in a gracious and mature manner, we may be giving them one of the most important gifts of all. Remember, the joy you find in giving is felt by others as well."
>
> —Anonymous

1. Preparing an estate plan is good Christian stewardship—saying thanks to God, expressing your love and concern for family, and showing charity toward others.

2. Remember, if you have no will or trust, state laws will determine who will inherit your property at your death. State laws do not include your church or any other charity as a beneficiary.

3. Consider naming the church as a beneficiary in your will or living trust. The gift could be a set dollar amount, a percentage of your estate, the remainder after other gifts are made, or part of the estate left if designated heirs are deceased.

4. Did you know that there is no limit on the size of a charitable gift to the church at the time of your death? No matter how large, the gift is deductible for federal estate tax purposes.

5. Think about the part you want to play in our church's future. You have the opportunity to support this ministry in many ways. Naming the church as a beneficiary in your estate plan, or making an endowment gift, can assure your continued participation in this ministry far into the future.

6. Giving to the church through your will or trust is the most common way to continue your support beyond your lifetime. When your estate plan is prepared, consider a gift to the church.

7. Life insurance is a way to make a larger gift to the church than you might otherwise be able to afford. Consider naming the church as a beneficiary of any insurance policy.

8. Our trustees and pastor enthusiastically support planned giving to our church. Contact them for more information.

9. We accept endowment gifts. The income will be used for special church projects. The principle of the gift is never spent and continues indefinitely.

10. Anyone can give an endowment gift. Any size gift may be made as an endowment. You may do this now or as part of your estate plan.

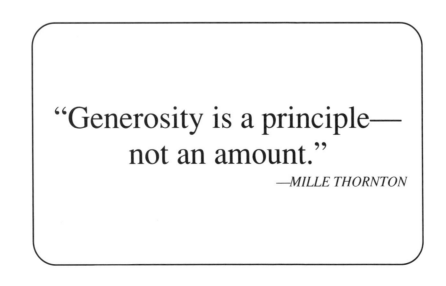

> "Generosity is a principle—not an amount."
>
> —MILLE THORNTON

 HANDOUT

Time and Financial Management

DAN P. MOSELEY

People who write and speak about time management and financial management consistently make the same point: In order to manage your time or your money, it is critical to know what you are currently doing with it.

If you want to understand what you value, simply keep a daily log. It will reveal with clarity what you believe in.

If you want to discover the one you trust, simply keep a log of your expenses. It will help you understand what you count on for meaning in life.

As you consider this prayerful exercise, write down your response to the following series of life needs.

How much of my time and money do I spend in the following activities?

Activity	Available Time 144 hours per week		Available Money $_____
TIME SPENT		**MONEY SPENT**	
Sleep	_____	Housing	_____
Preparing and Eating Food	_____	Food	_____
		Business Expenses	_____
Working for Money	_____	Utilities	_____
Reading and Watching News	_____	Leisure Activities	_____
Praying	_____	Church	_____
Leisure Activities (TV, Movies, Sports, Knitting, etc.)	_____	Community Needs	_____
Church	_____		
Service Agencies	_____		

Now, pray. Simply reflect upon this, and decide whether it is consistent with what you value in your life.

The closer we get to spending our energies and our money on those things that we value, the closer we are to an integrated sense of self that finds some peace and contentment.

PART SIX

YOUR CHURCH, TAXES, AND UNCLE SAM

For the Finance Team

Introduction

DONALD W. JOINER

Render Unto Caesar . . .

We live with a Constitution that announces a separation of church and state. But in reality, we live with a governmental system that has great influence on the economic affairs of our congregations. The most recent influences have appeared in a threatening manner as to whether the economic powers should treat full-time church leaders the same way they treat other professionals.

Who is an employee, and who is not? Many congregations treat all employees as self-employed contractors, whether they are clergy, organists, custodians, or a plumber who fixes the stopped-up drain. The federal government is beginning to audit those relationships, and fines have been levied.

When does a congregation need to file forms with the federal government, and which ones? When is income subject to taxation? What is the definition of a contribution, and what receipt is the local church obligated to provide to the donor?

An increasingly visible debate is engaged regarding clergy tax issues. Is a cleric an employee, or self-employed? Can the pastor really exclude a portion of compensation from income tax? The answer is—it depends. The criteria for determining the pastor's situation can be found in *The Abingdon Clergy Income Tax Guide,* which can be ordered annually from your bookstore or by subscription.

The goal of this section of *The Abingdon Guide to Funding Ministry* is to provide the finance leaders of a congregation with information about the actions the church should take when managing its funding ministry. Your church will thus behave in the same way as other nonprofit organizations. This publication is not engaged in rendering legal or tax advice. For advice and assistance in specific cases, the services of your own counsel should be obtained.

Fred Leasure works with churches in many denominations across North America, so he taps the issues most often asked at his seminars. Fred has an acute grasp of the relationships of the congregation and what the federal government requires of it.

Reporting and Filing for Churches

FREDERICK H. LEASURE

The constitutional mandate for the separation of church and state results in the church being exempt from many provisions of the law. Tax policy has exempted certain charitable organizations from specific taxes, because of the valuable services they perform for the "public good." Thus, many organizations have falsely assumed that "exempt" also refers to certain tax-reporting requirements. The church has both a legal and a moral obligation to comply with numerous layers of accountability, which have been designed to ultimately protect the interests and rights of the greater human community in a democratic society.

Fund Raising and Tax Exemption

As congregations have found it necessary to pursue more creative ways to fund ministry, they may have become subject to additional reporting and filing requirements, and perhaps some tax liabilities. This may be true at both federal and state, as well as local levels.

Unrelated Business Income Tax (UBIT)

A church that pursues revenue generating activities unrelated to its exempt purpose may be subject to taxation on this unrelated income (Internal Revenue Code Section 513 [a]). In order for this tax to be imposed, the following conditions may be met:

1. The income must be from an activity that is a trade or business (carried on for the purpose of producing income, whether or not profit results from the activity).

2. The unrelated business must be regularly carried on (including seasonally) by the organization.

3. The unrelated business does not significantly contribute to accomplishing the organization's exempt purpose (except for producing income).

When these conditions are met, the church must account for the financial results of the unrelated business activity on Federal Form 990T, and pay any federal tax that is due on the activity. It should be noted that rental proceeds from church-owned property are considered passive income, and are not subject to the Unrelated Business Tax. Also, Unrelated Business Income, properly reported and accounted for, does not jeopardize the tax-exempt status of the church. More detail on Unrelated Business Income Tax can be found in the instructions for Form 990T.

State and Local Sales and Use Tax

Many states now require congregations to collect and pay sales and use tax for the sale of nonreligious items. Simply because a church has carried on a sales activity in the past without being challenged does not necessarily mean that the sale of those items is exempt from state sales and use tax regulations. More information on state and local sales tax requirements may be obtained from your local or state department of revenue offices.

Property Tax Exemptions

Several states and cities have now imposed real-estate tax on property owned by churches. It should be noted that the imposition of the tax is usually based on the use of the property for nondirect religious purposes. In most states, a church's ownership of the real estate does not automatically qualify it for exemption from real-estate taxes.

Noncash Contributions

A noncash contribution would typically be a gift of real estate, securities, or tangible personal property. The gift of time and or talent cannot be deducted under the Internal Revenue Code. Individuals making noncash contributions to the church in excess of $500 ($5,000 for publicly traded securities) in aggregate for the year, will need the church to acknowledge receipt of such gifts by signing part IV of Section B of Federal Form 8283 (Noncash Charitable Contributions). If the church sells or otherwise disposes of contributed property (acknowledged on the Form 8283) within two years of its receipt, the church must complete Form 8282 within 125 days of selling or disposing of the property.

Cash Contributions

Beginning in 1994, any donor making a single contribution of $250 or more must be provided with a receipt from the church, in order for it to be taken as a charitable contribution. A canceled check without a receipt will not be sufficient. Likewise, if a donor receives something in return for a contribution (i.e., a dinner or other tangible item), the deduction is limited to the donation, less the fair market value of the item or service provided.

Lay People: Employees? Or Independent Contractors?

FREDERICK H. LEASURE

Some churches have attempted to escape reporting and withholding requirements by stating that the various lay people who provide services for the church (i.e., custodian, secretary, organist, etc.) are "independent contractors," not employees. Making this determination should not be done lightly and should take into account the following:

> Generally, the relationship of employer and employee exists when the person for whom services are performed has the right to control and direct the individual who performs the services, not only as to the details and means by which that result is accomplished. That is, an employee is subject to the will of and control of the employer, not only as to what shall be done, but how it shall be done. In this connection, it is not necessary that the employer actually direct or control the manner in which the services are performed; it is sufficient that he/she has the right to do so. The right to discharge is also an important factor, indicating that the person possessing that right is an employer. Other factors characteristic of an employer, but not necessarily present in every case, are the furnishing of tools and the furnishing of a place to work to the individual, who is subject to the control or direction of another, merely as to the result to be accomplished by the work, and not as to the means and methods of accomplishing the result, he/she is not an employee.
>
> *Internal Revenue Service Regulation 31.3401(c)-1(b)*

In evaluating these numerous tests of employee status, it is the position of the Internal Revenue Service that, in most cases, an individual would be considered an employee rather than an independent contractor. Though this does subject a church to another layer of reporting and filing requirements for its lay employees, this is a far more responsible position. Generally, it will be to the advantage of the lay employee, since it will provide Social Security coverage, as well as some tax advantages. Failure to properly classify an individual (layperson) as an employee can have severe consequences to the church. There is a potential for the church to be assessed a penalty and interest on any amounts not withheld. If the individual did not report the income, the church may be liable also for any unpaid taxes.

Lay People: Employee Benefits & Taxation

Indirect or noncash compensation provided by the employer for the benefit and convenience of the employee are typically known as "fringe" benefits.

The advantage of this form of compensation is that they can provide some tax-free advantage to the employee and therefore can possibly increase compensation to the employee at less cost to the employer. All fringe benefits are taxable unless they are specifically exempted by the Internal Revenue Code. The list of tax-free benefits includes the following:

Employee Discounts—up to 20%

Free Parking

Company Cars—personal use is taxable

Meals—provided for the convenience of the employer

Education Benefits—up to $5,200

Day Care

Medical Insurance

Group Term Life Insurance—first $50,000 for employee;

$2,000 for spouse and children

Though churches are exempt from nondiscrimination rules (except related to pensions), any benefits available to one employee should be made available to all. Likewise, you should consult the latest edition of the Internal Revenue Service Publication 525 (Taxable and Nontaxable Income) to determine any changes in limits and taxation of benefits.

Lay People: Pension Benefits

An employee of a nonprofit organization may take advantage of some of the specific provisions of the tax code reserved for such employees. One of the most commonly used plans is the Section 403(b) Plan, otherwise known as the Tax Deferred Annuity. Whether done through a commercial carrier or the denomination's Board of Pensions, the Tax Deferred Annuity provides for an employer contribution and/or a voluntary salary reduction agreement by the employee. The employee can have only one salary-reduction agreement per year per employer, and it must be prior to the receipt of compensation. Also, the funds remitted for the Tax Deferred Annuity must be on a church check, not a personal check of the employee. Since the employee does not receive this compensation until a later date (it is deferred), the income tax is deferred as well. However, some states do include this amount as current taxable income.

There are several rules to govern maximum contributions to a Tax Deferred Annuity Plan. An employee should be advised to seek competent tax advice in determining the maximum elective contribution.

Lay People: Reimbursements

An employee may be reimbursed for legitimate qualified out-of-pocket expenses (i.e., mileage, supplies, business meals, education, etc.). The Tax Reform Act of 1988 and subsequent regulations have considerably tightened the requirements for reimbursement. In order for payments to an employee to be considered reimbursement, and thus nontaxable, these three conditions must be met:

1. A reimbursement account must be established in advance of the expenditure.

2. The employee must account to the employer as to the actual expense, and the business purpose and expenditure is documented by receipt.

3. Unused balances in reimbursement accounts are forfeited or carried over into another year.

If any one of these three criteria is not met, the employer has an obligation to report the reimbursement as income on the employee's W-2. Failure to qualify reimbursements may create an adverse tax consequence for the employee.

Lay People: Federal Employer Tax Identification Number

All congregations must have a Federal Tax Employer Identification Number (EIN). Every report form to the federal government will require this number to be used to identify that particular congregation. If you do not have a Federal Tax Employer Identification number, contact your regional office of the Internal Revenue Service and request form SS-4 (Application for Employer Identification Number) with instructions. *Do not confuse this with other tax identification numbers that may be for state and local sales-tax purposes.*

When a congregation makes application for its Employer Identification Number, it need not make application for tax-exempt status under Internal Revenue Code 501(c)(3). As a local congregation, it is already covered under the group Federal Income Tax Exemption Ruling.

Lay People: Employee's Withholding Requirements

All lay employees must annually complete a Withholding Allowance Certificate (W-4). The information provided on this form will enable you, as the employer, to determine whether or not there are Federal Income Tax withholding requirements.

You will need to obtain a copy of Circular E, Employer's Tax Guide (Publication 15). This guide is free and is published annually. In it, you will find explanations of your obligations as an employer, relative to withholding a federal income tax. This publication will also provide you with the necessary tables to use in determining the appropriate amount to withhold from each lay employee.

You also may have state and local tax withholding requirements for your employees. You should check with the various taxing authorities to determine whether you have any liability in this area.

Lay People: Social Security (FICA) Tax Payments

The 1983 Social Security Act changed the view of churches as employers for Social Security purposes. Prior to this time, coverage for lay employees of a congregation was voluntary. However, it is now mandatory. Social Security taxes are levied on both the employer and the employee. As an employer, you must collect and remit the employee's part of the tax. A church must withhold this tax from wages in much the same way it does for federal income tax. The church also is liable for its share of Social Security taxes. Consult Federal Publication 539 for the latest information.

If your employee is participating in a Section 403(b) Tax Deferred Annuity program, the tax-deferred amount (both the employer contribution and the salary reduction amount) is not to be considered as part of the wage base for determining the amount of federal income tax to be withheld. It is, however, considered a part of the wage base for FICA computations. For more information, consult Federal Publication 571 (Tax Sheltered Annuity Programs for Employees of Public Schools and Certain Tax-Exempt Organizations).

Lay People: Unemployment Tax

Churches continue to be exempt from Federal Unemployment Tax. Some churches realize that lay employees (who are no longer considered self-employed contractors), are thus not protected in minimal ways from the economic impact of losing a job. Some churches therefore set aside funds on a routine basis to make available modest severance pay for church workers who lose a job, presuming no fault of the employee.

Citizenship Verification of All Employees

The Immigration Reform and Control Act of 1986 prohibits employers from hiring persons who are not American citizens or aliens authorized to work in the United States. Compliance with this law requires every employer to verify the identity and work authorization of every newly hired employee, and to maintain a record of this verification.

Immigration and Naturalization Service Form I-9 must be completed and kept on file for every employee. The form is self-explanatory and lists the various types of documents which an employer may use in establishing the identity and work authorization of an employee. Failure to comply with this requirement has a very severe penalty attached.

Ten Biggest Tax Mistakes Made by Churches

1. Not setting up an accountable expense reimbursement plan.
2. Adjusting housing allowances for ministers on a retroactive basis.
3. Improperly classifying employees as independent contractors.
4. Reporting the housing allowance to the minister on Form W-2 or 1099-MISC.
5. Not remitting payroll taxes to the IRS on time.
6. Failing to file Forms W-2 and 1099.
7. Not providing receipts for the donation of services or rent-free use of property.
8. Not reporting taxable fringe benefits and Social Security as additional compensation to employees.
9. Giving receipts to individuals for contributions without proper organizational control.
10. Failing to comply with the Fair Labor Standards Act for church-school employees, including preschools.

The Zondervan Church and Nonprofit Organization Tax and Financial Guide, 1993.

Lay People/Clergy: Payment of Withheld Taxes

You are required by law to deduct and withhold income tax from the salaries and wages of your lay employees. You are liable for the payment of the tax to the federal government, whether or not you collect it from your employees!

A distinction must be made here between clergy and laity. Unless a special request is made by a clergy person, no withholding of federal taxes can be made from compensation paid to a clergy person (Internal Revenue Code, Sec. 3401.a). This may or may not be the case with state or local taxing authorities.

Generally, Social Security (FICA) taxes and withheld federal income tax are reported together on Form 941 (Employer's Quarterly Federal Tax Return). These are quarterly forms and are due one month after the end of each calendar quarter. You may have to make deposits of these withheld taxes before the end of the quarter. Consult an updated version of Federal Circular "E" to determine how this may apply to your church. Failure to adhere to the deadlines for payments, as well as in filing the necessary quarterly and annual reports, will result in a penalty and possible interest being assessed to the church.

Annual Reporting Requirements

By January 31st of each year, you are required to provide all your employees with a W-2 form, indicating the amount of wages paid and income tax and FICA withheld. You also will be required to transmit the federal government's copy of these forms, using form W-3 (transmittal form for W-2s).

Beginning in 1992, some nontaxable items were required to be reported in box 17 of Form W-2. Employees' voluntary contributions to a Tax Deferred Annuity (Section 403[b]) through a salary reduction agreement, is one example of amounts to be reported in this manner. See the current instructions for the W-2 Form for a more complete discussion of this topic.

If there are those who are not employees to whom you have provided compensation that exceeds $600 in the year, you will be required to provide them with form 1099-MISC by January 31. The federal government's copy of these forms is submitted with Form 1096 (transmittal form for 1099s) no later than the end of February, for the preceding year's information.

Clergy: Reporting and Filing Requirements

FREDERICK H. LEASURE

A church has no withholding requirements for a clergy person, for either federal income tax or Social Security purposes. This may not be the case for state or local taxes. All clergy must file a federal income tax return, regardless of their filing status. Therefore, all clergy who have not received an exemption from Social Security have a personal obligation to file a 1040ES quarterly and pay self-employment tax.

Unless a special request is made by the clergy person, no withholding of federal taxes can be made (see Internal Revenue Code, Sec. 3401[a]). Therefore, regardless of the filing status of the clergy for federal income tax purposes, the church has no right or legal responsibility to withhold federal income taxes.

The annual reporting of clergy compensation must be made on either 1099 MISC or form W-2. The filing status chosen by your clergy will determine which form you should use.

1099 MISC

This form is used to report clergy compensation, if, for Federal income tax purposes, they have chosen to file as self-employed. The amount to be reported is:

Cash Salary + Allowances
Less: Housing Allowance Exclusion
  Health Insurance Premiums (if paid by the church)
  Tax Deferred Annuity Contributions
  Accountable Reimbursements

The amount reported should not include any reimbursements, the church portion of the pension contribution, health insurance, and/or group term-life insurance premiums paid by the church.

W-2

A W-2 should be issued to all clergy who have declared themselves to be employees, for federal income tax purposes. The amount to be reported is:

Cash Salary + Allowances
Less: Housing Allowance Exclusion
  Tax Deferred Annuity Contributions
  Tax-Free Fringe Benefits

The amount reported should not include any reimbursements, the church portion of the pension contribution, health insurance, and/or group term-life insurance premiums paid by the church. However, since 1992, Box 17 of the W-2 must list separately, by letter code and amount, the following items:

• voluntary amounts contributed to the tax-deferred annuity (403[b]) through salary-reduction agreements, and

• group term life insurance over $50,000

(See the current instructions for W-2 Forms to obtain letter codes and more detailed explanation.)

Clergy: Definition

Who is a clergy person? For the purposes of this discussion, the definition is provided by the Internal Revenue Service in its publication 517 (Social Security and Other Information for Members of the Clergy and Religious Workers):

> A minister of the gospel is an individual who is duly ordained, commissioned, or licensed to the pastoral ministry by action of a religious body constituting a church or church denomination, and given the authority to conduct religious worship, to perform sacerdotal functions, and to administer ordinances or sacraments according to the prescribed tenets and principles of that church or church denomination.

A person who meets this definition will qualify under the various unique provisions of the tax law that apply to clergy.

Clergy: Filing Status

The question being addressed is the filing status of a clergy person for federal income tax purposes only. All clergy who have not received an exemption from the Social Security system pay Social Security at the self-employed rate. The guidelines in determining whether a clergy person is an independent contractor or an employee are the same as those applicable to lay persons, as outlined earlier in this chapter.

In 1994, the Tax Court ruled on two cases that set important precedents for ministers on the employee vs. self-employed issue. In *Weber vs. Commissioner* (103 T.C. No. 19 Tax Ct. Dkt. No. 14475-91), the Tax Court ruled that a minister of The United Methodist Church was an employee, not an independent contractor, for Federal income tax purposes. In *Robert A. Shelly vs. Commissioner* (1994–432 Tax Ct. Dkt. No 5765-92), the Tax Court ruled that the taxpayer, a minister in the Christian Heritage Church, was an independent contractor. Both cases are important to all ministers because they address many of the factors in Reg. ¶1.3401(b) and Revenue Ruling 87-41, as applied to ministers.

Although the court acknowledged that some factors might suggest that Mr. Weber was an independent contractor, the factors indicating that he was an employee outweighed them. The court determined that the church's reporting ministers' compensation on a Form 1099-MISC instead of a W-2 was of little relevance.

In *Shelley*, the tax court ruled that the taxpayer was an independent contractor because his church did not exert "significant control" over him. Mr. Shelley was a pastor in the Christian Heritage Church, part of the International Pentecostal Holiness Church (IPHC). The IPHC was divided into regional conferences governed by a seven-member board and superintendent. In addition, the church itself was governed by a board of church members.

The court decided that Shelley was an independent contractor because no one supervised him or could fire him directly. The IPHC relies on the congregation to resolve any problems with a minister, and only the congregation has the power to dismiss a minister.

These cases set two important precedents. Most United Methodist ministers will probably be considered to be employees if their situation is similar to that of Mr. Weber. In addition, ministers in other churches with a similar organizational structure which exerts a similar degree of control over the ministers' duties will probably be considered employees.

On the other hand, ministers in churches with organizational structures which are more decentralized and provide only a general guidance of the minister's duties (like that of the International Pentecostal Holiness Church) will be treated as self-employed. (For more information, See p. 95 of *The Abingdon Clergy Income Tax Guide: 1995 Edition for 1994 Returns*.)

Clergy: Housing Allowance Exclusion

The Clergy Housing Allowance Exclusion (sometimes referred to as parsonage allowance, furniture and furnishings allowance, etc.) is a way for clergy to receive housing, whether it be in kind or by allowance, or a mixture of both, without having to pay income tax on this form of compensation. This is in recognition of the fact that even within a denomination, clergy are variously compensated in the area of housing. The Internal Revenue Service Code provides for an "exclusion," not a "deduction" from income. Section 107 of the Internal Revenue Code of 1986 provides that:

> In the case of a minister of the gospel, gross income does not include:
> 1. the rental value of a home furnished as part of compensation; or
> 2. the rental allowance paid as a part of compensation, to the extent used to rent or provide a home.

The only items the Internal Revenue Service has specifically said cannot be excluded are the cost of food and domestic help. The term "provide a home" has been broadly interpreted by the Internal Revenue Service to include such items as furniture, beds, cable television, lines, lamps, utilities, and expendables, such as paper products, light bulbs, and cleaning supplies.

Because of this broad definition, even clergy who live in fully furnished parsonages, with all utilities provided, still have the potential to have excluded from their salary an amount that represents their expenditures for items such as those listed above. This exclusion is available to clergy only as long as the local church passes a proper resolution.

A resolution for a housing allowance exclusion must be passed by the salary-paying body, prior to the clergy receiving the compensation. It is particularly important for a new resolution to be passed at the time of a change in clergy leadership. This greatly assists in the interpretation of the amount available for the incoming clergy in the short tax year.

Once the salary figure is set, the actual amount to be excluded from income under Section 107 of the Internal Revenue Code and designated as Clergy Housing Allowance Exclusion should be determined in consultation with the clergy person. This must be a dollar amount, not a percentage, and cannot exceed the fair market rental value of the clergy person's home (whether a parsonage or clergy-owned), with utilities so equipped and so furnished in that particular neighborhood.

Once this resolution has been passed, it grants authority to the church to exclude the amount designated from income on either the 1099 or W-2 Form provided to the pastor. It is the clergy person's obligation to support this exclusion in the compilation of his/her individual tax return, and also to report any unexpended exclusion amounts as "miscellaneous income" on that return. It is not the obligation of the clergy to document these expenditures to the local church; yet, adequate records must be kept by the clergy.

Clergy: Reimbursement vs. Allowance

The most equitable arrangement between a church and a pastor is for the church to agree to pay for usual and necessary professional expenses, such as travel, books, education, business meals, and so on. The definition of the distinction between reimbursement (accountable plan) and allowance is critical. Not only does it determine how it is accounted for, but it also determines how it is taxed.

Allowance

An allowance typically has the following characteristics:
1. It is identified as a specific amount in the church budget.
2. Expenses paid from the allowance may or may not be required to be substantiated to the local church.
3. The entire amount of the allowance is paid to the pastor, whether or not the actual expenses are incurred.
4. An allowance (with the exception of Housing Exclusion) is fully reportable as income to the pastor. It is up to the pastor to deduct appropriate expenses paid by the allowance on his/her income tax return. (For a pastor filing as an employee, these will be deductible only to the extent that they exceed 2 percent of his/her adjusted gross income.)

Reimbursement

A reimbursement *must* have the following characteristics to yield the desired resulting tax considerations:
1. It must be identified as a specific line item in the budget, before the expenditures are made.
2. Expenses that are to be reimbursed must be substantiated as to their business purpose and their amount.
3. Unused balances in a reimbursement are not paid to the pastor, but may be carried over into a new year's budget.
4. Reimbursements for professional expenses that otherwise would be deductible are not reportable or taxable to the pastor.

In the case of automobile expenses that are reimbursed by the church, the reimbursement may be for actual expenses incurred for business miles (not commuting), or on a cents-per-mile basis. If the latter is chosen, and the reimbursement exceeds the federal guidelines for that particular year, the excess must be reported as income. Typically, the IRS adjusts this rate for inflation on an annual basis.

If an automobile is provided for the use of the pastor, the commuting miles, as well as the personal miles, must be reported as income to the pastor. The amount to be reported as income may be determined by using either a cents-per-mile method or the federal tables based on the value of the vehicle.

Clergy: Taxation of Benefits

Indirect or noncash compensation provided to clergy (excluding housing and housing allowance exclusion) is taxable, depending upon the filing status of the clergy person for federal income tax purposes. All of the employee tax-free "fringe" benefits previously discussed are available to clergy persons who choose to file as employees.

The tax-deferred annuity program established under Internal Revenue Code Section 403(b) is available to clergy, regardless of filing status. Though the language of this section of the Internal Revenue Code is that of employer/employee, this benefit cannot be denied a clergy person simply because of denominational policy that establishes his/her filing status. Not all tax advisors agree about this matter, though this position

has been sustained by one tax court in a private-letter ruling regarding a pastor in the Assemblies of God.

Neither the amount a church contributes to a denominational pension plan, nor the amount designated as Tax Deferred Annuity through a salary reduction agreement with the pastor, is taxable compensation to the pastor. In the case of clergy, this is true for both self-employment tax and federal income tax. In order for a tax-deferred annuity to be established, an agreement must be made between the church and the pastor, prior to the receipt of compensation. Only one such agreement per employer per year is permissible. The same contribution limits set for lay persons apply also to clergy persons.

In the case of health insurance premiums and other health benefit plans that fall under Internal Revenue Code Section 414(c)(3), the payments made by the church are not taxable to the clergy, regardless of the filing status of the clergy, because the code states, "regardless of how compensated."

Substantiation Rules for Charitable Contributions

DONALD W. JOINER

The Omnibus Budget Reconciliation Act of 1993, unofficially known as the 1993 Tax Act, has charities asking questions. Rest easy, no rule states that a charity must report charitable gifts to the IRS.

Congress has worried for years that many deductions for charitable gifts on individual tax returns were not legitimate gifts. Some deductions never existed; other deductions were for more than the gift (especially if the donor received something in return).

The 1993 tax act includes legislation intended to address "charitable abuse." New Section 170(f)(8) provides that no income-tax charitable deduction will be allowed for a contribution of $250 or more, unless the taxpayer has a written receipt (a canceled check is no longer an acceptable receipt) from the charity. Separate payments will be treated as separate contributions.

Any type of receipt (postcard, letter, computer-generated form) will be acceptable to the Internal Revenue Service. If any goods or service are provided to the donor, the value of those goods or services must be noted on the receipt.

Many "rumors" exist that charities must report all giving to the IRS. This is not true! The burden is on the donor to obtain the appropriate receipt from the charity.

PART SEVEN

PROPERTY, PERSONNEL, AND COMPENSATION

For Trustees or Property, Personnel, and Pastor Relations Teams

Introduction

NORMA WIMBERLY

Christian stewardship is practical, visible, and documentable. Ordinary life, yet extraordinary because of a particular and profound theological perspective, can be lived in such a way as to be a transforming agent in the congregation, in the community, and in a culture where "too much is never enough."

Trustees, property managers, personnel and pastor relations committees, and financial officers of the congregation face daily the practical, visible, and documentable issues that "the rest of the world" deals with. Where better to model the church as leader than in these ordinary and vital areas?

Trustees are urged to utilize the following nine questions as an additional checklist to accompany those required by the domination and/or local codes, regulations, and requirements. The list is to be a nudge, a motivation for appropriate accountability.

John and Sylvia Ronsvalle offer an opportunity for reflection and a challenge to live a life of servanthood in their powerful "Discipleship for Affluent Churches"— one that is practical, visible, documentable—and one that can guide in the "ordinary" matters of keeping the church, its property, and its personnel viable.

Glenna and Roy Kruger, then Wayne Barrett, offer their expertise regarding pastor's compensation and benefits for additional church staff. Note the balance of tension between value and cost. We have an incredibly wonderful opportunity to model the spiritual dimension and importance of work, as well as to adhere to the legal requirements of employment.

Frank Keller, of the General Conference of the Mennonite Church, developed a practical but spiritual business perspective as a child. Frank's father grew lilac trees. In the spring, Frank and his brothers were responsible for taking lilac branches to town and selling them. Their father taught them three practical and spiritual lessons: God gives all—even the lilacs. (We are given pastors, secretaries, custodians, a building.) The boys were to tithe the money received. (We are to manage all of our property, personnel, and financial resources wisely). The boys were to be fair about the price, as well as polite to all their customers. (We are to be accountable for fair business practices, as well as compassionate).

The congregation, the community, and the culture actually do notice the way we live out our commitment. Pray that we will be wise stewards in all our affairs.

✓ CHECKLIST

A Year-End Checklist for Local Church Trustees

NORMA WIMBERLY

Here is a suggested checklist for the work of trustees in the congregation. You may want to complete this at year-end, then review it as the months go by, to see how well you are doing your job.

☞ 1. Is your congregation incorporated under the laws of your state? If not, have you discussed this year the advisability of incorporation?

☞ 2. Have you inspected your church property (including the parsonages) this year and made an inventory of the repair and maintenance needs?

☞ 3. Have you recommended to the committee on finance and the governing board a plan and budget for the maintenance and repair needs of your church property for this year?

☞ 4. Have you developed a long-term plan for depreciation and replacement of the equipment, furnishings, and facilities of the church and parsonage, and submitted it to the governing board for approval?

☞ 5. Have you had an annual review of insurance programs (workmen's compensation, fire, property damage, liability, etc.) by a qualified person?

☞ 6. Have you had an annual safety inspection of your church buildings and parsonages by your local fire department and/or insurance underwriters?

☞ 7. If you have responsibility for supervision or employment of custodial or other personnel, have you reviewed with the pastor-parish relations committee or the lay personnel committee the job analysis and salary schedules for these persons, and recommended needed changes to the governing board through the appropriate committee?

☞ 8. Have you reviewed the investment portfolio of your church with a qualified person, to be sure that the best possible return is being received on your funds and that the placement of your investments is in keeping with Christian responsibility?

☞ 9. Have you cooperated with the committee on stewardship and the committee on finance and/or the committee on estate planning in a program for informing the congregation about the possibilities for support of the ministry of the church through wills and bequests?

🤲 MEDITATION

Discipleship for Affluent Churches

JOHN AND SYLVIA RONSVALLE

The church in the U.S.A. has approached theology in the same way American English has developed. In other languages, usage has defined parameters. Foreign words incorporated into Chinese are seen as curiosities; in French, as decay. English, on the other hand, has taken the practical approach of borrowing liberally from any sources that worked. We take for granted such words as *kowtow* and *garage,* because they fit the need.

In a similar fashion, efforts at theology seem to be based on borrowing rather than on hard original thinking. The Europeans have had a justifiably profound influence. More recently, Latin American theology has made its impact with an emphasis on liberation.

However, can Christians in the U.S.A. justify living off the blood and tears shed in the development of oppressed peoples who seek liberation from a greedy few? What is more, is it even healthy? As mainstream Protestant churches struggle for identity, and, as theologian John Stott has suggested, evangelical churches have difficulty combining word and deed,[1] can either the Europeans or Latin Americans speak to the needs of the church in the U.S.? The present state of the church in North America may suggest that it is time to take responsibility for making a contribution to world theology out of our unique historical situation.

Economic Changes

For example, the U.S. exists in an economic condition first-ever in the history of the world. Since about 1950, a majority of people in some societies, including the U.S., have had their basic needs met, and extra money besides. The concept of discretionary income, nonexistent before World War II for most people, now is an important element in defining one's "lifestyle." Lifestyles are not even possible without discretionary income.

Poverty statistics only started being calculated in the 1960s. Available data for urban poverty—data for rural conditions is not available—suggests that, in 1941, 40 percent of the U.S. urban population lived in consumer units at or below the poverty line. This number of poor people in the cities was reduced to 24 percent by 1950 and was 13 percent at the beginning of the War on Poverty in 1963.[2] The statistics for total poverty in the U.S. would have been higher if data for both rural and urban were available. Currently, the percentage of the entire U.S. population in poverty, including both rural and urban, hovers around 13.5 percent.

Accompanying this decline in poverty has been a growth in wealth that amazes everyone. An article in one magazine was titled, "Money Hungry: Too Much Is Never Enough." The writer captured the current American culture in the opening paragraph:

> Never have we been more fascinated, more entranced, more seduced by money. The smell of it is everywhere, from the pages of the press to politics to museums to pulpits, fueling our passions and buoying the myth: With enough of it, we can change our lives for the better.[3]

The article quotes a society novelist who points to the many rich people spending more money than ever before. As a result of this increased affluence, new distinctions in wealth have had to develop. One million dollars isn't considered a significant fortune anymore.

And if there are new rich, there are also new poor.

We are not speaking here of the homeless, whose plight has become alarmingly well-documented. Rather, over the years, there has been a fundamental change regarding those who are able to keep a roof, however humble, over their heads.

There is a strong undercurrent in the U.S., in this "land of opportunity," that there is something dreadfully wrong with the person who is poor. So many people have worked their way up to being comfortable, that there is a moral judgment against poverty that makes it very hard to be poor with dignity anymore. What is worse, people who come from poor parents are many times not breaking the cycle of poverty. There is a feeling among the economic minority that there is something basically wrong with them. Poor people often judge themselves as harshly as does the society in general, making it very hard to change their circumstances.

The Extinction of the Church

The church in the U.S. has not developed a reasonable response to these changes. On the whole, the church in America remains in a pre-1950s mindset. While business employs advertising to sell the public everything from virtual-reality video games to hot tubs, the church continues to approach the majority of their parishioners as though they were barely surviving, asking them to spare what they can to keep the lights on.

On the whole, the church in the U.S. has avoided addressing the change in economic conditions that have defined life in these United States since World War II. For a while, that approach worked. The general move to the suburbs brought with it a building boom, including new churches. Throughout the 1950s, the percentage of income given to churches on average remained above 3 percent.

Then the affluence began to take hold. The churches, with little effort, had benefited from the overflowing growth. Once life in the suburbs became the norm, people found the momentum of economic change transforming many of their wants into needs. Perhaps no one could have anticipated how all-consuming the role of being a consumer could become. Money became a more awkward topic. The role of stewardship in the church shifted from returning a portion of one's income to God to paying the church's bills. Easy credit began to burgeon in the early 1960s. In a variation of owing one's soul to the company store, people began balancing their increasing incomes with their faster-rising credit-card payments. And the church remained silent as long as its bills were paid.

These trends are not innocent. Church contributions have not been able to hold their own in the competition for parishioners' wallets. Giving, as a percentage of income, has been declining since the early 1960s. Church members in 1991 gave a smaller percentage of their incomes to the church than did their counterparts in 1933, during the depth of the Great Depression.

Church contributions can be divided into two categories. Congregational Finances are the portion of contributions kept for the basic operations of the congregation. Benevolences are the church contributions which the congregation distributes beyond itself, including to denominational structures, international missions, and even local charities. Of these two categories, Benevolences has been hit hardest by these giving patterns. In fact, the trends suggest that by the year A.D. 2048, 0 percent of church-member income will be directed toward Benevolences. This would mean that, barring sufficient support from other sources, national denominational structures will be extinct by the middle of the next century.

Nor do congregations escape unscathed. The trend in giving as a percentage of income to congregations points to their demise in A.D. 2187, if current trends continue uninterrupted.[4]

The church cannot continue to tolerate the conversion of its members from stewards into consumers and expect to survive. The church in the U.S. cannot hope for the leftover crumbs from the general affluence and not lose its role in society altogether. Like it or not, the church must come to terms with the new affluence that permeates every facet of the society, including the people sitting in the pews and the ministers in the pulpits. If no society has combined such widespread church membership and attendance with this much financial success before, it is up to the church in the U.S. to develop a unique theology in response to its unusual experience.

Elements of a Discipleship of Affluence

Money remains an awkward topic. However, the fruits of ignoring money as an appropriate subject suggest that the church no longer can avoid dealing with the topic in a straightforward fashion, if it hopes to survive. The church in the U.S. needs to develop a theology which takes into account that the majority of its members are doing better than just barely making it financially, but rather can meet their basic needs and afford many comforts as well.

Yet, the solution is not to keep proposing building projects every three years. People are hungry for solutions that speak to their deepest needs. The church must help its members develop a response to this affluence that is consistent with the call of Jesus on their lives. The church needs to develop a theology that leads to a discipleship of affluence.

Personal Focus

One element of such a theological strain may well be a personal focus. Here, the suggestion is not a variation on the individualism which currently isolates well-to-do church members from one another and those in need. Yet, without a sense of well-being and self-worth, it is impossible for an individual to effectively serve others. It is no coincidence that Jesus defines the second most important commandment as loving your neighbor as yourself.

The church is in a position to help people come to terms with the wounds life has inflicted upon them. The counseling emphasis of the past decades has positioned the church to reach out in a practiced way to people who are in need. However, the healing process cannot be an end in itself. The church is in a unique position to put the healing process in context. What is the goal of becoming "well"—to be able to consume more effectively? Or to become whole enough to share oneself with others? Jesus' comment about losing one's life to gain it may be directly related to the question as to whether someone can find real inner healing unless an outward focus is part of the healing prescription.

Coping with Materialism

A second element of such a discipleship ethic addresses how one is to cope with materialism. Certainly, Jesus saw his followers' attitudes toward money as an important topic, even when the vast majority of his listeners were living at a survival level. How much more important, then, is a Christian attitude toward material goods when money has become such a defining factor in our society?

Yet the church has been silent on materialism in

general. Without a clear Christian agenda for serving others with their resources, Americans pursue accumulation as the newest virtue.

And they are paying for it—an estimated $30 billion in credit-card interest payments in 1991—not fees or purchases, but just interest payments![5]

General affluence without an agenda for serving others has led to a $244 billion legalized gambling industry.[6] In a world of starving people, Americans spent more than $30 billion on the diet industry in 1989.[7] And while Protestant overseas ministries based in the U.S. received $2.0 billion in 1991,[8] the soft drink industry claimed $44 billion in 1989.[9] The church needs to put these types of expenditures into a context larger than the immediate gratification preached by the general society.

> "Each citizen should plan his part in the community according to his individual gifts."
>
> —*PLATO*

A Positive Agenda

A third element of a discipleship of affluence must be a positive agenda for the church member's resources in a hurting world. This idea is complicated by a growing isolationism in the church. In workshops, when a variety of facts about world need are listed, the members of the audience respond with words like "overwhelmed" or "frustrated" or "helpless." The church must understand that it now exists in a communications-rich world. Henri Nouwen and his coauthors suggest that it is not that church people don't know or don't care about world need, but rather that they know too much, become overwhelmed, then become angry at their inability to solve these problems, and finally, become numb to them.[10] And as members turn away from the global mission of the church in frustration, there is a world of consumable goods calling to them to drown their sorrows in a sea of plenty.

The church has been an effective channel of education about world need, both physical and spiritual. However, the church must not only share information with people but also supply effective, broad-scale global strategies for meeting the needs presented.

A sense of positive initiative could become a distinguishing feature among church people in a society overcome by a sense of confusion. Reflections on the church universal, and even the strength of the international relationships available through church structures, could give congregation members a sense of cohesiveness in an otherwise overwhelming situation. Understanding their own potential for increasing the percentage of their income to their churches, in order to work through the established and effective channels the church has to offer might make an impossible task approachable. Reflecting on the bridges that exist between the church in the U.S. and the church in every nation may be a powerful response to the incredible amount of information that makes this world seem smaller and smaller, and yet more difficult to cope with.

Church people are more responsive stewards when . . .

. . . the church is meeting their personal needs.

. . . the church is actively involved in outreach.

. . . the church tenderly cares for each of its family.

. . . persons participate in and understand the decisions of the church.

. . . the leadership of the church is held in high esteem and is trusted by the membership.

. . . the church shows signs of new and exciting ministries.

. . . the church works diligently for full participation of all members in the life of the church and community.

The Nature of Servanthood

Finally, a deep sense of servanthood would reorder our priorities about affluence. Paul's letters to the Corinthians, a relatively wealthy church in the New Testament context, may yield important perspectives for affluent Americans.

Even more, the servant nature of Jesus would be a vital example of our discipleship. Philippians 2:1-13 could be a cornerstone for a theological response to general affluence. What does one do when one "has it all"? Jesus, though he had everything, chose the servant role. A clear lesson seems to be presented to those in the U.S. who would profess to be his followers.

A rougher lesson can be drawn from the church in Laodicea, in Revelation 3. Feeling that we are rich and healthy, we fool ourselves into thinking we need nothing. Yet, even the popular culture begins to recognize that something is lacking and society is adrift. Will the church be able to respond with a relevant answer? Acknowledging that we have power and comfort and security, servanthood may well be the only way to save ourselves from our success.

The Choice Before the Church

Without a self-defining mission that compels its members to submit their personal comfort to a greater cause, the church in the U.S. has become insular. Instead of addressing the needs of a hurting society, the church has turned in on itself.

It has been suggested that the subject of wealth and poverty is the second most talked about topic in the Bible. As Christians in the U.S. turn to the Bible as an authoritative guide, it may be difficult for the church to continue to avoid the Bible's message about what our attitude should be toward the general affluence surrounding us. To resist such a discussion could lead to the further marginalization of the church in the U.S., perhaps even its extinction.

In contrast, it may be that, in dying to its own fears and commitment to comfort, the church will find its life. For a servant church in the U.S. to develop a discipleship of affluence might well contribute a perspective to world theology that can help others to recognize their own potential to be faithful followers of Jesus Christ. At the very least, it might help the church in the U.S. to do so.

Notes

1. Thomas Wang, "With John Stott," *World Evangelization* 13, No. 49 (December 1987), p. 1.
2. Margaret G. Reif, *International Encyclopedia of the Social Sciences* (New York: Macmillan/the Free Press, 1968) 3:340.
3. Elizabeth Royte, "Money Hungry—Too Much Is Never Enough," *Self* (November 1988), p. 153.
4. John Ronsvalle and Sylvia Ronsvalle, *The State of Church Giving Through 1991* (Champaign, Ill.: empty tomb, inc., 1993).
5. Allen Sinai and Robert Brooker, *Debt, Credit Card Borrowing and the Economy,* Economic Studies Series, No. 45 (New York: The Boston Co. Economic Advisors, Inc., September 1992), p. 4.
6. Robert Whereatt, "As the Stakes Rise, So Do Fears of Fallout," *Menneapolis-St. Paul Star-Tribune* (September 23, 1990), p. A-1.
7. "Diets Incorporated," *Newsweek* (September 11, 1989), p. 56.
8. John A. Siewert and John A. Kenyon, eds., *Mission Handbook, 1993–1995,* 15th ed. (Monrovia, Calif.: Missions Advanced Research and Communication Center), p. 59; App., p. 2.
9. Annetta Miller with Vern E. Smith, "The Soda War Fizzes Up," *Newsweek* (March 19, 1990), p. 38.
10. Donald McNeill, Douglas Morrison, and Henri Nouwen, *Compassion* (New York: Doubleday, 1983), p. 53.

 PLANNING TOOL

Compensation and Benefits

GLENNA AND ROY KRUGER

In Paul's letters to the Romans and Corinthians, he underscores the spiritual importance of work and the worker. Paul tells his readers that all gifts and abilities come from God and that no one gift is more important than another in fulfilling God's will (Rom. 12; I Cor. 12). Paul exhorts his readers against thinking more highly of themselves, because of their gifts and abilities, than of others. All work is of equal importance in God's economy, no matter how the world might value it.

Every church has a unique opportunity and responsibility to be an exemplary employer within its community. To be an exemplary employer means grasping the opportunity to model, for the community, the spiritual dimension and importance of work. It also means complying with the applicable employment laws.

Paul also reminds the Corinthians of their obligation to appropriately compensate those individuals who are working directly for their church (I Cor. 9). How can we apply this principle today? We can develop a comprehensive compensation program which fairly acknowledges employee contributions, invests in employee professional development, and exhibits good stewardship principles.

Good stewards effectively use the resources entrusted to them. The importance of wisely analyzing the total value in purchasing good and services, rather than the initial cost, can be seen in Jesus' parable of the wise steward who build his house upon the rock. The cost of building on a rock foundation was no doubt more expensive than building on the sandy plain, but there is no doubt which foundation was more valuable over time. This concept of value versus cost is important to remember in the area of compensation and investing in our employees.

No subject raises such emotion in any organization as the topic of what to pay employees. No matter how committed employees may be to the mission of their organization, compensation is still a symbol of the value of that contribution. For church workers, the topic is particularly sensitive. Church budgets are usually tight, and salaries represent a major expenditure of funds. During difficult times, church workers may not receive adequate compensation.

In this article we will approach compensation and benefits in a systematic way. We hope to offer some new and creative ways of thinking about compensation. We will discuss salaries, benefits, and recognition programs. All these programs are part of a total compensation package which you can offer employees. You may find these ideas applicable to clergy and nonclergy positions, depending upon your denominational structure.

Benefits of a Systematic Approach

Why should you develop a systematic approach to compensation? Why not just pay each person based on what he or she asks for, or what the last person received, or on how many people are in the family, or whatever the chair of the board thinks is right? Here are several reasons why a systematic approach is beneficial for your church.

1. **Recruiting.** When you are recruiting for non-clergy positions, you are competing in the total labor market for the talent you need. Highly skilled individuals will have multiple opportunities. Although people don't go into church work for the money, you still need to understand what compensation is required in order to attract the appropriate talent. For example, well-organized and effective executive secretaries can make a world of difference in how well your church runs and how effective your pastor can be. In most labor markets, such talent is in demand. You will need to offer a competitive salary for that position in your community.

2. **Fairness.** The lack of adequate compensation can demotivate. If workers are feeling exploited by low wages, they may not achieve their best performance. They also may spend energy on making ends meet, rather than on fulfilling the mission of the church.

3. **Turnover.** There are many reasons why people leave jobs. Salary is often not the primary cause of turnover. Nevertheless, if your salaries stray too far out of line, retention also will become an issue. Turnover is expensive—recruiting costs, training costs, and loss of knowledge about the organization add up.

4. **Legal Issues.** Although the government does not become involved in the employment relationship of clergy to their churches, nonclergy employees are protected by all employment laws. As a good employer, you will want to be sure your compensation system does not discriminate. The Equal Pay Act of 1963 covers employers with only two or more employees. This law provides that there can be no difference in pay rates based on gender for equal work. Equal work is determined by analyzing the skills, effort, responsibility, and working conditions of the two jobs. You may pay different salaries based on seniority or performance. You also may pay higher salaries for positions that require greater levels of skill, effort, responsibility, and/or exposure to adverse working conditions.

In job descriptions, you will find information about the skills, effort, responsibility, and working conditions required to do the job. Here are some ways to interpret these terms.

Skill: Education and experience required. Examples are seminary degree, previous experience as a church choir director, word-processing skills, written communication.

Effort: Complexity of problem solving; complexity

or sensitivity of personal contacts; multiple tasks that demand simultaneous attention; meeting deadlines; mental or physical demands.

Responsibility: Decision making; policy involvement; amount of supervision given or received; amount of structure and standard practices in place; use of judgment; cost of failure to perform.

Working Conditions: Extremes of temperature; exposure to hazardous conditions.

Title VII, the Civil Rights Act of 1964, is a broader law which covers all aspects of employment, including compensation. Under this law, employers with 15 or more employees may not discriminate based on race, color, gender, national origin, or age.

In developing a compensation system, we pose some planning questions to consider.

Planning Total Compensation

As you develop your total compensation program, ask these questions:

1. Which positions will be included in the compensation plan? Nonclergy only? What are the motivational and financial needs of your employees?

2. What is your budget for all types of compensation? Have you budgeted for more than just cash salaries?

3. What is the appropriate mix of cash, benefits, and motivational benefits?

4. What level of administrative support is available to implement and manage these programs?

5. What is your plan for communicating the program to employees and involving them in the decision-making process?

In planning for compensation, churches should avoid the following temptations:

1. Do not try to duplicate larger, for-profit organizations. You can't afford it.

2. Do not do too much, too soon. Taking away benefits is the worst experience you can imagine!

3. Do not copy other organizations without knowing why. Each work force is unique, so borrowing ideas is great as long as you have done your own analysis.

4. Do calculate your costs up front. You may be surprised at how much your total compensation plan costs.

5. Do not underestimate an employee's personal motivation. You can't put a dollar figure on it, but

people often work for churches for spiritual reasons.

6. Do not take advantage of Number 5. Even though employees may be dedicated to the ministry, they still have financial and medical needs.

Now you are ready to take the next step in developing your compensation program. Make sure that your job descriptions are up-to-date.

Writing Job Descriptions

Use your descriptions to compare similar positions within your own and other organizations. It often helps to have the ideas of two or three people in your church when designing a job. Set aside some time to discuss the purpose of the position. Why will (or does) this job exist? The key question to ask over and over: What is the work to be accomplished? This is not the time to write: "Must type 70 wpm." You don't know that until you know what is to be typed, with what frequency, for whom, and on what kind of equipment.

When you are writing descriptions for existing positions, collect information about the work from current employees. Here are some suggested questions:

JOB DESIGN QUESTIONNAIRE

1. Describe the purpose of your job. How does it support the mission of the church?
2. Describe the three activities that take up most of your time.
3. What percentage of your time is spent on each of these three activities?
4. What takes up the rest of your time?
5. Are you responsible for the work of others?
6. Do you have work-related contact with any of the following: parishioners, the outside community, suppliers, applicants, potential parishioners?
7. Describe the nature of the contact (e.g., share information, influence them to act).
8. What specific skills or knowledge are needed in order to perform your job?
9. What equipment is used in performing your job?
10. Are there any special physical demands in this job?

With this information, you can write a job description. Here's an example of a job description for the senior pastor's secretary at a medium-sized church:

SECRETARY TO THE SENIOR PASTOR RESPONSIBILITIES

Responsibility #1: Gives administrative support to the senior pastor.
1. Types pastor's correspondence, sermon notes, memos, and other communication.
2. Answers pastor's telephone, takes messages as needed.
3. Maintains files on committees, budgets, and other resources needed by the pastor.

Responsibility #2: Serves as a focal point of communication about all church events.
1. Writes articles for and edits church newsletter.
2. Answers questions from the public, other staff, and parishioners about church functions, policies, and resources.

Responsibility #3: Provides clerical support for churchwide activities.
1. Types "order of worship" and ensures printing in time for service.
2. Relieves receptionist during breaks and lunch.

Now that you know what the secretary is asked to do, you can list the skills required to accomplish these tasks.

SKILLS

1. Must be proficient in using common word-processing packages for the personal computer, including use of graphics.
2. Must be able to demonstrate clear writing ability, including correct grammar and spelling.
3. Must be well organized to handle multiple duties.
4. Must communicate clearly with a variety of people and be sensitive to the confidential nature of much information.
5. Must support and believe in the mission of the organization.

Next, use the job descriptions to compare your salaries with those in other organizations.

Salary Surveys

When doing your comparisons, be sure you are comparing all the responsibilities of the position, not just the job title. Job titles often are created to meet the needs of a particular organization or individual. The content of the job may vary greatly from your position with the same title. Try to match at least 80 percent of the activities listed in the job description.

Your denomination may have specific recommendations for the pastoral and professional roles. For clerical, administrative, and maintenance jobs, you can call your state Bureau of Labor or local industry associations. These organizations may have research that they will share with you. Other churches and nonprofit organizations may be willing to exchange information with you about what is being paid for positions (not the salary of a named individual).

For example, using the secretary to the senior pastor position, you should be able to compare your description to a similar role at another church or nonprofit organization in your community. Gather as many comparisons as possible, so you can obtain an accurate picture of the average and range of salaries for this type position within your community. A comparison of only one or two examples may give a skewed picture of salaries. Perhaps the secretary at the church down the street has been there for twenty years and is paid well above average, in recognition of her experience. This does not mean that you should pay all employees the *average* wage. You will need to decide what you can afford and how the experience level of an individual compares to those in your survey.

The work of doing these comparisons and making the salary decisions can be given to a special committee made up of lay people and staff, or to your Personnel Committee if your church has one. Try to find individuals in your congregation who have experience with this type of project in their workplace. Or you could hire an outside consultant in compensation to do the work for you. If you can afford to do this, it has many advantages. The consultant offers expertise as well as objectivity, and may be perceived by employees as unbiased and more fair.

The next step in developing a compensation system is determining the total salary-benefit package that will be offered to employees on an ongoing basis. This includes professional development and recognition programs, and annual increases in salary and benefits.

Recognition and Professional Development

People work expecting a paycheck and some benefits, but they are motivated to work productively by a variety of factors. Churches should be intentional about recognizing the hard work of their pastors and other employees. Ministry can be stressful, involving long hours and sacrifices. Be sure to acknowledge their efforts. There are many benefits you can offer employees that will cost little or nothing.

Some persons are motivated by the need to achieve. You can respond to this by posting announcements of job openings to give employees and volunteers the first opportunity to express interest in available positions. You also can send employees to seminars that will enhance their skills or knowledge. Workshops and courses often are available through your local college at a very reasonable cost. If you can afford to give tuition support to an individual in completing a degree program, this could be a good investment. Churches may have limited opportunities to promote employees, but you certainly can offer talented and motivated employees the opportunity to work on new, challenging projects. This could mean a redesign of their jobs, with an upgrade in salary, which is another form of promotion. Achievers appreciate having their good performance acknowledged and receiving surprise awards of recognition immediately following the conclusion of an outstanding project. You could consider such things as Employee of the Month, dinner-for-two certificates, flowers on their desks, or other tokens of appreciation.

Some individuals have a need to influence and control their environment. Give these employees increased responsibility. Design their jobs to be challenging and involve them in problem-solving task forces.

Some people want to be liked and be part of a group. These people respond well to formal plaques and pins, length-of-service awards, social events such as picnics or holiday parties, celebrations, staff meetings or retreats, or fully paid membership dues in a work-related association.

In designing your program, you will need to analyze your work force and try to provide a mix of rewards that will touch as many employees as possible.

One important compensation decision involves the annual salary increases you will give.

Annual Increases in Salary

You will need to examine several factors in arriving at a decision in making and administering these increases. Ask other churches and nonprofits what level of raises they are planning to give their employees. This will give you information on the average salary increases being given to workers in similar circumstances. Your own denominational offices may have information from surveys they have conducted. If you live in a metropolitan area, you may have access to government cost-of-living index numbers. If so, use these only as a guideline. These are based on a predetermined list of purchases and may not necessarily reflect the lives of your employees. Cost-of-living indexes are best used for checking inflationary trends over time. Finally, look at your own ability to pay salary increases, and the additional government mandated costs, such as Social Security. This may be a subject for joint discussion between the Personnel Committee and your Finance or Budget Committee.

Once you have determined the amount of increases you want to give, choose a method for distributing them to employees. The method used by most academic and other nonprofit institutions is to give all employees the same percentage increase. Employees are presumed to be collegial and motivated primarily by the mission of the organization. This system has the advantage of being extremely simple to administer, and it avoids the prospect of trying to explain why one person received a slightly higher increase than another. Unless you have a very well-developed performance-appraisal system, we suggest that you not try to give "merit" increases.

Whatever method you use needs to be supported and accepted by the congregation and your employees. Most congregations delegate the task of making salary decisions to a committee or the church business manager. Be sure appropriate review occurs, so you have checks and balances to lessen the possibility of controversy.

Many nonsalary benefits should be considered also when determining what you can afford for total compensation. The following section discusses some of the more popular forms of benefit programs.

Benefit Forms of Compensation

Many nonsalary benefits allow churches to offer a compensation package that more adequately meets the individual and family needs of their employees. It would be extremely difficult to match the compensation programs offered by profitable businesses. Through the wise use of nontaxable, nonsalary benefits, churches can provide employees with a higher level of compensation than just an increase in salary. You might want to consider some of the following items to provide your employees with basic security and recognition of their hard work:

BENEFIT OPTIONS

_____ medical coverage for employees and dependents
_____ dental coverage for employees and dependents
_____ vacation pay
_____ sick pay or personal leave
_____ holiday pay
_____ disability insurance
_____ life insurance
_____ retirement plan
_____ sabbatical leave
_____ tuition reimbursement

Many of these programs may be available through denominations that have eligibility policies in place. Nothing in the law requires you to offer fringe benefits, though you must pay Social Security and Workers' Compensation. However, having once decided to offer other benefits, you must do so on a nondiscriminatory basis. The criteria for eligibility must be on an objective basis, such as hours worked, and not on gender, or any other discriminatory basis.

Workers' Compensation

Analyzing your workers' compensation program offers opportunities to practice good stewardship by researching options for cost savings, while still providing security for your employees. The way you buy the insurance, your requirements for coverage, and the benefits available will vary by state. Check with your state Bureau of Labor for your state rules. You may be surprised at the cost involved, particularly in states with liberal benefits. You can help to control the costs by taking the following steps:

1. If you have options about where to buy coverage, shop around.
2. Be sure your employees are properly classified, since you pay a rate based on the probability of injury to that job classification.
3. Investigate the cost of having some workers paid through a temporary service, where insurance costs can be pooled with a larger group.
4. For jobs with a high incident of injury, such as janitors, screen carefully, to be sure applicants realize the nature of the work.
5. Institute a safety program. A committee of employees can walk through the church once a month, looking for possible hazards (electrical cords strung across aisles, boxes blocking fire exits, loose handrails), then report the problems to the appropriate person for action.

Safety training may be available through your community college or hospital, for employees who do heavy lifting or work with chemicals.

Now we are ready to discuss a few administrative details that you should plan for.

Administration of your Compensation Plan

You should have a policy about the frequency of pay reviews, so that everyone is treated equally. Your policy should address whether pay reviews will be done on the anniversary date of hire, or on a date during the year when all employees are reviewed at the same time. This is known as a focal-point review. Its advantages are that the review process is done all at once, so no one is forgotten, and it means that everyone is reviewed under the same circumstances, rather than being influenced by how generous contributions were that month. The first time you use this method, you will need to prorate individual increases, based on the number of months since the last review of each person.

COMPENSATION POLICY

PURPOSE: To outline responsibilities and procedures for compensation decisions.

JOB CLASSIFICATION: The Personnel Committee will be responsible for developing job descriptions and analyzing jobs, in cooperation with the appropriate supervisor and/or lay committee. The Personnel Committee also will research and monitor appropriate salary levels for each classification.

JOB OFFERS AND PAY INCREASES: All compensation offers to new hires and pay increases to existing employees require the following approvals:

For nonclergy: Direct Supervisor, Personnel Committee, Business Administrator.
For clergy: Personnel Committee, Executive Committee of the Board.
All employees will be reviewed annually during the month of June. Pay increases, if granted, will be effective July 1. The budget for pay increases will be jointly established by the Personnel Committee and the Finance Committee.

OVERTIME PAY: Overtime pay of one and one half times normal rate will be paid for hours worked in excess of 40 hours per week by nonexempt employees. All overtime must be approved in advance by the supervisor. A work week is defined as Sunday through Saturday. All hours paid, including holidays, vacation, and personal leave time will be included in calculating total hours per week.

Your compensation policy also should name the authorization procedure for increasing salaries. No one individual should have that authority, without review by a committee or board.

Compensation systems require constant updating, since salaries rarely remain stagnant, and your jobs will be continually changing. Appoint a person or committee to review every aspect at least once a year.

Included is a sample compensation policy. You can write yours to fit your own denominational practices.

Communicating About Compensation

Some people feel the best thing to say about compensation is nothing at all. This decision is usually a mistake. Employees are concerned about fair and equitable treatment and about reaching a dead end in their career. When they lack information, they speculate, often making a situation worse than it really is. If you are embarrassed by your compensation system, not talking about it does not make it better. Do the best you can to make it fair, and then explain your system to your employees. This should be done by someone who thoroughly understands the system—perhaps the chair of the Compensation or Personnel Committee, or the business manager. Of course, you will not reveal the salary of individuals, but you should explain how the salaries are being compared, what benefits are available, and other ways in which their efforts will be recognized. Does that mean every employee will smile and say it's wonderful? No. At least you have been honest and employees can make their own decisions based on good information.

Compensation and benefits are a major portion of any church budget. Good stewardship means wise use of these resources. Careful planning will enable you to provide for employee needs, establish long-term partnerships with employees, and be a good example in the community. A systematic approach will enable you to accomplish this.

 PLANNING TOOL

Planning the Pastor's Compensation Package

WAYNE BARRETT

When it is time to begin those dreaded discussions about next year's compensation, here are a few crucial issues to remember.

First, help your congregation appreciate the difference between cost to the church and compensation to the pastor. When discussing these items, separate compensation issues into one column and cost items into another. You may come up with lists of budgeted items like this:

Pastor's Compensation	Church Cost
Salary	Pastor's travel
Parsonage utilities	Office expense
Parsonage insurance	Publications & books
Parsonage mortgage	Pastor's continuing ed.
Pension	Entertaining & gifts
Hospitalization	Vestments

Occasionally, we encounter church budgets that list all these items under a single heading of Pastoral Support. Church members often have the impression that all this money goes directly into the pastor's pocket. Separating these items right away can make the entire negotiations much smoother, since erroneous assumptions are addressed immediately.

Next, work together on the goal of maximizing the net income of whatever compensation the pastor will receive. This means recognizing that it's not what the church pays the pastor that matters—it's what the pastor gets to keep. Tax efficiency can make a big difference in the bottom line of any compensation package.

Clergy may receive money from the congregation with any of three different tax liabilities: (1) totally tax-exempt; (2) subject to Social Security tax only (SECA); or (3) subject to both income and Social Security taxes. See the following chart, which shows how this might work.

You will note that the tax liability can vary from 0 percent to 43.3 percent! This should suggest to your compensation team that shifting compensation from "salary," where the tax liability is highest, to a policy of reimbursement for professional expenses (which is tax free) can dramatically increase the value of the compensation—at no extra cost to the church.

Type of Payment	Income Tax	SECA	Tax Exempt
Salary	yes	yes	no
Parsonage (Rental Value)	no	yes	no
Travel allowance	yes	yes	no
Reimbursed Professional Expenses	no	no	yes
Hospitalization	no	no	yes

Suppose, for example, that your congregation plans to give the pastor a raise of $1,500. If all of it is subject to both income tax (say at 28%) and SECA (currently 15.3%), the pastor will get to keep only $900 of your raise. But what if the entire $1,500 is used to establish a Professional Expense Reimbursement Account? If the entire $1,500 were used for professional expenses—books, periodicals, entertainment and business lunches, the pastor would owe no tax and receive the entire $1,500—a 66 percent increase over the $900 the pastor could keep if the raise were salary. "He who has ears to hear, let him hear."

A tax-wise alternative to reimbursement of professional expenses is an allowance for furnishings. Parsonage dwellers know that there are many expenses related to housing, even if the parsonage is provided full of furniture. All housing-related expenses (furniture, appliances, utilities, cleaning supplies, lawn care) are subject to the IRC Section 107 "Housing Exclusion," provided the housing compensation: (1) is established in advance; (2) is actually spent on housing/furnishings; and (3) does not exceed applicable Fair Rental Values. Note that receiving funds as a Furnishings Allowance avoids the income tax but is subject to SECA.

Don't forget the tax advantage of establishing a long-term savings plan as a Tax Deferred Annuity (403b plan). As long as this is set up as a "salary reduction" plan and the church treasurer sends in all contributions directly, the pastor will have no current tax liability. Note that this is different from an IRA. While the pastor can make an IRA contribution without the cooperation of the church, the price the pastor pays is an immediate Social Security (SECA) liability. This can cost the pastor up to $300 for a $2,000 IRA contribution. The same money in a Tax Deferred Annuity has no current tax due.

Finally, don't be afraid to negotiate, for negotiations need not be acrimonious. It is merely a process for sharing information and expectations, in a mutual effort to solve a problem. Be up-front about your expectations. (Be realistic too!)

PLANNING TOOL

An Accountable Reimbursement Plan

WAYNE BARRETT

In recent years, the distinction between professional "allowances" and reimbursement of professional expenses has become all the more crucial. Many "flexible" spending plans have been disallowed by the IRS, with devastating results. In most cases of disallowal, the entire amount of the account is considered taxable compensation. For pastors who must deduct business expenses on Schedule A, this often results in many extra tax dollars. We continue to recommend a policy of reimbursed professional expenses consistent with IRC 274. Below is a description of an "accountable" reimbursement plan which meets the requirements of the IRS.

"Money is never spent to so much advantage as when you have been cheated out of it; for in one stroke you have purchased prudence."

—SCHOEPHENOUR

A Policy for Reimbursement

The most equitable arrangement is for the church to agree to pay for usual and necessary professional expenses for the pastor to carry on the ministry of the church. This, when properly executed, results in no taxable income for the pastor and extra expense for the church only for the actual cost of church business. However, new tax regulations make it more important than ever that these transactions are handled properly. Let's take a look at what is old and what is new in expense reimbursement.

It always has been necessary to make a clear distinction between an "allowance," which always has been taxable income, and true "reimbursement," which is not considered income in the first place. An "allowance" is money that is intended to be distributed to the pastor, irrespective of actual expenditures. For example, your church may provide a "travel allowance" of $3,600, paid out $300 each month. This tradition is, and always has been, just the same tax-wise as if it were salary. The "allowance" must be included by the church treasurer in preparing the year-end 1099 or W-2 form, and the pastor must declare the full amount as taxable income.

But reimbursement is a policy, not a price tag. The congregation agrees to pay for professional expenses at a predetermined rate: cost for purchases, cents/mile for travel, and so on. As the pastor incurs expenses, a voucher is submitted, documenting the expenditure. Upon receipt of the voucher, the congregation grants the pastor a check in the amount due. Because this transaction is not interpreted as compensation (IRC 162 & 274), this amount need not be reported as income.

Recent Changes on Reimbursement Policy

New regulations from IRS substantially tighten the requirements to meet the definitions of "reimbursement" under IRC 274. Currently, the payor (the congregation in most cases) serves as a sort of "auditor." The reimbursement voucher must, to the payor's satisfaction, address the essential elements of true reimbursement:

1. What the expense was (who was entertained, what was purchased)
2. When the expense occurred
3. Why the expense is business-related (why the item purchased was necessary, why the person was entertained, etc.)
4. Where the event/travel occurred
5. How much was expended (how many miles were traveled, etc.)

All five of these elements must be recorded to satisfy the requirements of a reimbursement relationship. Where confidentiality issues apply—protecting the name of a parishioner visited at a mental health facility, for example—the pastor may note that such documentation is available but withheld at this time. The IRS officials we have consulted have endorsed this important professional issue of confidentiality.

Four additional reimbursement issues to remember in establishing your policy:

1. "Use it or lose it"—any unused balances remaining in the budget must be forfeited. A critical distinction between an "allowance" and "reimbursement" is that allowances are always fully disbursed while only actual costs are reimbursed.

2. If the congregation is unable to offer additional money "on top of salary" for professional expenses, an important tax benefit may be achieved by reducing the salary by an agreed-upon amount and establishing a corresponding reimbursement account in the church budget. All the above policies apply. The pastor receives the money without tax liability, as long as payments are made only upon receipt of an expense voucher.

3. Expenses (other than mileage) in excess of $25 must be accompanied by a receipt.

4. Meals and entertainment expenses may be reimbursed at 100 percent of cost. There is an important distinction between deductibility and exclusion. While such expenses are limited to 50 percent of cost for income tax deductions, reimbursement may be made in full with no tax liability.

Copyright © 1984 Robert Portlock

"Hello, Father Faber. We were just discussing your request for a salary increase."

PART EIGHT

CHURCH AND STATE UPDATE

For the Finance and Pastor Relations Teams

Introduction

D O N A L D   W .   J O I N E R

Recent trends in American law reveal that legal planning and prevention can save clergy, churches, and denominations tens of thousands, sometimes even millions of dollars, otherwise spent on legal fees, court costs, penalties, and taxes. No minister can know all there is to know about the law as it relates to the church. However, all ministers should include as part of their education about church finance a sensitivity to new developments in the law that might affect them and the churches they serve.

This section of *The Abingdon Guide to Funding Ministry* is not legal advice for particular legal problems. Only attorneys licensed to practice law in particular states can and should be called upon to offer such advice. Nor is it a broad overview of the law and the church. Instead, this chapter discusses some of the most recent and critical developments in the law affecting churches and clergy, and what ministers (lay or ordained) should know about those areas when planning their church's finances.

Outside of criminal and domestic relations, law is divided into two broad areas: (1) litigation, the process of lawsuits; and (2) transactional law, which usually involves tasks like drafting contracts or determining tax liability. Significant developments in each of these two areas have particularly impacted the clergy and churches. This edition of the *Abingdon's Guide to Funding Ministry* addresses a litigation issue that has captured more headlines and caused more concern to all churches in the 1990s than any other issue: the clergy, the church, and sexual misconduct. It is an issue about which all clergy should be acutely aware in the years ahead.

Next, this section discusses a transactional issue: how churches might save on state sales tax when planning a construction project. The section also includes a brief report on the Religious Freedom Restoration Act, signed into law at the close of 1993, which promises to have an impact on almost all churches and religious organizations in coming years.

 LEGAL CLINIC

The Clergy, the Church, and Sexual Misconduct

Lawsuits, Lawsuits, Lawsuits!

THOMAS F. TAYLOR

On November 12, 1992, the *Wall Street Journal* published an article titled "Churches, Ministers, Finding Themselves Hit by More Lawsuits." Quoting from authorities knowledgeable in both law and ministry, the article explained that numerous types of lawsuits are increasingly being levied against religious workers and their organizations. In 1993, the media focused particular public attention on lawsuits against clergy and churches for various kinds of sexual misconduct. The types included child molestation, seductions of adult parishioners and counselees, and sexual harassment. As the news reports detailing these suits increased, many argued that they may unfairly affect some clergy. Some media report that the Roman Catholic Church has paid out hundreds of millions of dollars in settling such claims in the last ten years.

Few argue that a clergy person who has broken the law should be able to hide behind the cloth. However, if media attention merely sensationalizes these suits, emphasizing multimillion dollar settlements and jury verdicts, many fear that innocent clergy may become the targets of popular allegations. Not only might innocent ministers be forced to pay large defense costs associated with unmeritorious suits, but the damage to the reputations of innocent clergy that accompanies these lawsuits is often irreparable.

The following overview is focused on three of the most important issues in dealing with both true and false accusations of clergy sexual misconduct: Church Liability for the Misconduct of Clergy; Preventing and Addressing Acts of Sexual Misconduct in the Church; and Damage Control After False Accusations of Sexual Misconduct.[1]

Church Liability for the Misconduct of Clergy

Acts of sexual misconduct are committed by people—individuals—not denominations or churches. Yet, it is usually the denomination or church that victims turn to for recompense. This is because churches usually are insured or simply have more money than individual ministers. No denomination appears to be immune from the increasing claims of sexual abuse by clergy. No church can stop these lawsuits from being filed. But churches can minimize the risks of such claims by changing the kinds of circumstances that often lead to such lawsuits. If churches wish to avoid lawsuits for alleged wrongful acts, then they should understand the legal theories under which they may be held liable for acts of clergy sexual misconduct, and the factual circumstances that underlie those theories.

Victims generally have sought to hold churches and religious societies liable for the sexual misconduct of their clergy under four main theories: (1) *respondeat superior;* (2) agency; (3) negligent hiring; and (4) negligent supervision. The following briefly defines each of these legal doctrines.

1. Respondeat Superior

"Respondeat Superior," or "let the employer answer," means that an employer will be held liable for the acts of its employee, if those acts were within the employee's scope of employment. In the context of churches, most courts have held that, in order for conduct to be within the scope of employment, the conduct must be "in accordance with the principles of the church or in some way in furtherance of the purpose of the church or religious cociety, foreseeable or characteristic of the church or religious society."[2]

These same courts have determined that sexual misconduct by clergy is not within a minister's scope of employment.

Although it may seem obvious that churches do not employ clergy members to abuse parishioners, some courts have not defined "scope of employment" so narrowly. Some have held that even abuse which arises out of the confidential relationship that exists between ministers and their parishioners is within the scope of employment. Indeed, as the number of claims increases, some commentators believe that courts subscribe to this broad definition of "scope of employment." Therefore, churches must continually do all they can to limit opportunities for abuse in such confidential relationships.

2. Agency

Plaintiffs bringing actions under an "Agency" theory are claiming that clergy (the agents), or even board members or trustees, are acting on behalf of the church and thus binding the church by their words or actions. This theory has been generally rejected by courts where denominations can show that they have no control over the actions of individual churches or clergy in those churches. However, churches must never assume that they will be immune from a successful claim under this theory. Because many churches maintain at least some control over their clergy, denominations should clearly define, in written policy and procedure documents, or in correspondence to their clergy, the areas in which the clergy are not authorized to act on the denomination's or church's behalf.

Churches should repeatedly make clear that any sexual misconduct by clergy members, whether verbal or physical, is not authorized or condoned by the church. If any such conduct is reported, the church should immediately denounce the misconduct, make clear that the minister, if truly guilty of the act, was not acting on behalf of the church, and follow through with any disciplinary procedures provided in the policies.

3. Negligent Hiring

Plaintiffs also bring claims against churches under the theories of "Negligent Hiring." This issue may arise, for example, when a church hires a person to work with youth, and the worker molests one of the young people. "Negligent Hiring" means that the church did not exercise due care in hiring an offending worker, or the church did not adequately screen the applicant to discover criminal propensities. Although these actions have had only moderate success, allegedly injured parties continue to file lawsuits on this theory. All churches must continually guard against such claims by establishing procedures and policies that will help them spot and deal with such potential problems before they hire someone that puts them at risk.

4. Negligent Supervision

Churches can use reasonable care in hiring workers, yet still be liable if the church fails to exercise due care in supervising that worker, under the theory of "Negligent Supervision." Churches have been sued and deemed negligent for acts ranging from the sexual abuse of minors, to injuries or deaths occurring during church camping or sporting activities. Churches most likely will be found liable for negligent supervision if a court determines that the church failed to exercise reasonable care in supervising its employees, thereby creating an unreasonable risk to parishioners. Also, if the church knew or should have known that a clergy member's conduct would subject third parties to an unreasonable risk of harm, a church may be liable. Again, written policies and implementation through training could minimize the risk that such claims would succeed.

Walking the Straight and Narrow:
Preventing and Addressing
Acts of Sexual Misconduct in the Church

Sexual misconduct by clergy and church workers has historically been taboo—ignored or dealt with in secret. The recent deluge of cases against the Roman Catholic and other churches, however, demonstrates that churches no longer can afford to ignore the current increase in claims. Churches must face this issue head on, for the well-being of their parishioners and for the churches' survival.

The key to avoiding clergy sexual misconduct, and the resulting liability, is to establish clear policies and procedures that openly and forcefully address the misconduct. Even if some injurious acts still occur, a church may not be liable for an incident, if a court later determines that the church took reasonable precautions through its policies and procedures to prevent the injury. Churches should consider instituting at least the following policies to avoid incidents of, and liability from, sexual misconduct by ministers and church workers.

1. Look under the sheep's clothing.

One way to be more sure of an employee or clergy member is to do a formal background check before the hiring decision. Background checks should include calling past employers to inquire about history of aberrant behavior. Especially if an applicant is to work with youth, children, or other more vulnerable groups, churches are urged to telephone state and local police in past geographic residences of an applicant, for a criminal background check to identify potential abusers. By making a thorough background check, churches can avoid the claims often later raised by plaintiffs that the church "negligently hired" or "negligently supervised" a church worker.

2. Education

Churches should make clear statements about their positions on all kinds of sexual misconduct, and should openly discuss, both with parishioners and with clergy, the kind of conduct acceptable and not acceptable to the church. This provides an opportunity for churches to express their beliefs and concerns with respect to sexual misconduct, and to make clear the high level of moral conduct the churches expect from their clergy.

In addition, churches should instruct their ministers to avoid situations that may even suggest improper conduct. So far, most sexual misconduct claims against clergy and churches have stemmed from alleged occurrences in the counseling setting. Thus, churches should instruct their clergy to give special attention to the time, manner, and place of counseling sessions between clergy and counselee. Red flags of caution should occur to church workers counseling under emotionally charged circumstances, as when dealing with a troubled marriage or suicidal counselee. Ministers should consciously avoid acts or suggestions which could be construed as undue or unfair influence over an emotionally wrought person. Most ministers approach counseling relationships with the best of intentions. But in the present legal climate, ministers cannot be too circumspect when counseling any parishioner.

3. Balance the interests of all parties.

Because often the truth of sexual misconduct claims is not immediately clear, churches must balance and be concerned for the interests of all parties—that is, the alleged victim and the alleged abuser—until one party's version is proven true. Churches might consider the policy of setting up the following groups for each party, in the event of an allegation of sexual misconduct:

a. Support for the Victim: The facts from many recent sexual-abuse cases reveal that although true victims of clergy sexual misconduct need the support and understanding of their church, they often are ignored, disbelieved, or even held in contempt for accusing the minister. Even if a church is unsure of exactly what occurred, churches would do well to take the complaining party seriously. It could set up a support group to prevent victims from feeling abandoned. The existence of such a support group may encourage those who truly have been victims of sexual misconduct to report the incident to the church, when they see that the church will not ignore their claims or immediately discount their credibility.

b. Support for the Accused: Charges of sexual misconduct can permanently destroy the reputation of any minister. Ministers are not excluded from enjoying the benefits of due process under the United States Constitution. The Constitution guarantees that they are innocent until proven guilty. At the same time the churches select a group to support an alleged victim of sexual abuse, they also should designate a group of individuals to support the accused minister, to help direct him or her emotionally, legally, and spiritually through the ordeal. If the allegations turn out to be false, such groups can aid in preventing the falsely accused from feeling embittered and betrayed. If the accusations are true, the support group may be instrumental in encouraging restitution and repentance.

4. Encourage clergy and parishioners to report to objective third parties outside the local church.

When accusations have been made, churches should encourage clergy members and accusing parishioners to avoid face-to-face confrontations. Because of the highly charged nature of the controversy, such confrontations often become ugly enough to obscure justice. Parties should consider reporting any accusations or defenses to church leaders outside of the local parish. Any attempt by clergy members to approach their accusers alone may be viewed as an attempt to cover up misconduct or use the position of trust to coerce a retraction. In addition, such confrontations can create situations where other types of misconduct, such as rage or even violence, can occur, although (or perhaps especially if) the original claim was false.

5. Deal with reports quickly.

Churches must deal with reports of abuse immediately. If the accusation is true, this will help churches avoid liability by quickly disaffirming any "agency" relationship with respect to the misconduct. More important, immediate action may protect truly abused parishioners from further abuse and offer swift vindication to the victim.

If the accusation is false, rapid reporting and collection of information, before evidence is disposed of and memories fade, is more likely to defend innocent clergy members from false accusations.

6. Document investigations.

Churches should carefully document investigations into allegations of sexual misconduct. The evidence gathered during such an investigation can be essential also in the guilt or innocence of an accused. Either way, documentation is a critical element and should be meticulously handled by churches that are investigating allegations of sexual misconduct. Also, a well-documented investigation may help protect denominations and churches from claims of wrongful termination, if they are forced to fire or dismiss a minister for misconduct. Conversely, it may aid churches in supporting and protecting clergy members who have been falsely accused. If lawyers are retained to conduct the investigation, much of their material may be privileged also and protected from discovery by the attorney-client privilege and/or attorney work product doctrine.

7. Finally, in all situations, remember the Apostle Paul's admonition to "test everything; hold fast to what is good; abstain from every form of evil" (I Thess. 5:21-22).

Damage Control After False Accusations

The thought of being falsely accused of sexual misconduct makes most of us a little queasy—especially when we are the accused. How does one best respond to such an accusation? If you become angry, people will accuse you of being defensive. If you remain calm, they will say you are suspiciously under-reacting. And since most of us react irrationally, unpredictably, and often imprudently, propelled only by rushes of adrenaline when such accusations threaten our livelihoods, advice like, "Just be yourself," is usually unhelpful and shallow. So what is the best way to respond to such false claims?

On January 12, 1994, an article in the *Wall Street Journal* advised employers in the secular workplace how to best respond if falsely accused of sexual harassment.[3] Many of the observations and directives from professional career advisors and consultants quoted in the article are also applicable and valuable advice for clergy wrongly accused of any kind of sexual misconduct. The following highlights some of those suggestions that are especially applicable to church workers:

1. Don't retreat into hopeless despair. Your job and your reputation can survive even a crisis of this magnitude. (Remember, many in the church may be on your side before you even offer an explanation or response.)

2. Keep a cool head. Angry outbursts diminish your leadership authority and may give your accuser credibility. "Rage," notes one Ph.D. career strategist, "is too often associated with guilt."

3. Instead of anger, you will better retain your dignity and the respect of others if you restrict your emotional displays to astonishment, hurt, and grief.

4. Whatever your response, don't ignore or scoff at unfounded charges of sexual misconduct. Take the accusations as serious. They are.

5. Avoid face-to-face confrontations with your accuser. A fatherly pat on the shoulder in an attempt to make peace may give your accuser an opportunity to yell, "Get your hands off of me!" Such situations often distort the true intentions of the party trying to make amends. Nothing you say will make a lying accuser change his or her mind now.

6. Report false accusations to a superior immediately, no matter how seemingly insignificant. Preempting a public report of a false accusation against you will bolster your credibility and let the world know that you want the true facts out in the open from the beginning. Don't wait for a formal complaint to be filed.

7. When you report to your superior, take as much documentation as you can quickly compile regarding your accuser. Try to reconstruct all relevant meetings or contacts with your accuser. (This is another good reason for ministers to document all important events in their ministry as a matter of course.)

8. As soon as you are accused, take a short time alone or with a trusted friend to collect your thoughts and emotions. Then, respond quickly to the charges in the above prescribed ways.

Conclusion

As with all things, the present intensity of sexual misconduct claims against clergy probably will pass. But things may grow much worse before they get better. A church's best defense against true accusations of sexual misconduct is to attempt to prevent the acts from occurring by proactively avoiding circumstances that often precipitate the wrongdoing and the resulting lawsuits. Similarly, false accusations can be dealt with more quickly and effectively if ministers, before possibly being falsely accused, anticipate how they should respond. To all church workers, strive to be upright, of course. Beyond this, however, strive to be careful—we need and cannot afford to lose you.

Notes

1. Mr. Taylor acknowledges the significant contributions in preparing this article, of attorneys Mark O. Morris and Brian Hulse, both of the law firm of Snell & Wilmer.

2. Joseph B. Conder, *Liability of Church or Religious Society for Sexual Misconduct of Clergy,* 5 ALR 5th 530, 535 (1993).

3. *Wall Street Journal,* "Control the Damage of a False Accusation of Sexual Harassment," J. A. Lopez, p. B1.

4. Ibid.

 LEGAL CLINIC

Sales-Tax Savings on Construction Supplies

THOMAS F. TAYLOR

Here's a possible tax-savings tip for churches or other tax-exempt organizations that intend to start construction of a building or addition. The issue is whether a tax-exempt entity, such as a church, can legally use its tax-exempt status to purchase construction materials for a new building or addition, and thereby avoid paying state sales tax on the materials. While a contractor who purchases the materials normally would need to pay sales taxes, tax-exempt entities may not be required to.

Sales tax is based upon state law. Thus, as with all state-law questions, you should consult an attorney licensed to practice law in your state before attempting any state-tax-savings strategies. Most state tax commissions attempt to interpret strictly all statutes governing exemptions against the taxpayer, in an effort to limit the scope and number of the exemptions. State tax commissions, however, are still subject to the jurisdiction of state courts and may not always get what they want.

The law in some states may allow your church or religious organization to erect a building or addition, without paying sales tax on the materials for the project. For instance, in *Thorup Bros. Construction, Inc. v. Auditing Division of the Utah State Tax Commission* (Civil No. 920184, filed September 15, 1993), the Utah Supreme Court effectively overruled the Tax Commission, which had taken the position that a Catholic high school was not exempt from paying sales taxes on materials used in the construction of an addition to the school.

In *Thorup Bros.,* a Catholic high school contracted with Thorup Brothers Construction to build additions to the high school. The high school purchased construction materials to build the additions and then donated the materials to the construction project. The high school used its tax-exempt status to purchase the materials without paying sales tax. Thereafter, Thorup Brothers agreed to credit the high school for those materials. Later, the Tax Commission audited Thorup and claimed that it should be assessed additional sales tax of $26,328.30.

Through an appeal process, the high school eventually took the case to the Utah Supreme Court. The Court held that Thorup was not subject to sales tax on the high school's purchase of the construction materials, reasoning that the high school was the true owner and consumer of the materials. The Utah high court reasoned that the sales were exempt because of the school's complete control over the construction materials, from the time of purchase until they were used in the project. Thus, at least in Utah, the *Thorup Brothers* decision is generally favorable to churches that desire to purchase construction materials and thereby avoid sales tax on their projects.

Even though the Utah Supreme Court allowed the purchase of the materials free from sales tax, some risk of assessment under such circumstances still may exist, since a tax commission may claim that facts related to cases like the *Thorup Bros.* case are limited to the facts of that case only and are not directly applicable to other contracts. Also, some states may focus more heavily on use and consumption of materials, rather than ownership of them. See, for example, *Tri-State Generation, Inc. v. Department of Revenue* (636 P.2d 1335 [Colo. Ct. App. 1981]). Here, a nonprofit utility corporation was required to pay use tax on construction materials for a power line, because a controlling Colorado statute specified that such tax assessment was based upon "use."

If your church is in a state whose law comports with the *Thorup Brothers* case, and it decides to purchase its own construction materials for a project, in an attempt to avoid paying sales tax, your church could maximize its opportunities by doing the following:

1. Directly issue purchase orders for all construction materials and request to be invoiced directly for the same. (The church can interact with the contractor to determine what materials should be ordered.)

2. Pay all suppliers directly by issuing church checks to the supplier.

3. Obtain insurance in its name which covers "materials, equipment, supplies, and temporary structures on the premises" of the project. The church must assume the entire burden of risk of loss on the materials purchased by the church.

4. Obtain warranties on materials that run directly to the church.

5. Retain and store any surplus materials for repairs or replacement to its project on the church construction site.

6. Consistently assert in all written and oral communications with the contractor or any other party that the church is the purchaser and owner of any construction materials in question.

7. An agent from the church (presumably someone elected from a church building committee) should be designated to inspect and directly supervise the purchase and receiving of all construction materials purchased on the church tax-exempt number. (This agent still may work with the contractor to assure that all materials meet construction specifications. However, the agent should not rely solely on the contractor for such assurances.)

8. Explicitly reserve in its contract with the construction company the right to purchase and donate any materials to the construction project that the church chooses.

9. Finally, the church and construction company may choose to agree, in writing, that the church indemnify the construction company for any actual payments of sales tax incurred, if the state tax commission challenges the construction company on unpaid sales tax for the construction materials, and ultimately prevails. If the parties so agree, the construction company should agree to resist and defend itself against any such effort by the tax commission. Presumably, the construction company will want to be reimbursed for its costs.

The above process may initially appear overly cumbersome to many. Each church will need to determine, based upon the size of its construction project and the amount to be saved, whether this process is worth pursuing. Even if the procedures are followed, no one can guarantee that a state tax commission will not audit and attempt a reassessment. However, if the law of a given state is consistent with the decision of the Utah Supreme Court, and if a church follows the forgoing recommendations, it could well maximize its chances of saving significant amounts on unpaid sales tax, and of prevailing, even in the event that a state tax commission challenges the exemption claimed by the church. Again, if your church is embarking upon a new building or addition project, consult an attorney in your state to see whether you might enjoy some tax savings on that project.

 LEGAL CLINIC

Religious Freedom Restoration Act

T H O M A S   F .   T A Y L O R

On November 16, 1993, President Clinton signed the Religious Freedom Restoration Act (RFRA) into law. This federal statute creates a statutory right to practice the free exercise of religion.

"But," you ask, "didn't we already have a guarantee of free exercise of religion under the United States Constitution?" Although the free exercise clause under the First Amendment of the Constitution already existed, ostensibly for the same purpose as

RFRA, many had become dissatisfied—indeed, outraged—with the way the Supreme Court had interpreted the First Amendment in recent years.

In *Oregon v. Smith* (494 U.S. 872 [1990]), the Supreme Court abandoned the previously held requirement that the government show a compelling state interest before it may impose or place a burden upon the free exercise of religion. In *Smith,* the high court found that Oregon's drug laws, which included a ban on the use of peyote, did not violate the free exercise rights of Native Americans who used peyote in their religious rites. The *Smith* decision resulted in thunderous objections from across the religious and political spectrum. From Pat Robertson's ACLJ, to the ACLU, First Amendment fans stormed Congress to change the effect of the decision. They eventually succeeded.

Many advocates for RFRA argued that *Smith* had set a precedent for allowing the government to make greater inroads into religious liberties of all kinds. Indeed, it appeared that the high court was headed in that direction in *Smith,* when it stated, "Disadvantaging minority religious practices is an unavoidable consequence of democratic government." Such language sent chills down the spines of proponents of individual rights, causing them to proclaim that the sky was falling on our religious liberties.

However, post–*Smith* decisions by the Supreme

"Through our voluntary organizations and the giving that supports them, ever more Americans worship freely, study quietly, are cared for compassionately, experiment creatively, advocate aggressively, and contribute generously. These national traits are constantly beautiful and must remain beautifully constant."

—*BRIAN O'CONNELL*

Court regarding minority religions made it unclear whether the Court was ready to adopt completely such a narrow understanding of the free exercise clause as was articulated in *Smith.* For example, in *Church of the Lukimi Babalu Aye, Inc. v. City of Hialeah* (113 S.Ct. 221 [1993]), the Supreme Court invalidated municipal ordinances designed to suppress the Santeria religious practice of ritualistically sacrificing animals. The *Hialeah* decision may be used to temper the effect of the Court's holding in *Smith.*

What is the greatest benefit to religious believers under RFRA? Certainty. The above decisions by the Supreme Court reveal that we live in uncertain times, when it comes to the freedom of our religious practice. The RFRA statute provides stability and, at least for now, renews our confidence that our freedom to practice our religions remains. Subsequent interpretations of RFRA by courts will tell how much certainty we have obtained.

 LEGAL CLINIC

Fund-Raising and the Law

F. STUART GULLEY

Promissory Estoppel in Fund-Raising

Have you ever wondered whether any legal protections are available to our institutions, if a donor makes a multi-year pledge and, at some point during the course of pledge payment, reneges? This is an interesting question to consider, as our institutions seek larger and larger gifts for major projects, which could result in significant and embarrassing financial loss to the institution, if a pledge went unfulfilled.

Should a donor renege on a pledge, the institution may be able to enforce it through the legal principle of promissory estoppel. Promissory estoppel essen-

tially means that a donor is estopped (barred or prevented) from claiming that she or he is not legally obligated to fulfill the pledge, because it is only a promise. Generally, pledges to our institutions are promises. They are not binding contracts, meaning that the charitable institution cannot demonstrate consideration, an important principle of contract law.

Because the courts want to protect and encourage philanthropy, they often have invoked the principle of promissory estoppel when a donor threatened to renege on the pledge, even though the pledge is not considered a binding contract. A seminal case in promissory estoppel theory occurred in the mid-

1920s, when Allegheny College sued the estate of Mary Yates Johnson to claim a portion of a $5,000 pledge that Mrs. Johnson had made to a capital campaign at the college.

In 1921, Mrs. Johnson designated that her pledge be used as an endowment in her name to support ministerial students attending Allegheny College. Soon after making the pledge, she gave the school $1,000 toward the balance, but in the next year she notified the school that she repudiated the remainder of the pledge. Unwilling to take the woman to court while she was still living (who among us would want the publicity, which could scare off other donors?), the school waited until her death and brought suit against the estate. In its suit, the school claimed that it had relied on the promise/pledge of Mrs. Johnson, and that for this promise not to be fulfilled would be an injustice to the institution and future ministerial students. The court agreed and awarded Allegheny College the remaining $4,000 from Mrs. Johnson's estate.

To invoke promissory estoppel successfully, the following conditions must be met: there must be a pledge; the institution must show that it relied on the pledge; and finally, the institution must show that failure to fulfill the pledge will result in an injustice to the institution.

As representatives of our institutions, it is our job not only to raise money, but to help protect the institution from unexpected changes of heart and/or mind of the donor. When we secure in writing all the circumstances of the pledge—what it is for, how much it will be, and what timetable will be followed for payment—we place our schools and churches in the position of satisfying all the elements of promissory estoppel theory.

Cy Pres *Doctrine in Fund-Raising*

What would happen if your institution received an estate gift which it could not use, because to do so would be illegal, impractical, or impossible? Many congregations have faced similar situations. For those who work for institutions that receive federal funds, for example, it is illegal to award scholarship money on the basis of gender or race. It may be impossible to

use a bequest if it is left for a program that no longer exists. Or it may be impractical to use a bequest if it is intended for a purpose not in keeping with the mission of the institution. When this happens, the institution may turn to the court and request that the gift be redesignated, under the stipulations of the *cy pres* doctrine.

Cy pres is a French term meaning "as near as possible." Courts have *cy pres* power to redirect the use of a decedent's gift for purposes as near as possible to the original intent of the donor, when it can be shown that the bequest, for the reasons stated above, cannot be used.

Cy pres doctrine is an ancient doctrine and has at least one root in the early Christian church. It was a common practice of the early church for individuals to make donations of property to the church as penance for their sins. In exchange for the gift, which would come to the church at the death of the individual, the church promised to pray for the soul of the individual after death, as assurance of gaining and maintaining an advantageous position in the kingdom of heaven. If a gift became unusable, the churchmen who sat as judges in the chancery would agree to redirect the use of the gift for a worthy purpose. By this method, the soul of the donor in the afterlife was not jeopardized, and the church continued to benefit from the gift.

There are three prerequisites for the *cy pres* doctrine:

1. a valid charitable trust must be established;

2. the decedent's original purpose must have failed due to impossibility, illegality, or impracticality;

3. the terms of the trust must have evoked a general charitable intent which exceeded the decedent's specific intent.

The *cy pres* doctrine should be a reminder to all fund-raisers that we should encourage donors to be clear about the intentions of any gifts they may leave in a will. Moreover, we should urge our donors to make a gift-over provision in their will. A gift-over provision grants the institution receiving the gift the authority to use a bequest in the most prudent manner possible in the event the donor's original and primary intentions should be impossible, impractical, or illegal at the time the gift is realized.

PART NINE

RESOURCES FOR FINANCIAL GIVING

For the Church Library or Resource Center

Introduction

NORMA WIMBERLY

Today, worshiping communities are blessed with a wealth of books and other resources to support the funding of ministry. None of us could possibly read, reflect upon, and use all of them.

The editors asked each of the contributing writers to *The Abingdon Guide to Funding Ministry* to name one or two books they believe are "classics," books that had a major impact on their lives and ministries. The bibliography provided here is intended as support as you continue to develop your personal perspective on funding ministry.

The resources listed include material for financial commitment programs to be used by local congregations, as well as a listing of campaign management firms. (These lists are provided for information, and do not imply an endorsement or recommendation.)

Don and Norma pray that your adventure in funding ministry is exciting, satisfying, and filled with spiritual wonder. The Apostle Paul reminds us that stewards are required to be trustworthy (I Cor. 4:2) rather than successful. We hope you will be trustworthy, keep the faith, and believe that success is possible in God's way, and in God's time.

Book and Resource Reviews

Barrett, Wayne C. *The Church Finance Idea Book.* Nashville: Discipleship Resources, 1989. pb. 157 pp. ISBN 0-88177-065-5.

Explains ten strategies for commitment campaigns, yet the author offers hundreds of other techniques and methods. Addresses financial administration, fund-raising, capital projects, and planned giving.

————. *More Money, New Money, Big Money.* Nashville: Discipleship Resources, 1992. pb. 159 pp. ISBN 0-88-177-120-1.

In this follow-up to *The Church Finance Idea Book,* Barrett shows that every congregation has significant sources of new and untapped income. More money: increasing results from current sources; New money: discovering new and untapped sources; Big money: learning to cultivate major gifts and bequests.

Block, Peter. *Stewardship: Choosing Service over Self-interest.* San Francisco: Berrett-Koehler Publishers. pb. 264 pp. ISBN 0-881052-28-1.

While this book was written for application to business and industry, the church leader will quickly see that the church's word has been used more faithfully and appropriately than the church uses it. Throughout, one sees biblical stewardship principles (without calling them that) put to work within the setting of everyday life in business and industry. An eye-opener!

Decker, Bert. *You've Got to Be Believed to Be Heard.* New York: St. Martin's Press, 1992. pb. 272 pp. ISBN 0-312069-35-9.

This book speaks directly to perhaps the biggest problem in stewardship. We haven't learned how to communicate our message. Bert Decker shows that effective communication involves our personality in all its manifestations.

Grimm, Eugene. *Generous People: How to Encourage Vital Stewardship.* Nashville: Abingdon Press, 1992. pb. 153 pp. ISBN 0-687-14045-5.
Grimm closes his book with "A Checklist for Vital Stewardship," questions for congregations to ask about the presence and effectiveness of their financial stewardship programs. The author's narrative stresses the importance of biblical foundations, clear definitions, planning, the individual's need to give, a variety of approaches to commitment, and pastoral leadership.

Joiner, Donald W. *Christians and Money: A Guide to Personal Finance.* Nashville: Discipleship Resources, 1991. pb. 128 pp. ISBN 0-88177-096-5.
In a world of market pessimism on the one hand, and get-rich-quick schemes on the other, we need a clear sense of the Christian principles for sound financial planning and freedom. Writing in a practical and down-to-earth style, Don Joiner explores these and other questions that concern Christians and their money. Each chapter includes focus questions and exercises that bring learnings home to personal experience. An appendix provides suggestions for sharing the study in a group setting.

Lawson, Douglas M. *Give to Live: How Giving Can Change Your Life.* La Jolla, Calif.: ALTI Publishing, 1991. pb. 195 pp. ISBN 0-9625399-9-6.
Lawson's book addresses the spiritual malaise of North America, explores the spiritual, emotional, and physical benefits of giving, and offers ways to get involved—-with both time and money. The author's "Giving Path" is outlined to cover giving as a vital part of living all of life, from early childhood through the several stages of adulthood.

Levan, Christopher. *The Dancing Steward: Exploring Christian Stewardship Lifestyles.* Toronto: The United Church Publishing House, 1993. (Distributed in the USA by the Ecumenical Center for Stewardship Studies.) pb. 171 pp. ISBN 1-55134-004-6.
In this intriguing and challenging material, two dramas are designed for use in worship, with a study guide at the end of each chapter. Chris goes to the heart of the matter and allows us an opportunity to explore not only the issue but also possible alternatives for faithful persons and congregations.

Mather, Herbert. *Becoming a Giving Church.* Nashville: Discipleship Resources, 1985. pb. 56 pp. ISBN 0-88177-023-X.
This booklet shows how our financial giving is rooted in the congregation's faith and life, its self-worth, its members' sense of shared mission, and their vision and plans for achieving goals.

Meeks, M. Douglas. *God, the Economist.* Minneapolis: Fortress Press, 1989. pb. 257 pp. ISBN 0-8006-2329-0.
The author assesses our current situation through theological critique and offers the lens of God's "law of the household." Economics, politics, and theology march hand in hand as Meeks centers his argument on a social conception of the Trinity.

Moore, Gary D. *The Thoughtful Christian's Guide to Investing.* Grand Rapids: Zondervan Publishing House, 1990. pb. 336 pp. ISBN 0-310-53131-4.
Here is a complete course on investing from a Christian perspective by a stockbroker who lives what he believes. This book includes ways of giving through estate planning.

Needleman, Jacob. *Money and the Meaning of Life.* New York: Doubleday, 1991. pb. ISBN 0-385262-41-8.
Needleman carefully investigates the meaning of money in the context of spiritual growth. The book is filled with dialogue between professor and students.

Nouwen, Henri. *Life of the Beloved.* New York: Crossroad, 1992. pb. 119 pp. ISBN 0-8245-1184-0.
In this brief volume, Nouwen describes the spiritual journey as a process containing four movements: we are taken, blessed, broken, and given. Of interest here is the focus on giving as an essential component of the Christian pilgrimage, helpful to those seeking to undergird Christian stewardship with a spiritual and liturgical foundation.

Primavesi, Anne, and Jennifer Henderson. *Our God Has No Favorites: A Liberation Theology of the Eucharist.* San Jose: Resource Publications, 1989. pb. 107 pp. ISBN 0-89390-165-2.
Providing theological background for the Eucharist, this book weaves together the threads of human equality and worth before God with the use of our resources in empowering people to proclaim and live the gospel.

Schaller, Lyle E. *21 Bridges to the 21st Century: The Future of Pastoral Ministry.* Nashville: Abingdon Press, 1994. pb. 160 pp. ISBN 0-687-42664-2.

Of particular interest is chapter 11, "How Many Income Streams?" Schaller insists that the Seven-Day-A-Week Church can count on financial resources from ministries that occur at times other than Sunday morning—a simple thesis, but one that many congregations can implement immediately.

The Spiritual Discipline of Tithing. Grand Rapids: Reformed Church Press, 1993.

This packet has all the necessary items to conduct a 3-session, 6-hour retreat, with tithing as its focus. Includes a step-by-step leader's guide, worship bulletins, handouts for participants, and two videos which contain tithing meditations, biblical-foundations study, and a cultural-awareness segment. Available from RCA Distribution Center, 4500 60th St. SE, Grand Rapids MI 49512; Tel. 800-968-7221.

Stevenson, Kenneth. *Eucharist and Offering.* New York: Pueblo, 1986. pb. 327 pp. ISBN 0-916134-77-6.

Stevenson offers a detailed and helpful study of Eucharist and sacrifice, which draws together both a history and a theology of the church's understanding of the sacrifice of Jesus and the offerings of the people.

Vallet, Ronald E. *Stepping Stones of the Steward.* Grand Rapids: William B. Eerdmans, 1989. pb. 185 pp. ISBN 0-8028-0464-0.

Taking the words *journey* and *steward* as metaphors of the Christian's life, and using 14 of Jesus' parables as a springboard, Vallet explores various dimensions of Christian stewardship—which is much more than a pledge drive. The 14 stepping stones correspond to the 14 parables as recorded in Matthew and Luke.

Watts, John G. *Leave Your House in Order.* Wheaton, Ill.: Tyndale House, 1979. pb. 189 pp. ISBN 0-8423-2152-7.

This book is exactly what it purports to be: a guide to planning your estate. It includes helpful forms to assist estate planning.

Wimberly, Norma. *Because God Gives.* Nashville: Discipleship Resources, 1986. pb. 24 pp.

Searching the Old and New Testaments, this booklet offers a variety of passages related to giving. Included are questions for meditation and discussion.

_____. *Putting God First: The Tithe.* Nashville: Discipleship Resources, 1988. pb. 56 pp. ISBN 0-88177-058-2.

Usually we give only our leftovers to God, because we forget that all creation belongs to God. The author helps individuals and small groups learn about tithing in Old Testament times, and what Jesus has to say about giving with a joyous heart. One section offers testimonies from persons in all walks of life concerning their adventure with the tithing principle.

Campaign Resources and Suppliers

Campaign Management Firms

American City Bureau
1721 Moon Lake Blvd.
Hoffman Estates IL 60194
708/490-5858

Cargill Associates
4701 Altamesa Blvd.
Fort Worth TX 76113
817/292-9374

Church Fund-Raising Services, Inc.
4869 Darwin Court
Boulder CO 80301
303/443-1260

Ketchum, Inc.
1030 Fifth Avenue
Pittsburgh PA 15219-6293
412/281-1481

Kirby-Smith Associates, Inc.
5 Fawn Drive
Quarryville PA 17556
800/762-3996

Office of Finance and Field Service
General Board of Global Ministries
475 Riverside Drive, Room 320
New York NY 10115
212/870-3837

Resource Services, Inc.
12770 Merritt Drive, Suite 900
Dallas, TX 75251
800/527-6824

Ward, Dreshman & Reinhardt, Inc.
P.O. Box 448
Worthington OH 43085
614/888-5376

Campaign Resources

Discipleship Resources   *Celebrate Giving*
P.O. Box 6996   *Celebrate and Visit*
Alpharetta GA 30239-6996   *Celebrate Together*
800/685-4370

Stewardship Resources   *Pony Express*
P.O. Box 75205   *Iron Horse Express*
Oklahoma City OK 73147   *One in Christ*
                               We Are the Family

Abingdon Press   *Off and Running*
P.O. Box 801   *Letters for All Seasons*
Nashville TN 37202-0801   *Give to Live*
800/672-1789

LeWay Resources   *Called to Serve*
56 Drendel Lane   *Celebration Sunday*
Naperville IL 60565   *Special Delivery*

Net Results   *Consecration Sunday*
5001 Avenue N
Lubbock TX 79412-2993
800/762-8094

Envelope Suppliers

National Church Supply Co., Inc.
Box 269
Chester WV 26034
800/627-9900

Postal Church Service
8401 Southern Blvd.
Youngstown OH 44512-6789
800/228-6101

Duplex Envelope Co.
3801 Carolina Ave.
Richmond VA 23222-2203
800/446-3035

These lists are supplied by the Stewardship Team, The General Board of Discipleship, P.O. Box 840, Nashville, TN 37202. 615/340-7075.

Biography of Contributors

Terry Allen is Senior Pastor of First United Methodist Church in Troy, Michigan. He is an active writer, lecturer, and advocate for stewardship ministries as a Stewardship Associate of The General Board of Discipleship, The United Methodist Church.

Wayne C. Barrett is Executive Director of The United Methodist Foundation of the West Michigan Conference. He is editor of the *Clergy Finance Letter,* a personal finance journal for American clergy. The Reverend Barrett is author of *The Church Finance Idea Book and More Money, New Money, Big Money* (Discipleship Resources). He previously pastored churches for thirteen years.

Brian K. Bauknight is pastor of Christ United Methodist Church in Bethel Park, Pennsylvania. He has served as leader for the United Methodist Large Church Initiative, as designated preacher for The National Radio Protestant Hour and as guest preacher for various summer assemblies. Dr. Bauknight is the author of *Right on the Money: Messages for Spiritual Growth Through Giving* (Discipleship Resources) and *Of Gardens and Grandchildren* (Dimensions for Living).

Hilbert J. Berger has served as a stewardship leader with the North Indiana Conference as well as with United Methodist general agencies. He is the author of *Now Concerning the Offering* (Discipleship Resources), *Exploring the Faith with New Members*, and other articles illuminating faithful stewardship. He has pastored several growing churches in Indiana. Dr. Berger is presently retired from the pastorate but continues his work as a speaker and consultant.

Mary Boyd is Administrative Assistant to the Stewardship Unit of The General Board of Discipleship of The United Methodist Church. Mary is Music Director of Alpha United Baptist Church and an active member of the spiritual community in Nashville.

Kenneth H. Carter, Jr. is pastor of Congregational Care, Christ United Methodist Church, Greensboro, North Carolina. A member of the Western North Carolina Conference, he has served urban, rural, and suburban congregations. He is the author of *The Pastor As Steward* (Discipleship Resources) and a variety of essays, reviews, and study materials. He is president of the Southeastern Jurisdiction Association of Stewardship Leaders of The United Methodist Church.

Dan Conway serves as Secretary for Planning, Communications and Development for the Archdiocese of Indianapolis. Mr. Conway is responsible for facilitating the strategic planning efforts of the Archdiocese and other agencies of the Church in central and southern Indiana. He also serves as a consultant to dioceses and other Church-related organizations in the area of planning, communications and fund-raising.

Deborah Fisher is Senior Pastor of Our Savior's United Methodist Church in Schaumburg, Illinois. This congregation more than doubled in size from 1989 until 1993.

Kenneth R. Gallinger is in ministry at First United Church in Port Credit, Ontario, Canada. He has been actively involved in New Church Development of the United Church, is past Chair of Muskoka Presbytery and past President of the Toronto Conference. He has written for a variety of journals and periodicals and has led several events for the Ecumenical Center for Stewardship Studies. He hosts "Spirit Connection" for Vision TV in Canada.

F. Stuart Gulley is the Director of Development for the Candler School of Theology, Emory University. He was formerly Director of Admissions and Student Placement and has been active in the Candler community since beginning his theological education there. An ordained elder of The United Methodist Church, Mr. Gulley serves on the Board of directors of the Appalachia Service Project.

David Heetland is Director of Development for Garrett Evangelical Divinity School in Evanston, Illinois.

Gregory G. M. Ingram is Senior Minister of the Oak Grove A.M.E.C. Church in Detroit, Mich. His book *S.A.T. (Spiritual Aptitude Test for African Methodism* is widely used in teaching new members and for nurturing others in the church. Other books by Dr. Ingram include *A Matter of Obedience*, a must-have resource on tithing.

James P. Johnson is president of the Christian Church Foundation of the Christian Church (Disciples of Christ). That unit seeks to ensure the continuing ministries of the denomination by providing opportunities for the stewardship of accumulated resources through planned giving. The Reverend Johnson's ministries include education, consultation, management and coordination of development for total assets of over $50 million. Before joining the Foundation, he pastored churches in Missouri and Kentucky.

Donald W. Joiner is director of The Planned Giving Resource Center with the Stewardship Unit of the General Board of Discipleship of The United Methodist Church. He previously served as Associate Council Director for the Detroit Annual Conference and as a pastor. He is the author of *Christians and Money;* coauthor of *Celebrate Giving, Celebrate and Visit*, and *Celebrate Together* (Discipleship Resources).

Richard B. Kelly is Business Administrator of Vestavia Hills United Methodist Church in Birmingham, Alabama. For 23 years, prior to his current position, he was in the Information Services Division of McGraw-Hill. He is a certified Church Business Administrator through courses at Emory University.

Renard J. Kolasa is an attorney in Farmington Hills, Michigan, specializing in tax and business law. He has worked extensively in the areas of estate and gift tax planning, retirement planning, charitable giving, employee benefits, and small business law. Mr. Kolasa is Chancellor of the Detroit Annual Conference of The United Methodist Church.

Glenna Kruger and Roy Kruger are members of First Baptist Church of Portland, Oregon. Glenna has worked as a human resource manager and consultant for over 21 years, and currently as Human Resource Development Specialist for a Fortune 500 corporation. Roy is a research and program evacuator for a nonprofit educational research organization. Previously he was a professor of marketing and management and has worked with academic institutions, small businesses, and government agencies in research and evaluation.

Alec Langford is a minister of counseling in Indianapolis, Indiana.

Frederick H. Leasure is the Executive Director of The United Methodist Foundation of Western Pennsylvania. He has served on the faculty of the Community College of Allegheny County's CPA program as well as The United Methodist Planned Giving School. The Reverend Leasure is the author of a variety of articles for denominational publications and received the 1991 Fund Raising Executive of the Year Award. He has served as president of the National Association of United Methodist Foundations.

Don McClanen is Executive Director of Ministry of Money in Gaithersburg, Md. It was his inspiration and calling that formulated this special ministry. A writer and world traveler, Don is dedicated to helping people come to terms with the struggle of faith and money.

Herbert Mather administers the work of the Stewardship Unit of The General Board of Discipleship of The United Methodist Church. He previously served on the staff of the South Indiana Conference and as a pastor. He is the author of *Becoming a Giving Church, Gifts Discovery Workshop;* coauthored *Celebrate Giving, Celebrate Together*, and *Collaborating in Ministry* (Discipleship Resources); and wrote *Letters for All Seasons* (Abingdon Press).

Gilson Miller is senior pastor of Newburg United Methodist Church in Livonia, Mich. The plays reproduce in this *Guide* were part of a longer stewardship study in preparation for his D.M. program.

Dan P. Moseley is Senior Minister at Vine Street Christian Church in Nashville, Tennessee.

Thomas Petty is Treasurer/Director of Administrative Services of the Northern Illinois Conference of The United Methodist Church. The Reverend Petty formerly pastored churches in Illinois. He is a Certified Financial Planner.

Ronald Reed is an Episcopal cleric who has served in a leadership capacity in every level from local to denominational levels. Although he is called on to lead in many denominational and ecumenical capacities, he is also a proficient writer in magazines for all denominations.

Thomas Rieke is Director of The Network for Charitable Giving in Oakland, Calif. His many stewardship responsibilities have included being Assistant Secretary to The General Board of Discipleship of The United Methodist Church. In addition to his theological degree, a law degree has been of great benefit in his work. As a speaker he is called on by many denominations throughout North America. His many writings include *How To Give Away Your Debt* and *Opportunities in Stewardship*.

Paula K. Ritchie is former Vice President and Director of Stewardship Interpretation for Church Finance Council of the Christian Church (Disciples of Christ). In that capacity she was called on to lead many workshops in stewardship education, as well as writing for her denominational resources.

John and **Sylvia Ronsvalle** founded empty tomb, inc., in 1972 to coordinate diaconal efforts of churches in Champaign County, Illinois. They currently offer research information and training to address the crisis in worldwide mission giving. The couple live and work in an impoverished urban area, building bridges between area Christians and the poor. The have traveled worldwide to study needs and avenues of outreach.

Betsy Schwarzentraub has been a Stewardship Associate with The United Methodist Church for ten years and is a clergy member from California. A former pastor for sixteen years, she is now a church consultant to denominational leaders and individual congregations.

Dale Stitt is an ordained minister with the Christian Church (Disciples of Christ). He currently serves as the Director of Program for Ministry of Money—one of the missions of the Church of the Saviour in Washington, D.C. His ministry has included local pastorates and leadership responsibilities on the regional and national level of the Christian Church with a specific focus on Christian stewardship.

Donald G. Stoner has served as Director of Planned Giving for the Commission on Development of the United Church of Christ since 1983. Previously, the Reverend Stoner served as pastor of two congregations, on the staff of the Illinois Conference of the United Church of Christ and with the Development Office of Elmhurst College. He has been an active participant in the Ecumenical Center for Stewardship Studies.

J. L. (Jim) Tarr was Executive Director of Boy Scouts of America. Originally from Oklahoma, Jim has traveled extensively with the Boy Scouts as an executive, a board member of a number of corporations, and as a fund raiser. He is currently a consultant in the formulation of endowment funds and planned-giving programs.

Thomas F. Taylor practices law in litigation in Salt Lake City, Utah. He is the son of a minister and has held positions in ministry and religious education. From 1985 to 1987, Mr. Taylor was Assistant Minister at St. Michael's Lutheran Church in New Canaan, Connecticut. He also has served as visiting lecturer for the Religious Studies Department at the University of Illinois in Urbana. Presently, he is Director of Adult Education at the First Presbyterian Church in St. Lake City, and a lecturer for the Utah Institute for Biblical Studies, a Salt Lake City affiliate of Regent College, Vancouver, B.C. Mr. Taylor writes and speaks on nexus areas of law and religion.

William Ralph Taylor is a minister of The United Church of Canada since 1969 and has served congregations in the Newfoundland and Labrador Conferences. The Reverend Taylor has been on staff in Middle Judicatories and with the General Council of the United Church of Canada. (He has agreed to serve there "as long as it supports the people in the pew and the person in the pulpit.")

Norman J. Tellier has served as Coordinator of Gift Planning for the Reformed Church in America since 1987. He is an ordained minister and has been a pastor in churches in the Albany, New York area. He completed the Certified Financial Planner Professional Education Program of the College for Financial Planning in Denver, Colorado.

Karen E. Warren is pastor at Central Central Christian Church in Elkhart, Indiana.

J. Phil Williams is currently the Executive Director, Ecumenical Center for Stewardship Studies in Elkhart, Indiana. Prior to this position, he served as Interim Senior Minister at Central Christian Church (Disciples of Christ) in Elkhart, two years with the Presbyterian Church (USA) as Associate for Stewardship Training, and several years as Stewardship Minister with a middle judicatory staff of the Christian Church. He is a member of the Ecumenical Center for Stewardship Studies.

Patricia Wilson-Kastner is the director of the Church of St. Ann and the Holy Trinity in Brooklyn, New York. She presently serves as President of the Board of St. Ann's Center, is Dean of St. Mark's Deanery of the Brooklyn Archdeanery on the Diocese of Long Island, and is Vice-President of the founding board of the George Mercer Memorial School of Theology. Dr. Wilson-Kastner is a member of the Standing Commission on Ecumenical Relations and is part of the International Anglican-Methodist Dialogue group. She is the author of numerous books and articles.

Norma Wimberly is a freelance writer, teacher, and consultant in the area of Christian stewardship. For several years she served on the staff of the Stewardship Unit of The General Board of Discipleship of The United Methodist Church. Ms. Wimberly is the author of *Dare to Be Stewards, Earth Care, Putting God First: The Tithe,* and numerous articles for a variety of publications.

Laura E. Wright is the retired staff officer for stewardship of The Episcopal Church. She is a lifetime Episcopalian and New Yorker, and still attends the parish church where her parents and grandparents were married. Ms. Wright continues to serve the church as a consultant in stewardship education and programs.

INDEX OF FUNDING TOOLS

Thank You for Purchasing
The Abingdon Guide to Funding Ministry.

We hope this resource has helped you in funding your ministry, and we would like your advice. How can the Guide be improved? Please send your comments to the address below:

1. Where did you purchase or secure this volume of the *Abingdon Guide to Funding Ministry?*
   Please mark a choice:
   ☐ bookstore   ☐ catalog, mail, or phone order
   ☐ booktable   ☐ subscription
   ☐ other _____

2. Are you primarily a
   ☐ pastor
   ☐ finance or stewardship team member
   ☐ worship team member
   ☐ business administrator
   ☐ pastor-relations team member
   ☐ nonprofit business executive
   ☐ other _____

3. How easy or hard is it to find what you are looking for in the *Guide?*

4. Which two sections of the *Guide* do you or will you use most?

5. Which sections of the Guide do not interest you or anyone else in your congregation or organization?

6. Which sections have potential use for your church work, but did not prove to be very helpful in funding your ministry?

7. Since you are in charge, what would you change or add in future volumes of the *Abingdon Guide to Funding Ministry?*

8. Would you purchase another volume of this *Guide?*

Please send your comments to Editors, *Abingdon Guide to Funding Ministry,* Abingdon Press, P.O. Box 801, Nashville, TN 37202-0801.